CARP AMID THE STORM

by Tim Paisley

"Serenity is not freedom from the storm,
but peace amid the storm."

Debenport.

Angling Books Ltd.
1 Grosvenor Square
Sheffield S2 4MS

First Published 1992 by
Angling Books Ltd.,
1 Grosvenor Square,
Sheffield S2 4MS

British Library Cataloguing in Publication Data

Tim Paisley
Carp Amid the Storm
1. Carp Angling
I   Title
799. 1'752

ISBN 1871700 65 5

Produced and Typeset by
Steve Wilde of One and Only
and Angling Publications Ltd.

Printed by
Wm. Gibbons & Son Ltd.

Dedicated to

all carp fishers, past, present and future,
but especially to

my mate Bill Cottam for his support
through the difficult years.

Roger Smith and Ritchie McDonald
who gave me the guts to change direction.

Greg Fletcher, who shared some of what follows.

Dave Preston, who introduced me to a carp fishing paradise.

Pete Curtis, for his paintings and drawings.

Jim Gibbinson, Pete Springate, Terry Eustace
and Kevin Clifford – in admiration.

Fred J. Taylor and Maurice Ingham
for their friendship – and the past.

Steve and Sandra for inspirationally interpreting and deciphering
beyond the call of duty.

And that special carp person and best friend I've ever had
Mary Paisley

Contents

(e)

Foreword

A few years ago, I sat at a desk in England to write a foreword to a book I had never seen. From 5,000 miles away, however, I felt I knew the American author well enough to write it and I literally demanded the privilege.

I was unaware of the existence of "Carp Amid the Storm", otherwise I might have pulled rank and demanded a similar privilege of author Tim Paisley. I feel I know him well enough. As things turned out, however, I now find myself sitting at a desk in Wanneroo, Western Australia, some 10,000 miles from where it is to be published, writing a foreword because he has asked me to do so. And I am proud.

A mere 10,000 miles can make no difference in terms of content and although this effort on my part beats the previous foreword record by double, in terms of distance, I *do* have the manuscript by my side and I *have* read it.

Colin Dyson, one time Editor of "Coarse Angler", wrote once that "This man Paisley *can* write." Not perhaps in those exact words but the message was clear. Tim Paisley *can* write. (He splits the odd infinitive occasionally but we can, perhaps, forgive him for that since very few modern journalists appear to bother these days!)

Writing apart, it could be said that Tim Paisley and I have few common interests but, on reflection, perhaps we do.

We are, in effect, "so different - yet so same".*We enjoy good food, good wine, poetry, the outdoors, the dawns, the sunsets, waterside wild life, jokes against ourselves and the company of our fellow man. We both have a profound respect for our quarry and we both enjoy fishing. It has to be said, however, that we enjoy fishing at entirely different levels. His is of the intense and passionate kind that I once pursued myself and it shows in his works. Mine is now only intense and passionate on very rare occasions. I seldom "put in the hours" because I do not believe my modest results justify it.

My lack of modern carp fishing experience makes me one of today's also-rans but I like it that way. I confess, however, that I have learned a great deal about the new approach from Tim Paisley. I am never going to be seen seriously carp fishing again but the long days and nights I have spent with the author and his happy band will stay with me in memory for all time. So too will this book.

It is, you see, "so different – yet so same". "So different" because it is *not* about how to do it but rather about how it was (or was not) done. A book of memories and joys and disappointments, of success and failure, anticipation and realisation, of dreams and reality. "So same" because it is about carp and carp fishing and carp people. "So different" because its pages are not littered with photographs of bleary eyed carp men displaying their catches. "So same" because it holds just enough of them to do the subject justice and whet the appetite. "So different" because there are actual drawings of people, fish and places. "So same" because there are the few essential, technical diagrams to clarify certain aspects of the text.

The author makes no apology for including previously published articles. Nor need he. They had to be part of the book and it would not have been possible to improve on their original presentations. They will all stand being read again – and again…

It has been said of me that I have developed into an old story teller. I accept that as a compliment and believe that my enjoyment from reading stories helps me better to tell them.

Tim Paisley is a story teller and this is a book of stories from his own special repertoire. I have enjoyed reading them.

There are, alas, all too few books available today that dwell upon the sheer love of carp, amid the storm of fierce how-to-do-it competition. We should give thanks for this one.

It is my kind of book and I am proud to be part of it, both here and briefly in the later chapters.

Fred J. Taylor

* *"so different - yet so same"*

Quoted from Tom T. Hall's (country singer) "L. A. Blues."

Euphoria in the early days of carp fishing infatuation at Snowberry Lake.

This is more by way of an explanation than an introduction, really. In chronological terms *Carp Amid the Storm* is the fourth book published in my own name, following in the wake of *Carp Fishing, Carp Season* and *Big Carp*. In reality it was my first book, and much of the material dates back to before those three books were written. What follows is an apparently random collection of material by one author writing under two different names – Matthew Black and Tim Paisley. Much of the book was written in the seventies, the bulk of it in the eighties, and some of it in the nineties. Nearly half of the chapters have already been published, which means that over half of the book hasn't been published before, and while a few of you may question the inclusion of previously published material in here, I make no apology for it. Some of the chapters in question were actually written for this book, then released early for a variety of reasons. Others have been included because they are among my favourites and I want them to have a permanent home. I suppose wanting them preserved is a form of vanity. Perhaps, but on the other hand the vanity can't represent too great an ego, because the fifteen previously published articles/chapters included here represent about ten percent of my published article output! In other words over one hundred and fifty articles didn't make it into here.

On the other hand I think I should apologise for the fact that two of the chapters have already appeared in books, "Hooked in Reed Warblers", which was actually written for this book but was first published in "For the Love of Carp", and "Blank at Fox Pool", which appears in Ritchie McDonald's book "Ritchie on Carp". The latter piece I just had to include because it described a week which had a great effect on my carp fishing outlook over the succeeding years – and the cast list and events were not without some significance, either. Perhaps I'm being a bit over defensive about the inclusion of published material. It is an accepted practise in literary circles: much of Yatesy's book Casting at the Sun had already appeared in article form – and I wish that Rod Hutchinson would produce a collection of some of his published material, particularly the "Along the Way" and "Back Along the Way" articles.

A number of readers may be confused because some of the chapters were originally published in the name of Matthew Black, which is not my actual name. Yes, I'm confused about that, too, but having explained the scenario in the Introduction to "Carp Season", I won't try your patience by going through all that again.

The fact that much of the material was written quite some time ago means that many of the views and thoughts expressed have altered - particularly my somewhat cynical feelings about permanent relationships. Much of the material was written at a time when I was unattached, and couldn't imagine meeting anyone who would be willing to put up with my strangely structured carp life and my unlivable-with temperament! Meeting and marrying Mary has proved me wrong, but the fact that I'm now happily married doesn't change the way I felt then. You can't change history by changing words on paper so some of my comments about then aren't at all in conflict with the way things actually are now. It's just that I've been proved completely wrong since I wrote them. In addition the fact that all the chapters were written independently of each other means that there may occasionally be some repitition – and very probably some contradiction! – in the thought processes and philosophies expressed.

In terms of the previously published material there may be some surprising omissions to those of you familiar with my work. I know the first Matthew Black piece is the favourite of many of you, but it embarrasses me now – as do many of my earlier Matt Black pieces – so it had to go. On the other hand, one of my own favourites, "Listen Girls", I omitted because I felt it was of too limited appeal, although as a piece of writing I was not at all displeased with it. Perhaps in another ten years I'll be so desperate for material that I'll be anxiously ferreting through the remaining published pieces for a "Second Best of…" volume. (Joke, chaps, relax.)

My thanks to the great Fred J. Taylor for doing me the honour of writing the Foreword to this book. He is a great man and I feel fortunate that we have become close in recent years following our collaboration on the Dick Walker Memoir. Ironically, our paths must have been within months of crossing at Snowberry in the seventies: at the time I had no idea I was fishing for carp Fred J. had himself stocked and fished for.

Thanks also to my friend Pete Curtis for his beautiful cover paintings, and the lovely line drawings which add so much atmosphere to the book. His illustrations add a timelessness to the text which to me is an essential ingredient in the expression of carp fishing emotions: I'm grateful to Pete for the endless trouble he has taken to bring his illustrations into line with my requirements. The fact that Pete doesn't know the waters described means that on a couple of occasions he has had to use a degree of artistic license in converting the written word into a visual impression. That's a very minor point, but I mention it in case anyone who knows the waters concerned becomes disorientated. The words and the pictures are there to convey events and emotions, not accurately record and catalogue them.

This is perhaps an overlong introduction to a book the readers will make their own minds up about, anyway, but I suppose the explanations are a sort of defence mechanism. Other authors will understand that. This is by way of saying "I know the book's got shortcomings but this is the book I want it to be". So that's the way it is. I hope at least some of you like it as much as I do!

Tim Paisley

It began during the war when I watched my oldest brother and a friend conjure roach out of the friend's garden pond. I think it was the sense of mystery that intrigued me, the wonder of those lovely fish suddenly appearing out of an inert, impenetrable, alien medium from nowhere.

The intrigue was dampened, rather than fuelled, in the forties with forays to a smouldering pit in nearby Cowslip Field. I once caught a handful of quality roach from there, took them home and ate them. Why else would you catch fish?

What I used for tackle in those far off forties' days I can't imagine, because I can't remember owning any.

The fishing died for rugby, soccer, tennis, cricket, athletics and egg collecting, to be revived in my teens by my best friend, Stuart. We fished the local ponds for stunted roach, Farrington Lodge for perch, then aspired to the giddy heights of fishing the Lancaster Canal in the Garstang area "for tench". We occasionally caught roach – if we were lucky.

The pull of the water was growing and one Friday night I camped alongside the Lancaster Canal overnight – to bait the swim for the following morning. The first barge through redistributed the groundbait.

We fished in Ireland for two weeks, and caught bream and rudd in some numbers.

Then we took up golf and, shortly after, life's whims sent us our separate ways.

Nine years later I fished again – in Norfolk – for bream, with maggots. I caught eels. I had the nouse to change to breadflake – and caught bream.

The fishing fire was rekindled and Tim Jnr. and I started fishing local Sheffield waters, including Dam Flask, Underbank, Marshalls, the Rivelin Valley Dams – and the Robin Hood Pond.

One Sunday morning at Marshalls there was a man fishing for carp. Nothing happened for a long time – then he lost one. I was impressed by the significance of the event, his stillness and his resigned stoicism at the loss.

I started fishing "for carp".

First bait was potato. Daughter Suzy wanted to know how you kept the potato warm once it was in the water.

Never caught a carp on potato.

Switched to breadflake, and on a steamy late May night in 1971 I caught a huge single figure carp – and became involved.

Four years later I went to Snowberry – and became addicted.

Caught my first double there in 1975 – or 1976.

For five years I had a love affair with Snowberry – and its carp – and flirtations with Roman Lakes, Butterley, Codnor, Cuttle Mill and Harlesthorpe Dam.

Caught my first twenty at Cuttle in 1977 (or maybe 78).

Met Fletch (Greg Fletcher) in 1978.

Left Snowberry behind and fished Elsecar, Harlesthorpe and Wentworth before the start of the Carp Society broadened my horizons and opened my eyes.

Fished Stockley Road with Mike Wilson in September 1981.

Fished Longfield with Fletch, Diedrich, Winkworth and Ritchie McDonald in March 1982 – and saw Ritchie catch the leather at 34lb.

Travelling On...

Fished Waveney with Clive, Malc, Rod Hutchinson and Lennie Middleton in July 1982 on the first Carp Society Junior Fish-In.

Went back to Waveney in November 82 and caught 'Big Scale' at 32lb. My first thirty.

Was invited by Dave Preston to start the 83 season on a water in Shropshire – and started a love affair with the area and its waters. The mere which Dave and I fished became known as The Mangrove.

Went down to Kent in September and fished the Tip Lake, courtesy of Bob Morris and Leisure Sport. Met Fred Wilton for the one and only time.

Went back to D Lake in October and caught 'Big Scale' and 'The Leather' at 31.06 and 31.13 respectively.

1984 was the year of 'Carp Season' and the few days on the magnificent Erehwon has become an enjoyable, annually unsuccessful event.

For three and a half years I was unemployed, penniless, without transport, fishing very little – and very inefficiently when I did. I read, wrote, reflected on life, produced 'Carp Fisher' – and made plans.

In 1987 one set of plans led to Bill Cottam and I forming Nutrabaits.

In 1988 another set of plans led to Carpworld getting off the ground – and 'Carp Fishing' was published by Crowood Press.

Later the same year, 'Carp Season' was published by Angling Publications (formed by Steve Wilde and I). And I met Mary.

In 1989 Mary and I got together. I formed an official Mangrove syndicate and took over the running of Birch Grove.

Since then we've fished the Mangrove and Birch, with occasional forays to Drax, Horseshoe, Chigborough – and anywhere else that Society Fish-Ins may take us.

How many doubles, twenties and thirties have I caught in all that fishing? Thirties – four: they don't take much counting. The rest: I haven't a clue.

Have I loved every minute of it? Not really. In fact, I've quite hated some of it and have given up on a number of occasions – once for as long as two days.

Any regrets? Dozens, but they are forgotten now.

Ambitions? 25lb common, 30lb common etc., a huge Mangrove fish; a Birch Grove 25+, then a thirty…

But it doesn't matter if I achieve none of these things: being there is enough.

Most vivid memories? First carp. First impressions of Snowberry and the mysterious world of carp fishing it represented at that time. Meeting Greg Fletcher, Nigel Talling, Micky Sly and Rod Hutchinson. First thirty. Fishing Elsecar. First sight of The Mangrove. Fitz catching Pinky. Meeting Stoney. Fishing Horeshoe. Mary's 25lb+ from Birch Grove. Fred J's visits to Birch…

And a thousand and one others of people, sunsets, dawns, arriving, departing, blanking, catching, travelling, travelling on…

I was always aware that there were carp – as anglers are. They were fish in other people's waters, occasionally caught by other people. I just fished, quite brilliantly in my eyes, not even mediocrely in retrospect, and, looking back, I'm not quite clear in my mind if I caught my first carp by accident or design.

In the course of just fishing I was granted the long coveted privilege of fishing Marshall's Pond in Loxley Valley. It was *the* local water, in that it was well stocked, and contained carp which people fished for, as opposed to myths which were known to be present but which no one dared waste precious hours of their life on. I was fortunate enough to obtain a day ticket (days were actually half days then) and turned up at first light on the appointed Sunday morning. It was busy, as Sunday mornings are, and I may or may not have caught; that part of it escapes my memory. The lasting impression of the day was that twenty yards to my left there was a man fishing for carp. It was the first time I had witnessed such a phenomenon. My eyes kept being drawn to his quill float, erect and apparently permanently motionless, fifteen yards out into the pond. He made me feel uneasy and slightly inadequate – but unconvinced for all that. But there was a quiet, heroic fatalism to his approach that suddenly made what I was doing seem a bit pointless and inadequate. There was more character in his fishing, partly because of his calm acceptance of his inactivity, and partly because there was a stillness and mystery surrounding what he was doing that contrasted dramatically with the mundane predictability of my own efforts.

He hooked a fish about ten o'clock. The other anglers knew the score and resignedly reeled in while the battle was fought – although watching someone else play a fish in open water doesn't look like a battle: until you know the feeling yourself you can't fully appreciate the significance of the bent rod and the line remorselessly cutting through the water. The man fought his battle, and lost, the hook pulling out as the unseen fish circled deep in the margins. Outwardly he took it well, with a stoical display of calm resignation. I was impressed, and almost certainly a disillusionment with my own stereotyped splodging set in that morning. My approach to fishing changed, although I can't remember if I specifically started fishing for carp. My efforts may have centred on tench because I'm sure I still thought of carp as being uncatchable.

Close season fishing was allowed at Marshall's, as it was at the Robin Hood pond, situated further down the valley towards Sheffield. I was a member of the latter, and it contained carp and tench. On a late May night in that same close season I was fishing the Robin Hood pond. I was probably also escaping. There is a part of me that has to stand apart from life on occasions, and the fact that I was fishing late at night suggests that that was one of those occasions.

It was raining; a fine rain that was just heavy enough for me to have the umbrella up. The air was soft and mild. It was quarter past eleven, unusually late for me to be at the water's edge, but there were fish out there, holding me, dragging a succession of last casts out of me.

The water was like oxtail soup, khaki coloured in the searchlight beam of the torch. The red tipped quill would sail out, following a lump of bread flake into the circle of light. The float would lazily cock, and after every cast it would be towed out of the circle of light into the darkness. Each increasingly determined strike would be rewarded by the float hurrying back towards me, the hook baitless – and fishless. It was frustrating, and I began to feel a bit panicky. I should have been home, but the continuous action on the big bread flake baits was unprecedented.

Recast, sink the line, watch the float rise into the circle of light and slowly make itself comfortable. Tense the muscles of the right forearm, with the fingers opening and closing round the reel seat. Float up – flat. Strike? Wait? Did I know about tench and lift bites then? Yes, I probably did, but I'd never connected with one. The float started to drift to my right and vanished into the darkness – from memory for the thirteenth time. The twelve foot Fibatube match rod cut through the torch beam – 'and stopped abruptly in mid journey!

The pond was small, weedy and treelined, and whatever I had hooked visited most of it within a few seconds of our relationship. I can remember little or nothing about the fight, except that it never for one moment occurred to me that I would land whatever was busy making a fool of me out there in the damp blackness. I must have known it was a carp straight away. The tench just fought – admittedly doggedly, but quite fairly and unalarmingly. This thing didn't fight, it just swam at great speed in three or four different directions at once. Being new to fishing in the dark I didn't known about watching the rod tip, and if I had done I wouldn't have been able to see it anyway: the night was as black as the ace of spades and the umbrella was limiting my vision. I vaguely remember pulling the fish out of the reed bed opposite – which spoke volumes for the quality of the Bayer Perlon 3lb line (mist grey) – and being agreeably surprised that nothing gave. The fish set off in another direction or two.

Some time later I landed the fish. Well – that's my version of the event. It's just possible that the fish had seen all there was to see in the pond and had decided to broaden its horizons. Whatever the reason it joined me on the bank, and I was quite stunned by it.

It was a carp; a pretty mirror of about six pounds and in superb condition. *Now* I cannot believe how big that fish seemed then, so I simply cannot convey the impression of hugeness of that moment. But it was big, and it was disturbingly beautiful. I didn't understand at the time but I now know that I am moved by mirror carp, and I think my excitement was tinged with emotion that night. A distinctively scaled mirror carp brings it home very sharply that a carp is an individual entity, an isolated being in its own right. I was captured in that moment, as many had been before, and many have been since. I was captured by the whole circumstance of the night, and the landing of the fish – but the experience was far more than an angling one. There was a realisation of an affinity in the encounter with that magic mirror, an affinity that makes complete sense of the nonsensical need to spend as much time as possible on the banks of carp lakes.

I had caught a carp doing everything wrong. I read books, picked brains in tackle shops, and set about fishing for the small head of carp in that Loxley Valley water doing everything right. And it didn't take long for the message to sink in that it was almost as easy to catch carp by accident as by design.

I know that many of us have become carp anglers through the accidental capture of a carp, or as the result of seeing one caught. That being the case, the unsuspecting and ill prepared innocent is almost certainly an angler already and, to a lesser or greater extent, finds refuge from his office, factory, shop, building site, wife or whatever, by the side of his favourite water. Why carp fishing then takes over from the pursuit of the previous quarry is a very personal thing.

If you become involved by catching a carp accidentally, then initially it will almost certainly be the carp itself which is the fascination. If you start your carp fishing by actually going on a session, then you may well be aware of, and be attracted by, the timelessness and serenity of carp fishing from the word go. I have taken two 'normal' pleasure anglers on carp fishing trips at different times and, at face value, they both acted identically to start with. They accepted my advice about setting up with good grace, they looked at the ball of bait with a quizzical expression of disbelief, sniffed it and made the mandatory noises of even greater disbelief, politely thanked me for casting it into the required area for them, then purposefully ignored the carp set up and got on with the serious business of fishing the margins with a single maggot, or caster, and a size twenty hook. The carp rod was looked on as a useful decoration to the swim, but of little further significance. Not having previously caught a carp, or seen one caught, they felt that there was little chance of their roach bashing being interrupted. Of those two anglers, one is now a confirmed carp man and the other still fishes the margins for whatever comes along.

I honestly think that the mental attitude that carp are almost impossible to catch makes the early carp sessions the most enjoyable of all – in a painful sort of way. There is the mystery of the unseen and unknown, coupled with the magical beauty of the unattainable. But it's like anything else; the harder the attainment, the more rewarding the prize. And the greater your own contribution – in terms of thinking and effort – to the attainment, the more meaningful it will be in the long term. That is not to say that you will not get a great deal of pleasure from catching a twenty pounder on your first carp fishing trip. You will be ecstatic, and will probably think that you are the kiddie. If you continue to think that then your carp fishing life will, sadly, be a brief and unpopular one. If you are able to look back from five years on and recognise the early success as a stroke of good fortune then you will probably remain a carp angler.

Over the years you get many rewards from carp fishing – and not all of them will be concerning the capture of fish – but the innocent pleasure of those early amateurish efforts, when any progress takes on a major significance, will be a precious memory. When Browning wrote "…and never could recapture that first fine careless rapture" he certainly didn't have carp fishing in mind, but the line conveys just what I'm struggling to say now.

I tend to think of my own switch from pleasure to carp fishing as being instant, but on reflection I'm not absolutely sure that it was. It certainly was in <u>attitude</u>, but probably not in commitment, as I can vaguely remember trying to perform the impossible feat of fishing two floats simultaneously for some time after I caught my first carp. One float was three yards out in front of me, in a weedy tench swim, and the other six or seven yards out away to my left "for carp". Presumably the inefficiency of what I was doing was soon borne in on me, or the need to catch carp overtook the need to just catch, and I changed to

Conversion

more 'orthodox' two rod carp fishing arrangements.

The memory of the capture of my first carp – already described – is indelibly imprinted on my memory, as are many subsequent captures. That impressionable event occurred at a small, tree fringed mill pond in the Loxley Valley, on the outskirts of Sheffield, and for a number of seasons thereafter I was content to pursue the small head of single figure carp in that picturesque, secluded water. Of course 'small head of single figure carp' is a rationalisation from some years on: at the time the water was probably just as likely as Redmire to yield a big carp.

In those early days I still thought that a fishing session lasted as long as a flask of coffee, and even a marathon twelve hours at the waterside seemed a very unsocial occurrence. In writings on carp fishing I think that there are some areas that are best left to the reader's imagination, and I would suggest that the private lives of carp anglers, and specimen hunters generally, fall into this category. As a rule, carp fishers do not make ideal husbands, though I'm equally sure that there are many splendid exceptions to that unnecessarily sweeping generalisation. But carp fishing can be an addiction, and addicts make poor bed-fellows, whether the addiction be drugs, gambling, women, mountaineering – or carp.

I cannot think that I was an addict at that stage, or that I even had any inkling that I was likely to become one. The water I fished was only five minutes from home, I didn't indulge in marathon sessions, and I only used to fish a couple of times a week at most. The time spent fishing for carp – and my results at that time – bear witness to the fact that I was not an addict, but I'm equally sure that after I had hooked that first carp, I was never quite the same again. Perhaps I fought the addiction for a couple of years before giving in, or perhaps it was just that I had no conception of what was going on in the carp fishing world outside, and the lengths that other people were going to to catch carp. But just as that first carp diverted my thoughts firmly onto carp fishing, my first trip to Snowberry Lake in Buckinghamshire signposted my decline towards addiction and precipitated a rejection of the confines of domesticity.

I first went to Snowberry on the evening of the fifteenth of June, 1975 for the opening night of the season. Apart from the beauty of the countryside and the lake itself, here was a whole new world. A world of grim faced, knowledgeable, confident men who apparently knew exactly what they were doing. A world of matching carp rods, matching rod rests and buzzers, brolly camps and huge landing nets. I went down with high hopes, but after a walk round the lake my heart sank. How could I compete with this collection of giants from the carp fishing world?

My tackle was very basic, but did include a recently built glass carp rod made up, of course, from a 10ft. Richard Walker Mk. IV blank… Looking back that 'of course' is significant. To a beginner like me Dick Walker was still synonymous with carp fishing. It was a magnificent blank and many of today's eleven and twelve foot rods have a feel of a Mk. IV with something added at the bottom end or in the middle. I tried my best, of course, but I did not catch. I had one butt ringer in the early hours but had never fished open bale arm before and… I'll not go on.

I had my twelve hour session and reluctantly left that stunning setting at noon the next day, carpless. When we left the brolly camps were still there and

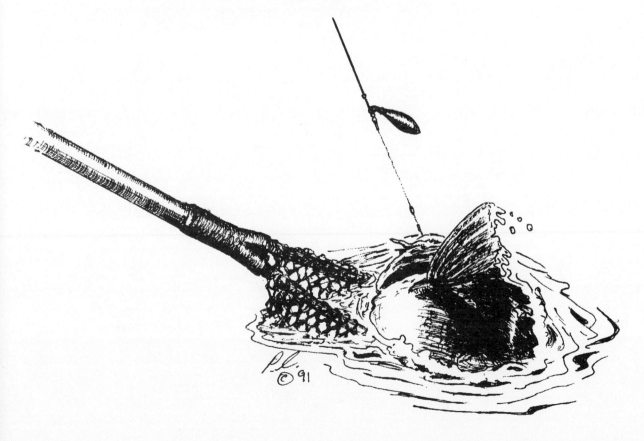

the grim faced men were asleep in them, or stretched out on their bed chairs by their rods. Carp cruised around on the surface in the hot June sun and I had to return to an office desk up north. Clearly I was missing out on something. At that moment the time restriction of the previously accepted norm of a short session was already breaking me in half. The permanent feel of the brolly camps pitched at the water's edge immediately aroused a massive restlessness in me. Physically I left the water, but my thoughts, and perhaps something more, were left behind in the beautiful sun filled amphitheatre of that tree guarded lake.

The long shadow of addiction had been cast on me, and it was a welcome shade. Overnight twelve hours became less than a minimum period for a session. I had to get back down to that water as often as possible to be in the presence of its carp and relax in its peaceful, dreamy atmosphere. I had got to start catching those carp that had been beyond me on that first trip. There was a feel to carp fishing that immediately captured part of me, and at that time Snowberry personified the carp fishing that I wanted to be part of – and was to do so for a number of years.

'Serious' carp fishing was upon me, though I certainly can't claim to have become a better citizen through the involvement. Addicts make poor bed-fellows.

Is a first season about events, or are the impressions you are left with more important? Or perhaps looking back from eight or nine years on, it is almost true to say that the important thing has been the impressions left by the events. Certainly the memories are indelible and golden, although the indelibility has little to do with any successful carp fishing exploits on my part.

The affair born of love at first sight of Snowberry was never, at any time, affected by disenchantment. I would still fish it now if I had the time and the money. It really is a lovely place. The principal impressions of that first season are of people, and atmosphere, and of becoming aware that I had an enormous amount to learn to become even a run of the mill competent carp angler. The somewhat forbidding atmosphere of the silent, grim-faced brolly camp inhabitants of the first night did not turn out to be a true impression at all. In fact, I did not see many grim faced men at the lake in the four years I spent there. We all have our off moments, obviously, but as carp lakes go it was unusually open and friendly.

I had joined the lake with a view to catching a double figure carp. From a distance it seemed a reasonable target and undoubtedly attainable. There was a fair head of doubles in the lake. Having said which, I will immediately record that I didn't catch one of them that season. I did catch thirty carp between 5lb and 9lb 13oz. On the other hand, Nigel and Ken had over twenty doubles each and other members had double figure fish in ones, twos and handfuls, over the season.

Why had Nigel and Ken landed over twenty doubles while I had caught none? The question had to be answered honestly if I was to profit from the season in terms of carp catching. It was not down to any particular swim because I tended to fish one that did produce its share of ten pluses. Terminal arrangements were pretty standard in those innocent days and while this would be about the time that Lenny, Keith and Kevin were starting into the boiled baits and hook out set ups, I'm quite sure no one at Snowberry was using them during the period I fished it: in carp fishing terms Snowberry was sheltered from the advances which were already making an impact on the mainstream carp waters. I was forced to the conclusion that I was either a lousy angler or my baits weren't good enough. None of us will accept that we are lousy anglers, and I'm not, so it was down to the bait.

I'm not going to include any technical sections in this book for the simple reason that technical works very quickly date, particularly in the fast moving carp world. Feelings are much of a muchness from generation to generation, but it really is not possible to make some mention of carp fishing without reference to the all important aspect of bait, so I'll digress onto the subject for a couple of paragraphs.

Snowberry was a carp only water, so I started on maggots and caught a great many carp on them, and had a few on crust. After those two worthies blew out six weeks into the season, I struggled and the majority of my fish came in those first few weeks. Sultanas didn't go, peanuts, tic beans – no success at all, although I have no recollection of how persistent I was with each of these baits. I'm sure that I did quite a prolonged pre-baiting programme with peanuts because I felt they should be the big one, but I never had a twitch.

Now I was aware that one of the golden rules of the carp fishing world is that you don't ask. Other anglers were catching double figure carp and I was

convinced that, given the bait, I would get one. Clearly it was time to delve into the mysterious world of specials. Would that I hadn't bothered, because they've kept me penniless since! At that time, my knowledge of exotic paste baits started and ended at Kit-e-Kat. I had used it at the Robin Hood Pool, with instant success, but I recognised that every carp angler who set foot on Snowberry would also know about the stuff and that it was, therefore, best ignored. (This faulty philosophy has cost me a great many fish over the years. It takes a long, long time for a bait to blow, but in those early days I thought that if I knew of a bait it must have already been fished out). What else was there?

I had been reading about carp fishing for some time. Dick Walker in his timeless 'Stillwater Angling', 'B.B.', Sheringham et al in my oft read 'Confessions'. Sheringham's early 1900's treatise on baits, tongue in cheek as it was, still remains, in context, the best summary of carp baits that I have come across. Who else? There wasn't the present wealth of carp fishing literature available in the mid seventies, and there was certainly very little openness about baits. My only contemporary source was Jim Gibbinson's 'Carp', not the original hard back, but the simpler Osprey book in the Angling Library series. It was there in black and white, an outline of baits. The one that captured my imagination was cheese paste; the one that didn't was luncheon meat. Jim didn't rate it. Rod Hutchinson has said somewhere that books should be a background to your thinking and not do your thinking for you, or words to that effect. I'll drink to that. Jim is very authoritative and I was over-influenced by his reference to luncheon meat to the extent that I developed a mental block about it for the rest of that first season.

In fact, tinned meat baits, the full range of luncheon meats, Bacon Grill, Spam etc., are among the best carp baits of all time, were accounting for many of the double figure fish to come out of Snowberry that season, and scored heavily on every carp water I fished in the seventies. Tinned meat was a very difficult bait to compete with on some waters and my enthusiastic amateur concoctions at Snowberry were of no great interest to the carp at all. All that is not intended as a criticism of Jim, but it does indicate the dangers of relying on any carp fishing writer who is, firstly, only offering an opinion and secondly, and more importantly, is possibly heavily influenced by factors he may not wish to disclose. (In other words Jim probably had something a great deal more effective than luncheon meat as a bait when he wrote 'Carp'!)

I've wandered a bit, but in doing so I suppose I've put my finger on the fact that the first Snowberry season was very formative, in that I became bait orientated, but beyond that the background to it all is of prime importance. Snowberry was steeped in atmosphere: the atmosphere of an easy, relaxed relationship with the other users of the waters and the atmosphere of a beautiful, isolated lake, shrouded in trees and mystery and dating back over a hundred years. The water is referred to as Carp Pool on maps going back to the nineteenth century and has, at times, a silent, haunted feel to it that conveys a resentment of intrusion.

Escapism plays a large part in our attitude to carp fishing, and there are times when we've got to get to the water for a while for reasons other than catching carp. I re-thought that thought many times as I turned off the busy A5 into the farmyard at the top of the track leading down the fields to the water. Arriving in the dark hours was a stunning experience. Two hours plus of a noisy car engine and a steady stream of car headlights, suddenly replaced by the absolute black stillness and eerie silence of the car park under the massive trees. It was worth the trip for that moment alone – for about five minutes – then the sudden restlessness of the need to test the carp's reactions to the latest in the long line of baits took over.

Verbal descriptions of carp lakes are singularly unsatisfactory, so I won't attempt to paint a picture of the water with words. Imagine it as you want it and that is Snowberry. Huge trees, heavily wooded on one side, an overgrown island at very moderate casting range, the odd weeping willow and a few lily beds. Put them together the way you want them and it will be about right. I couldn't have improved on the combination that time, nineteenth century man, and nature had come up with.

I can only describe my involvement with the water from a carp fishing angle, which is as most of you will want it. My affection for the place goes far beyond carp fishing though, because it undoubtedly had a strong influence on my life at a time when I was very much in need of a new reason to believe.

There is a poster on my kitchen wall which shows a restless sea crashing against a tree lined shore. The caption is *'Serenity is not freedom from the storm but peace amid the storm'*. That was Snowberry then and it is carp fishing now; the peace amid the storm; the escape route where I can turn off from the unwelcome intrusions of a well ordered society which makes too many demands on a person as disorganised and individual as myself – and I think the same can be said of hundreds, or thousands, like me.

Mentally, I keep going back to Snowberry – and physically, because I call in each time I pass. It does none of us any harm to make strong recall of our early carp fishing days. The capture of the big fish has been made easier by the publicising of their whereabouts, Fred Wilton's baits, the rig which sprang from the original thinking of Lenny Middleton, and the shrinking of the lakes with the arrival of carbon fibre, which has made all of us ton up casters. Except that there is still a world of carp men who are plugged in to none of these things and just want the seclusion and the atmosphere. I get asked "How many twenties this season?" and my soul contracts, it really does. I am not a big fish man, I am a carp fisher. If I catch the odd big fish I will share the pleasure of it with close friends and the grapevine will devalue or overrate it, as it thinks fit. If the tale is worth the retelling, then I will write about it. But I have written about as many blanks and small fish as I have big fish, I think because my motivation to go carp fishing springs from a number of sources – which in turn means that the need to convert experiences into words does so, too.

So if I do write about the capture of the odd big carp, it is with a feeling of apology. I spend an enormous amount of time planning the downfall of carp and putting those plans into effect. I know what a disrupting effect carp fishing has had on my private life, and I have always been nervous of influencing otherwise model citizens into jeopardising all they hold dear in pursuing the big fish full time.

There is more to life than carp fishing, I'm told. I spent thirty odd years in search of whatever that something is, then found it on the banks of carp lakes and in the company of the carp fishing fraternity. Perhaps this book will go part way to conveying what the massive love of carp fishing is about, or perhaps it won't. I'm told that Dick Walker once asked Kevin Clifford, "How many

twenties do you want to catch?", the implication being that there is more to fishing than catching carp. But it rather ignores the undoubted fact that, for the vast majority of us, there *is* far more to carp fishing than just catching carp.

I have wandered far from the first season at Snowberry and now I'll leave it altogether. I fished the nine months through, double-less, no doubt frustrated, absolutely captured and highly suspicious of luncheon meat. The first day of the following season rendered much of that sentence obsolete.

The more enthusiastic you are, the longer the close season lasts. The close season of 1976 was the longest on record and no subsequent break from carp fishing has altered that statistic. I think its duration was stretched unendurably by the fact that I was engaged in the (for me) highly unlikely activity of carrying out major alterations of a structural nature to the kitchen, much to the wife's surprise and my own mortification.

The kitchen alterations were a voluntary venture, presumably representing a recognition that carp fishing was getting out of hand and that I needed to spend the close season punishing myself for the breaches of the matrimonial rules the coming season was about to escalate. I was trying to ease my conscience knowing that I would not be answerable for my actions once the middle of June arrived. Never was a middle of June more welcome; the punishment of the comprehensive re-structuring of the kitchen was too severe a sentence, although every back-breaking minute of it seemed worth the effort once the morning of June 15th arrived. From memory, Openers was the Monday night and I was to spend the rest of the week carp fishing. It would be my longest session up to that point.

I make frequent references to long sessions, and mine have become longer and more frequent as time has passed. I should perhaps make it clear that I do not think it is absolutely necessary to fish long sessions to catch carp, or to obtain enjoyment from fishing for them. The combination of a going bait, known feeding times and a local water can lead to excellent short session carp fishing, and one of my best seasons, in terms of catching carp, was based on that type of fishing. There is some feel of carp fishing there, too. The anticipation, the physical and mental satisfaction and the fulfilment of the fish. But one essential ingredient is missing; the timelessness of a succession of days of nothingness, which is part of the great attraction of carp fishing for many of us: the great escape.

I knew where I wanted to fish and the journey down was fraught with the fear that there would be someone in the camp site swim. An early afternoon arrival revealed an empty lake. The place looked wild and unkempt like a beautiful woman who has just climbed out of bed and is still half asleep. It was hot and still, and heavy with the drone of insects. The carp were flaunting themselves openly all over the lake, some moving quite close to the bank where I was setting up. It was idyllic.

Some time during the dark months of winter, Julie and I had taken John Curry and his wife Eileen out to dinner. Who is John Curry? John ran Fourways Fisheries and the Snowberry Syndicate and ostensibly the reason for taking him out to dinner had been to thank him for his kindnesses during the previous season. In fact, it was to try and discover the full SP about a bait that I had been getting wind of. Dinner cost an extraordinary amount of money, the information about the bait was given willingly – and the full recipe was published in Anglers' Mail the following week! (This was the Wilton bait.) A sequel to the dinner in the winter was that Julie and I were invited to the Curry's for an evening meal on the first night of the season, the conclusion to be timed so that we would be back at the water for midnight. We feasted royally, drank wine to excess and made it back in time for the ritual start.

Eventually midnight on the fifteenth of June arrived, as it always does. All the impatient anticipation was rendered meaningless, and that thought has

stayed with me. Since that session my anticipation of midnight on the fifteenth has become a long term pleasure: impatience is no longer part of the close season equation. In advance I had given much thought to choice of baits, presentation etc., but all the careful planning was rendered meaningless by the four million baby carp which had survived the winter from the previous season's spawning. From the moment of casting out the indicators were never still and the soft paste baits were vanishing as fast as I could rebait and recast.

Daylight broke, I was living through the development of a hangover, I hadn't caught a carp and the combination of a dry landing net, tiredness, hangover and small carp shredding the baits was already making the session a nightmare. I was a failure, nothing was going right; and if my anticipation of the

coming season has matured, the unnecessary anxiety over not catching immediately is still with me, much as I fight it.

About nine o' clock my mind started working.

The water was not very busy; there were perhaps six other anglers on it. The swim at the opposite corner of the island, the Planks swim under the weeping willow, was unoccupied and there were carp showing off that swim in front of the island willow. There were always carp under that willow, I was later to learn, and if you wanted to find out if a method or a bait was working, the quickest way to do so was to stick it under the fronds where they brushed the water.

I took one rod round with me and contrived to set up on the planks, which

at that time presented problems. It was a tight swim, although it's much more fishable now because over the years a number of us have made major structural alterations to it as it temporarily became our second home. I started off with a rock hard ball of bread paste – I did, honestly – and I started to get twitches, one inch lifts of the indicator. I left the bait out there an hour, during which time the indicator would lift occasionally. At the end of an hour I reeled in and was surprised to find that the bait was intact. Small fish would have made some impression on it; the indicator lifts were down to carp.

I recalled that deep in the recesses of my basket (old habits died hard), were two tins of luncheon meat, purchased, and almost used, the season before. If ever there was a moment when the pink persuader was needed, this was it. Small fish resistant (joke), irresistible to carp, previously unfished by me: I was convinced before the bait went out. Subtly I cut off a lump the size of two Swan match boxes together, stuck a shock absorber on the hook and attempted to heave the lot out to the willow. As casts to the hot spot went, it was singularly inaccurate and went in five yards to the right. There were fish there; it would do. I put the rods in the rests. The carp twitches had prompted me to take a second rod round to the temporary swim and that was cast nearer to the willow, but unintentionally short. Normally I would have recast both rods, but the limited supply of luncheon meat dictated a necessity for settling for less than perfection in the bait positioning stakes.

The Planks swim faced south and got the full impact of the sun once it had cleared the big tree on the edge of the island. I was starting to develop that nackered feeling where the edges of reality become a little fuzzy. I had brought a packet of King Edwards to toast the start of the season and was, by now, chain smoking them. The Curry's curry from the previous night was still festering inside me and starting to add to my discomfort – and I was fishless.

Relax, relax, it will happen. The cramped position exaggerated the attack of carp man's tummy and I undid my belt to ease the pressure. God, that was better. The lake started to doze in the heat of the sun and there were no signs of activity to the ten or twelve rods that were fishing. The hum of the distant traffic merged with the hum of the squadrons of insects which were just becoming alive to the fact that there were a number of unexpected meals sitting around. The early urgency was passing out of me. Ten hours into the season. I'd get my double figure fish sooner or later. But I'd like it now, then I could concentrate on anticipating my next ambition of winning the pools.

The indicator moved two inches. The anticipation heightened. Two inches was not a small fish twitch, not when it was slow and unhurried like that. I pulled it back, which was not easy with the swim laid out the way I'd got it. Five minutes and it twitched again. From memory, the lead up to the take was a protracted one, but eventually the yellow bottle top made a leisurely journey towards the second ring and a heavy resistance met the answering strike.

For a long time the first fish of each season took me by surprise in terms of the pressure they put on the tackle. I was always taken aback by the fierceness of the fight, and this fish was no exception. There were lily pads to my left so, of course, that was where it headed, and apart from the antics of the fish, I'd got another major problem on my hands. As I stood up and struck I remembered that my trousers were unfastened.

I think it must be conceded that playing a kiting fish is a two handed affair, and that playing a kiting, lively, first double figure fish is a serious two handed affair. The Planks swim is a little like the Pontoon at Cuttle Mill, in that you are in the full focus of the floodlights, and as I struck I heard someone on the wood side say, "Tim's in", or words to that effect. My trousers started to slip and I wasn't in a good position to prevent them. I didn't want to suffer any great loss of face through having my trousers fall down, but I had to give priority to the landing of this long sought prize.

If you really concentrate and focus all your willpower, it is just possible to keep your trousers up by using your hips and your thigh muscles. (If ever any of you have seen the Gymnasium snippet from an old Spencer Tracy film, you will know what I mean. I'm digressing again, I know, but it is relevant and it was one of the most hysterically funny things I've ever seen. Mr. Tracy, who was not noted for his comic roles, was the anchor man in the middle of the bottom row of a human pyramid in a gymnasium display at school, some American PTA function. The pyramid assembled itself, the bottom row braced itself under the weight from above, at which moment Mr. Tracy's wife and daughter took their places in the audience and the elastic in his shorts broke. From there I will have to leave it with your imagination.)

If this fish had at any time made its way into the open water to my right, I would have had a long enough breathing space to do something about the errant trousers; and even if I'd been able to assume my normal fish playing position, crouched down at the water's edge, it would have helped. But the carp stayed determinedly left, and there was a line of reeds about four feet high along that side of the swim, masking me from the fish, but not from the audience around the far bank. Eventually it got fed up with life under the willow and came grudgingly to the net. The first good fish of the prolific summer of 76 rolled into the net. It looked big. Was this it? Was this the longed for, long sought double figure carp? I hastily adjusted my attire before lifting the whole shooting match out of the water and staggering through the willow to the bank with it.

The fish was a mirror of nine pounds twelve ounces. I had three more carp in the next hour, all on luncheon meat, all weighing over ten pounds.

Originally I went to Snowberry armed with the knowledge that 'carp ran'. The full significance of this was lost on me at the time as I had never witnessed a full blooded carp run; my fishing at the Mill Pool had been in snaggy swims and had all been shut bail arm or float fishing. If you saw reference to carp running in the books you rather got the impression that it was a leisurely indication which made setting the hook a casual procedure to be executed with aplomb. I even saw a series of drawings in an angling weekly showing a silver paper indicator rising and falling in an easy rhythm. This was what I was looking for at Snowberry.

The reality was slightly different.

There are moments in life which make an impression disproportionate to the apparent significance of the occurrence. My first carp run was one of those moments. It was one in the morning, first Snowberry season, pitch black, raw and anxious. I had buzzers, but I didn't like using them because they offended my sensitivity, worked but spasmodically and I rarely took my eyes off the indicators anyway. Indication was by means of silver paper cylinders on wooden spears (slightly roughened) at forty five degree angles. I was getting twitches on the bed of maggots, slight scrapings of the silver paper up the spears. The first time this happened I nearly wet myself. I was becoming convinced that I would never catch a carp and this was the first sign that the impossible might become reality.

Another rustle. I peered at the silver papers anxiously, and discovered that one was missing. I had a recount. One – there should be two. I found the other one in the butt ring and realised that the repositioning was also responsible for the hissing sound that I was trying to place. I picked up the rod, shut the bail arm, and the rod was almost torn out of my hands. Setting the hook was not a problem with maggots as bait. The feeding continued well into daylight and the gut churning phenomenon of the silver paper pinned against the butt ring with line pouring through it was just as disturbing a proposition in the cold light of day as it was in the dark hours.

There is almost as great an addiction in silver paper butt ringers as there is in carp fishing itself. Undoubtedly my experience over that first weekend of howling runs influenced me greatly. There was something remote, mysterious and primeval conveyed by the sight of an indicator heralding a flat out run; something almost threatening about it. For the next three nights I dreamed about silver papers in the butt ring. At work and in the pub I picked up discarded cigarette packets and lovingly shaped the silver paper innards into cylinders fit to grace any butt ring. For three weekends all I was interested in was butt ringers. Never mind the carp, just gimme runs.

Slow lifts of the silver paper to the butt ring were ignored, however hittable a take they represented. I'd got to be in that distraught state where shutting the bail arm becomes an act of naked courage, where the silver paper represented a carp hell bent on making the other side of the lake, or the nearest snag, and woe betide anyone who tried to prevent it. That was the message I got from cavorting silver paper.

Inevitably, the effect on my carp catching was not good. The carp were now feeding over-confidently on the heavy carpet of maggots and I knew nothing of rigs to make them bolt, so I either got slow lifts that stopped after so long, which were either short confident takes or line bites, or I got butt ring

howlers which were a prelude to the line going slack from bite offs. By the time I'd sorted that out, I'd stopped getting takes altogether and my struggles were beginning – for that season.

The second season was different. This was the beautiful summer of '76 and the carp managed to cure me of my great passion for butt ringers – they surfeited me with them. How those carp fed that summer. Vivid memories come flooding back of those long, hot days and clear, cold nights, when the inhabitants of that lovely lake fed right through the dark hours and on into daylight – until the sun's appearance over Little Brickhill called a halt to the orgy. And all summer through I wrestled with the demon that butt ringers gradually became.

I was using a succession of good baits and, in common with Nigel and Ken, I caught a great many carp between five and twelve pounds, but I missed, or lost, almost as many and the succession of missed takes and losses gradually built up into a dread of the sight of that silver paper in the butt ring.

There were extenuating circumstances. The small fish problem necessitated the use of brick hard baits. I was fishing against the island, which meant that the fish were often running sideways to me, and I was freelining for reasons of economy and because of a mistaken belief that the fish were becoming leger conscious. God, didn't we labour under some misapprehensions? The reasons of economy were that most of the runs came in the dark hours, which meant recasting to the island fringes anything up to a dozen times in a good night. Freelining with big baits was cheaper than legering because retackling just cost a hook and a bit of line. I'm slightly less cautious about the wastage of leads these days, and carry an actual bomb box in the car for replenishing supplies when I'm snag fishing.

In addition, I was fishing swims surrounded by trees which made striking a precise and calculated operation, rather than an abandoned thrash. Those of you who regularly fish among trees will appreciate that I am ignoring the fact that potentially there is another chapter covering disasters occasioned by not carrying out well rehearsed routines of striking in confined spaces. "I must strike sitting down, I must strike sitting down"… Half an hour later it's away and you're standing there trying to disentangle the rod tip from the overhanging branches. (There is a definite 'law of clearances' applicable here. Whatever length of rod you use, it will be just three inches too long to allow clearance on the strike).

All were contributory factors towards my growing state of confusion, and while I look back with tolerant sympathy, and smilingly dismiss my struggles as those of a beginner, I cannot swear that I would do any better now if faced with the same combination of problems. If you think that is dumb, remember that there is now one enormous difference between then and now; in current carp fishing the hook is outside the rod hard bait, which makes setting the hook ninety nine per cent easier.

There was a gradual evolution through a variety of stages of missed takes. I started by wrestling with it manfully and trying to let the power of the mind prevail over the inadequacy of the flesh. I would have to find a way of picking up line much quicker on the strike. As I was only fishing at thirty to forty yards, I had started out using the Mk. IV's, which had a medium action, from memory in the $1^1/_2$-$1^3/_4$lb test curve range. These were replaced by North Western $2^1/_2$lb TC's and ultimately by Fibatube 132's, $3^1/_2$lb TC Loch Lomond pike rods, all in an effort to pull a hook out of a rock hard bait forty yards out. It has been some consolation in recent years to discover that many others went through the same problems with the early rock hard baits. At least at that stage I was thinking – possibly not very well, but I was thinking. I do remember stepping up the line strength to balance the tackle to the 132's so I could safely strike with the clutch wound down tight.

At some stage of the season I studied Jack Hilton's description of what to do when confronted by a butt ringer, and learnt it off by heart: his words became a sort of ritual incantation to be muttered in a vain attempt to keep ice cool. Every time the silver paper attacked the butt ring I would heroically fight the engulfing wave of total panic and drone Jack's magic words – "Pick up home, push out rod to arm's length, feel line tightening…" I read as many authorities as possible on the subject of butt ringers and came to the conclusion that few, if any, had ever actually experienced one. They'd either never had one or they had three hands, because I always seemed to be one hand short in terms of carrying out the instructions to the letter. Or perhaps these people just weren't used to fishing for carp among snags and didn't recognise the importance of setting the hook as soon as possible. Even Jack Hilton's apparently simple instructions seem to be advocating the use of three hands.

I'm right handed so I've got the rod in my right hand, right? Pick up home, that's done with the other hand, in my case the left. 'Feel line tightening'. Now I've never been entirely clear as to just when and how this part of the procedure is supposed to take place. I've got the rod in my right hand, the reel handle in my left, somewhere out there in the pitch black a carp is powering off at an apparent hundred miles an hour plus – and I'm mentally lining up the angle of the strike so that I don't clatter the rod tip into the branch that I've clobbered on the last three runs. And somewhere in all this I've got to feel the line tightening.

I did try, but the difficulty was finding time to get a hand over the tightening line so that the strike could be timed to impart optimum force to pull the hook out of the rock hard bait – before the carp dropped it on feeling the resistance of the third hand feeling the line. I tried a variation on the theme and this involved frantically pulling line off the spool to get ahead of the carp before shutting the bail arm – if you follow. In theory, this should have worked well.

The first time I tried it, I failed to get the line over the bail arm pick up and the force of the strike set in motion the famous bail arm flap, rendering the strike ineffective. To be fair, the carp were determined to let me have a real crack at getting it right so it wasn't long before the silver paper again disappeared from its resting place on the grass and relocated itself in its second home in the butt ring. Keep calm kid, for heaven's sake, keep calm. This is not easy when you are being deafened by the sound of line hissing through the silver paper and the paper flapping against the butt ring. Pick up rod. No problems so far. Pull extra line off the spool. It wasn't always possible to keep pace with the carp during this part of the exercise; little commons don't run – they hurtle. If all went according to plan, the silver paper was by now well below the butt ring. Bail arm in, silver paper hurtling towards the rod butt. Feel line tightening by clapping left hand over the front of the spool to prevent a recurrence of bail arm flap. Silver paper stops six inches from the butt ring. The carp has either died of exhaustion, dropped the bait, or is contentedly chewing same in some jungle of a snag.

I tried clapping my hand over the spool with the bail arm open, but had to have treatment for line burns. I tried every permutation of actions yet devised to execute the simple act of shutting the bail arm and striking a carp run – with varying degrees of failure. In the end I settled for letting blind panic take over whenever the silver paper hit the butt ring. It worked as well as anything.

Many of you will think there is a great deal of exaggeration in all this, but there is not. When the runs were at their most prolific, and the baits at their hardest, I finally became so confused and dejected by the whole performance that I actually turned my back on a butt ringer and went off to bed without striking. That's a terrible confession, I know, and I still find it hard to believe that runs could have induced such a mental condition. It is usually lack of action that gets you to screaming point.

Yes, many of you will have read all this in disbelief. Problems with striking runs. How quaint. Of course, it's different now with the rigs and hook out. The job is, at worst, part done by the time you pick the rod up, and if you have problems with the occasional dropped run you just cram the butt ring with foam, or stick a back stop in behind a three ounce bomb. You and I have all the time in the world to crawl out of our warm sleeping bags, complete the job the carp has obligingly half done for us, then congratulate ourselves on our competence at setting the hook. And I for one would rather have it this way, make no mistake about that.

I mourn the passing of silver paper though. I loved that; the sight of two symmetrical cylinders side by side on their spears. The rustle of silver paper up a spear is as evocative a sound as ever it was and the hiss of the line through the paper heightened the excitement of the run somehow. But memory is playing tricks with me now. It's idealising something that was far from ideal. The paper was often soggy, which made it dull and silent – and it was a torment in a wind. I once sat and watched a pair of cylinders flapping round on their spears all one night, then discovered at first light that one of the spools was empty and the paper had 'unfolded' from round the line.

Distance lends enchantment, the saying goes. For some things, yes, but not in the case of the early Snowberry days. The whole thing was a beautiful, unfathomable mystery which filled my mind seven days a week. If carp fishing is a love affair now, it was a wild infatuation then, gripping me physically and mentally paralysing me. I love the carp fishing I do now: I was utterly consumed by my carp fishing of the early Snowberry days.

Hooking a carp with the bail arm shut is not quite the terrifying experience that shutting the bail arm on a fast moving carp is, but then again, it isn't really carp fishing. It's a way of catching carp which have, over the years, learnt that to rush off across the bed of a lake or pond with some choice tit-bit in their mouth is to court disaster, and they therefore avoid doing it if at all possible. This attitude on the part of the carp is a torment to genuine carp fishers. Those who tire of catching small fish are placed in a dilemma. Either they join the new breed of carp men and seek *the bait*, a ball of expensive chemicals so irresistible to carp that even the oldest and wisest cannot avoid one of the long resisted headlong dashes to perditions, or they learn to become anglers.

Learning to be an angler all over again naturally goes against the grain with most carp men. They are men of 'dogged infinite patience' who will happily sit for a week or two for a few butt ringers and a couple of decent carp – but sitting for a week or two waiting for butt ringers and *fishing* for a week or two are very different things. Certainly, your genuine carp fisher may move from his pitch occasionally to make the odd dawn and dusk sortie to the lily pads at the corner of the pool with a stalking rod, and if weather conditions alter dramatically he may even move pitch altogether, but part of the attraction of carp fishing is the slowness. Sooner or later the carp will turn up and on an open bail arm set-up, even if you do happen to be doing something else at the very moment of a take ('doing something else' is a science in its own right for attracting takes), the carp will continue its headlong dash until you have time to deal with it.

However, times, waters and carp's habits change, and no true carp man will go indefinitely without some tale to tell that finishes with the capture of a big fish. If the carp he is fishing for cease to give butt ringers, and he himself is reluctant to expend a week's income on a few balls of bait, then fish for them he must. This will, more than likely, mean blundering into the strange new world that shut bail arm fishing can be. To put it mildly, shut bail arm fishing for carp requires a greater degree of alertness than open bail arm methods. That is an understatement. On some waters shut bail arm fishing (twitcher hitting) requires razor sharp reflexes and constant vigilance, and on others it requires enormous patience and an ability to 'read' what the carp at the other end of the line are doing.

In the first article I ever wrote, which was on the subject of short tail legering, I naively suggested that 'a carp cannot move from stationary to flat out in four feet'. Oh, the innocence of my early carp fishing days! Technically, that may be true, but having now fished a much wider variety of waters I am inclined to think that on some waters they are as near flat out as makes no difference within a much shorter distance than that. On these waters twitcher hitting can be a very trying business, but on others the carp often give a series of predictable 'pulls' on the indicator which can lead to a successful strike by the exercise of vigilance and patience.

I can remember precisely what I was doing when I became mentally converted to the necessity of twitcher hitting. I was replacing a silver paper indicator on its spear in the planks swim at Snowberry Lake one Saturday morning in late September. It was the difficult summer of 1977 and the surfeit of butt ringers the previous season had given way to a famine. Those same carp which had so enthusiastically tried to commit hari-kari just twelve months earlier, were now giving butt ringers at a rate of roughly one every three weeks.

Twitcher Hitting

Jim Gibbinson in his Bysing Wood days, with a 14lb mirror, one of a catch of 10 doubles taken in an afternoon. That sort of result can give you a severe inferiority complex in your early carp days. If the truth be known it still does!

For three months I had been ringing the changes on baits, but always with the same result; as soon as the fish felt the indicator, it left the bait. I don't know how many times I had put silver papers back on spears, but that particular time was obviously the straw that broke the ass's back. It took three months, but eventually I got the message. The carp were obviously just not hungry enough to get silly and take risks, but apparently they were hungry enough to try each offering to see if there was a hook in it. Ideal twitcher hitting circumstances, I felt.

There was only one carp man writing authoritative technical articles in the popular press on carp fishing at that time, so I set about studying the gospel according to Jim Gibbinson. If the Kent boys could do it, so could I. And there it was in black and white:

"There are those waters where, for most of the season, you'll wait in vain if you wait for runs. You either gear your fishing to deal with twitch bites or you don't catch anything – it's as simple as that".

How succinctly put; what a pleasing turn of phrase this schoolmaster from Kent has. I read on. Hook length fifteen inches, link nine inches; more or less the rig I was using anyway. An emphasis on the use of buzzers occasioned a trip into Bletchley for new batteries and aroused reservations about the reliability of my old Herons. I had never attached any undue significance to the fact that they buzzed occasionally – they had always appeared to be activated more by fluctuations in temperature than by carp interference – but I spent much of the evening scraping rust out of the buzzer unit and that seemed to help. Bottle top indicators; no problem there, plenty of those. I have a strange assortment of indicators made from plastic tubing but I always revert to yellow bottle tops in daylight, they are somehow pleasingly aesthetically jarring against the rest of the matt-blacked ensemble. *"Indicator 18 inches below the rod".* My reflexes should be able to cope with that, but would the carp lift it that far? *"Gradually wind the bobbin up with each successive twitch till your reflexes are geared to cope with the tiniest movement".* That sounded like hard work, but I could see what he was getting at.

I liked the next bit. *"One afternoon I took six double fish in quick succession using the method just described…"* But he then went on to say that as far as twitcher hitting goes, he was not in the same league as Bob Morris, Cliff Webb and Robin Monday. The mind boggled. How many doubles were they in the habit of hooking in quick succession? I put away the magazine and went to bed to try and sleep off the sudden inferiority complex which had descended on me. Six double figure fish was a good season for me – not an afternoon.

Next day was nice. It was better than that, it was the sort of day that reminds you what life's about. The carp had not been feeding early so I was in no hurry, and it was after eight when I crept under the weeping willow and onto the Planks pitch. I had to alter the whole pitch to a twitcher hitting base, which meant re-arranging rod rests and seating arrangements so that I was sitting on the rods and not three yards behind them. I cast a floating bait out on an open bail arm while I changed things round, and had a run immediately from a mirror of about nine pounds. Perhaps I'd better leave a top bait out, that's how I had been catching most of my fish anyway – but six doubles in quick succession, that was a strong temptation. I went for three bottom rods and gave the floaters a rest. I was fishing small, flavoured, sardine baits against the island willow on two rods, having narrowed that down to the bait which the carp were ignoring least, and tiny bits of luncheon meat on the other. I sat there for an hour or two and nothing happened. It was very pleasant, a beautiful early autumn day; the sun was above the island trees by now and the day was warming up. It had been a disappointing season by Snowberry standards and there were only a couple of other anglers on the lake.

A buzzer sounded and the left hand indicator started to climb; my right hand had a cigarette in it at the time so the lightning grab for the rod butt was a bit delayed while I transferred it to my mouth – by which time the indicator had stopped. I consoled myself that it wasn't hittable anyway, but mentally chalked it up as one that Jim and the boys would have had. Clearly, cigarettes and twitcher hitting were not compatible. I would have to try and smoke with my left hand.

The sun moved round clear of the tall silver birch on the island and I was now in what should have been the main feeding time. A further twitch to the left hand rod; this must be the succession of twitches Jim wrote of. I wound the bottle top up to within six inches of the rod and grasped the corks in anticipation. The bottle top on the second rod shot up a foot then stopped. Then the same thing happened on the third rod. I looked like a learner going up the scales on a piano as my hand leapt from rod to rod.

Two o'clock and the sun was swinging across the top of the woods opposite and starting its slide towards Bletchley. The indicators had moved seven or eight times and I hadn't even struck yet. Bob Morris and his mates would fall about watching this performance. I adjourned to the caravette for a fresh supply of coffee and cigarettes and had a rethink.

I had read an article some time previously by 'Black Majician', Dick Weale, suggesting that you pull the bait back after each abortive twitch on shut bail arm set ups; I would try this. While Jim didn't mention it, it had worked well for me with freelined baits, and I had seen many references to 'teased twitchers' in carp mags. Perhaps Norfolk carp liked twitched baits and Kent carp didn't. I'd try that. I also cut down to two twitcher rods in an effort to speed up my reactions (I went back to a floater on the third rod and caught a seven pound odd mirror almost straight away). About an hour later, the indicator on the right hand rod moved up six inches, then stopped. I couldn't reach it from my seat so I moved round to the other side of the rods and pulled it back down to twitch the bait. Or at least I started to pull it back down; I'd become so immersed in what I was trying to do that I'd ignored the standard precaution of checking the line where it enters the water after a half take. I should have checked because I suspect that the carp was lying with the bait in its mouth. No sooner had I started to pull the bottle top down than it was torn from my fingers and cracked into the second ring – and the carp let go. I think I possibly swore.

The afternoon drifted on, I kept trying to remember to smoke with my left hand, and tied myself in all sorts of knots trying to stay alert while I poured coffee and lit cigarettes. Calls of nature were a hazard and on return from such trips I fully expected to see one of the indicators in the 'you have just had a take' position, one inch from the second ring, but this was one of those rare days when that frequent indignity was not heaped upon me.

No further movement for an hour; almost time to go round to the caravette for the football results (I really roughed it in those days). I wound the bottle tops up to within six inches of the rods and gave a sharp tug on each line to twitch the baits slightly. Just as I straightened up from the rods, the indicator on the right hand one slowly climbed the six inches to the rod. I struck on a tight line and made contact! The carp moved slowly and sedately down the lake to my right. I don't think it realised, initially, that it was hooked and as it was swimming away from the island towards the middle of the lake I wasn't in a hurry to antagonise it. After it had swum about thirty yards, I increased pressure: and the carp seemed to suddenly realise what was going on and turned directly away from me. I started back-winding to cope with the sudden run, but the line went slack.

Such moments are best experienced in splendid isolation. The beauty of the late September afternoon was forgotten and I threw the rod into the rushes to the right of the pitch without even winding in. I was very disenchanted with carp, twitcher hitting and life at that moment. I felt I had earned that fish and had lost him.

I went and had tea and listened to the football results – but Wednesday had lost yet again, so that didn't help much. I presumed that I had pulled out of the fish and it wasn't until I wound in later that I discovered that the line had parted above the hook. I am very careful about line and there was certainly insufficient pressure for a genuine break on seven pound BS, so I could only think that I had lost the fish as the result of a belated bite-off.

I started again at dusk and found the whole twitcher hitting business much easier in the dark with isotope indicators, in addition to which the carp seemed to be more willing to give a readable series of twitches after dark than in daylight. The final 'take', which was, at best, a lift of no more than five or six inches, was usually the culmination of an hour's twitching, and sometimes I had to repeatedly twitch the bait to revive interest (or to interest another carp). I had caught carp on shut bait arm rigs prior to that day, but had never managed to hook genuine twitchers before, so I was delighted with the two fish I caught during that evening, a mirror and a common, a little under twelve pounds each.

Fishing for carp with the bail arm shut is not easy. I don't know why it should be that carp vary so much in their taking patterns from water to water, but they do. Snowberry carp responded well to twitched baits and set off with the bait reasonably slowly, which made them an ideal congregation on which to practise twitcher hitting. But my experience is that Snowberry is an exception, rather than a rule, and out of the dozen or so carp waters I have fished with any sort of regularity, there is only one other where the carp's behaviour is anything like similar. On most others, takes are explosive. Until you have actually seen an indicator move the four feet from ground to rod in a snap of the fingers it takes some believing, but it happens commonly enough on hungry, hard fished waters where being hooked is part of a carp's way of life.

I have seen a number of theories put forward as to why carp do bolt off with the bait and I think that the basic reason is that it is startled – either it is startled by some outside agency, or it startles itself. Dick Walker gives a very pleasing explanation of the 'startles itself' theory in 'Still Water Angling':

"...a carp will look at it, go away, return, taste, eject, retreat, and so on for a very long time, usually finishing by taking the bait very gingerly and bolting in alarm at its own temerity."

What have carp which run with the bait got to do with shut bait arm tactics? Simply this. Don't be ruled by fishing shut bail arm methods. Some carp are probably genuine twitchers and will never run with the bait, but I suspect that others have twitching forced on them. Most twitcher rigs are based on short tail legering principles so that when an already suspicious carp suddenly gets this overwhelming urge to pick up a totally unnatural cube of luncheon meat, or ball of paste, it has got to convince itself that it is safe to do so. It will not increase the carp's confidence on picking up the bait to feel the friction of the leger-link swivel, the pull of fifty yards of line through the water, the resistance of the buzzer antenna and the weight of the indicator on the line.

If I'm confronted by twitching carp I try two approaches, the standard twitcher one, and also trying to increase the carp's confidence by removing all the paraphernalia off the line at the rod end and opening the bail arm. A loop of line hanging down from the spool is not difficult to watch in daylight, and very often a carp which keeps twitching a silver paper cylinder off a spear, or off a groundsheet, will run off in a state of confusion when it fails to encounter the anticipated resistance.

Jim Gibbinson is right, of course. There are some waters where the only way you will catch your share of the carp is to fish for them by sitting on the rods and learning to understand each movement of the indicator. If you do become a disciple of the gospel according to Jim, heed his concluding words well or you are in for a frustrating time:

"Don't be discouraged if you aren't successful immediately… …gradually timing, technique and confidence will come. And once mastered, it will produce a hell of a lot of carp that otherwise wouldn't have come your way."

Two Snowberry teased twitchers.

Ah yes. Here it comes, you will be saying; the monster that never was. Well, no, it's not quite like that. Yes, I've had my moments of heart-break when I've wanted the ground to open up and swallow me; when the line has gone slack after I've been connected to SOMETHING ELSE for anything from ten seconds to ten minutes and I've been left shaking, speechless and wanting to cry. But that's part of the game; we court great triumphs and risk great disasters and such are the frustrations of carp fishing that only the fortunate few taste the former without suffering their share of the latter.

No, this fish was different. For a start it wasn't all that big, although it may well have seemed so at the time at around… well, does it matter? The significance of a weight lies in the eyes of the beholder. It certainly didn't depart unseen because it spent some time almost in the net, and when it did come off I actually laughed because the fight had been… well, memorable. Not that my companion, who had been trying to net the fish, took the loss that lightly. She stomped off furiously into the woods without a word and I didn't see her for a couple of hours.

It was the start of the maize storm at Snowberry. I'd been feeding it in but it looked so unappetising that I hadn't the bottle to actually fish it. It really is incredible how dumb you can be when you look back, if you know what I mean. I think the certain knowledge that carp were hard to catch impaired my thinking for years. The first time I baited up with maize a couple of carp leapt over it within minutes of it going in.

"That's strange" I thought.

Carp didn't usually leap there. The thought never even crossed my mind that the leaping was possibly connected with the maize! To be fair, I didn't know at that time that maize was an acknowledged carp bait; there was a certain secrecy surrounding the subject then. Having said which there's not much point in baiting up if you ignore the vote of confidence the carp promptly accord you. I drove off home, still without an ounce of confidence in the maize, and it was a month before I finally tried to fish it.

When I did eventually get round to putting some on the hook I found that I'd got a major technical problem on account of the hardness of the stuff. I was boiling it for anything up to two hours but it still wouldn't take a hook, so after much thought I attached it to the hook with – I daren't tell you this – one pound line. No, I'm not laying any belated claim to the discovery of the hair because that wasn't how I was attaching it. I was sewing about eight or ten grains together in a ball and burying the hook in the middle of this ball. It sounds unbelievable and that just about sums up the results on the method – unbelievable.

I've always done a fair amount of float fishing for carp and that was how I started on the maize, laying on with this ball of maize under a quill float against the lily pads in the car park swim, shaded by the massive chestnut and flanked by a weeping silver birch and a gelder rose. (I looked that one up because the bush was so beautiful). It was mid-afternoon and I cast out with all the confidence and enthusiasm of an angler who has a lump of coal on the hook. I was out of the wind and the red tipped quill lay at half cock in the still surface. I was sitting on the wooden steps that lead down to the water at that spot and I don't suppose it mattered much that I'd got an inedible bait out there. It was idyllic.

The One That Got Away

Ten minutes after I'd cast out, the float stirred gently, went round in a tight circle, then stopped and returned to its original position. What happened there? Clearly, something was moving in the vicinity of the bait, although from the actions of the float I got the impression that it was fish moving against the line rather than paying attention to the bait itself. Still, it must have had something to do with the bait, surely?

The float stirring went on for a frustrating and patience straining twenty minutes and I was really beginning to doubt that it was a carp, when the float jerked a couple of times then slid smoothly under and away. I struck carp.

I had, at that time, had enough disasters with the overhanging chestnut to ensure that I stayed sitting down while I struck, but I still automatically braced myself for the crash of the rod tip on timber as I struck. There was none; I could concentrate on what was happening in front of me and, predictably, the fish was moving right at a fair rate of knots. I say predictably, but really, anywhere other than straight into the net was bad news in that swim. There were trees to the left, lily pads in front to the right and immediately to the right the fronds of the weeping birch hung down into the water, a feature which had attracted me to the swim in the first place.

You will all have experienced that particularly delicate moment when the rod is up from the strike and has to come down very quickly to keep the line away from the inevitable overhanging branch – but you can't bring it down too quickly because you have got to keep the pressure on. Anyway, the overhang won by a short head and the line snagged at water line, but came free when I buried the rod tip under water and heaved. The line came free but the fish was unimpressed and continued its journey down the bank to my right.

The gelder rose on my left prevented me getting enough real pressure on the fish to get it moving back towards me, but the spot it was trying to get to wasn't bad from my point of view. My troubles would start if it decided to swing out from the bank on the twenty yards of line it had gained, because it had enough line to make it to the lilies. No, I agree, it should not have had that much line at that stage, but when did you ever play a carp that did exactly as you wanted it to?

As it was clearly reluctant to come back towards me of its own free will, my only option was to go and join it – the twin obstacles in the path of achieving this objective being the previously mentioned beautiful weeping silver birch trunk three yards to my right and its brother chip five yards beyond. They were both too close to the water for me to manoeuver round the front of the trunk without getting a soaking, which wasn't part of my plans, so the only alternative was to pass the rod round the front of the trunk from one hand to the other, while maintaining pressure on the fish, keeping my balance and preserving my dignity. As I got the rod into my right hand it bent round even further and I had to rapidly regain a grip with both hands. I was now between the two birches and had room to get more pressure on and move the fish back towards me. It decided it wanted to go left anyway.

It was nice under the birches but the branches were rather low, and while I could keep sidestrain pressure on with the rod held low, I had considerable problems in terms of having the fish in front of me, or getting the rod up to land the fish. By this time the carp was clearly watching my every action with interest, because its next move smacked of the calculated cunning of a chess

player who has been studying his opponent's last move for an hour. The worst thing that could possibly happen, just at that moment, was that the carp reached the other side of the rather attractive fronds – which caressed the water some distance in front of me – and then come up to the surface; so that's what it did. How could it possibly know that that would lead to stalemate? I couldn't move it from there. I would have to go back round the tree to the original spot so that I could exert enough pressure to clear the line from the overhang.

I passed the rod back from right hand to left hand, which is a far dicier performance than vice versa when you are right handed. Now if the fish would come out to the left and the line would come clear of the fronds at the same time, I would be able to cram enough pressure on to get it on a short line. You'll have to understand that, at that time, I didn't know about exerting pressure in one direction to get the fish moving in the other – and if I had, this fish wouldn't have bought it anyway. The carp went back down to the right, the line came free of the overhang, and Julie arrived.

"Have you got one?"

I never did have the feeling that I'd 'got' that particular one, but confirmed that I was indeed attached to one.

The fish was considering its next move while attempting to return to its unknown position of some time previously, down the right hand bank.

I didn't fancy the scramble round the tree again and by now Julie was holding the net with the air of someone who expected to be using it in the next couple of minutes. She did a fair bit of carping in those days and her playing of a hooked fish did lack a certain finesse: she just used to hit them and then winch them into the net – it was brutal to watch – and couldn't understand why I was pussy-footing around with this one.

The carp was tiring by this time, mentally and physically, I guessed, and increasing side pressure started to bring it. The gelder rose on my left forced me to pump the fish to me with short sideways movements of the rod, but it slowly came along parallel to the bank towards the expectant net of my friend. It was clearly seen to be a double figure carp of quite beautiful scaling and possibly big enough to be a personal best, which would put it at twelve poundish.

The fish was under the trees, but coming nicely. Because it was still under the trees, I was having to keep my rod low to the water and – well this bit is hard to explain. The Herons were straight in front of me and, of course, I was focussing my full attentions on this Kasparov of the carp world. As I completed one of the short pumping strokes to bring the fish to me – it would be about a yard from the net at this stage – the line between the first and second rings somehow got caught round the tension screw at the side of the Heron. No, I don't know how, but it did. Now you will have to shut your eyes for a moment and imagine the predicament I was in then, because the fish was *right*, my rod tip was *left*, and the line was hooked round the buzzer head straight in front of me.

Twelve pounds of carp puts a fair bit of tension in the line, so there was no way I could unhook the errant line from round the buzzer screw without easing the pressure on the line, thus on the rod tip and, inevitably, on the hook hold. The carp sensed that there was something amiss and just lay completely still about a yard from the net, with my friend telling me to bring it a bit further in please because she couldn't quite reach it. She didn't quite phrase it as

42

reasonably as that. Her language failed to match her undoubted physical beauty at times.

Yes, I have worked out since what I might have done, but then I didn't expect to lose the fish. I worked out that if I reeled hard as I moved the rod from left to right across the top of the buzzer, I could keep the pressure on the hook hold and free the line from the Heron screw all in one movement, then sweep the fish into the net with the next pull of the rod. I put the plan into operation.

Of course the chess players amongst you will have worked out what happened next. As I made my move the carp made his. I kept the pressure on as I swung the rod from left to right and plucked the line clear of the adjusting screw. Unhurriedly the carp righted itself and moved from right to left. The bend came out of the rod, the hook dropped out, the carp swam back from whence it came, the net holder stalked off into the woods with a face like thunder and I sat there laughing and re-living the previous half hour.

How can you explain to a woman that that was the right end game? It was adjudicated a draw and the carp and I went our separate ways, both convinced that we'd won.

Snowberry
Remembered

I'm including this piece in the book because it's the only published article for which I've ever been complimented!My own feelings about it are bitter sweet. I like the piece and it brings back many happy memories of the Mill. The two characters central to the story were my old friends, Bob Sellars and Pat Brady. Bob is still with us. Sadly, Pat, who was a lovely man, older than most of us in the game (at the time) but as daft as anyone about it, died at his beloved Cuttle Mill shortly before the article appeared. In accordance with his last wishes, his ashes were scattered from the Pontoon by Bob and Pat's other closest carp fishing friend, Martin Preece. Pat is now a pleasant memory whose company and friendship I enjoyed. Here's to you, old friend.

A thousand years ago, when the earth was flat and twenty pound carp were still thought to be big, I fished a water called Cuttle Mill. It's a beautiful place with gentle people and the picturesque lakes are stocked with reasonably catchable carp. It was watched over by two lovely people called Albert and Lil Brewer and they brought pleasure and carp to deprived carp men who didn't cast a mile and a half, couldn't understand advanced biochemistry and weren't plugged into the 'carp waters' grapevine.

Obviously what follows is pure invention. It came in a dream and I woke up and wrote it as I'd dreamt it. Or was it the other way round? Did I live through the dream then have problems relating it to reality? Be it invention or reality, it is born of affection for a water I love and carp men whose friendship I value. I thank them for their agreement to this being published, but let no one think that I am laughing at them. I think too much of them and have laughed too many times with them for that. I do not assess people by their ability to catch carp, or to cast a hundred yards, or because they are model citizens. In truth, I know of few who are good at these things – and certainly none who have mastered all three. Friendship is an intangible thing which defies definition.

I was sitting on my bed-chair at the Mill on a warm, breezy, late July morning. Deeppocket was the best part of a hundred miles away in Middlesex. Addiction had given way to compulsion and he'd vanished for the summer. That's the good news, then it gets better.

You can't help liking the Pontoon. It's like being on the stage – great if you're good enough to carry it off, but you feel like a lemon if you get on there and don't catch. I can't ever remember having had that feeling there. I'd drawn the Pontoon to myself, or on my own. Whoever was going to fish the other side still hadn't arrived. (It's two swims for those of you who don't know the Mill.) Opposite me the sun was making an eerie appearance out of the mist over the Long Pool, and the early morning haze was roofed over by a pale blue sky. It was peaceful and unbelievably quiet. The baits were out, the rods were in their rests, I was gently drifting and all was very right with the world. It was half past seven and I'd been up the best part of three hours, mixing baits and having breakfast. I was experimenting with three different bait mixes, none of which seemed to be working.

Pat and Bob were due there for a couple of days. I'd been there two days and had been struggling slightly without Deeppocket's guidance on the bait mixes, but I'd changed the ingredients that morning. So I was sitting, drifting, at peace with the world, when someone fell into the water at the back of the Pontoon.

"That'll be Pat now", I thought.

I was right. This dripping wet figure crawled onto the Pontoon and said cheerfully, "Morning Matt".

Pat was used to such setbacks and took them in his stride. "Can you give me a hand to fish my stuff out of the water?"

I duly obliged. Let's be fair, the walkway over the water is fairly narrow, although I've never seen anyone else fall off it twice in one day. Not sober anyway. I consoled him on his bit of bad luck and he took it philosophically.

"It's a warm day. I'll soon dry out".

We exchanged the standard pleasantries that carp anglers trade when they haven't seen each other for a couple of months. He tried to look pleased about the fish I'd been catching and I tried to look concerned that he hadn't been catching. And all the time we were talking I had this gnawing doubt at the back of my mind about Pat's casting.

It was warming up on the Pontoon and he had put his chair up. He took his Barbour off and hung it over the back of the seat and I watched with detached interest as the whole shooting match did a slow motion back flip into the water. I quickly recovered it for him.

He tackled up then went to change. He hadn't cast out up to that point, which was fortunate because his casting was slightly unorthodox. He put the bait into the water by means of a round arm sweep. His bait started somewhere behind his left ankle and he swung round with the rod at waist height. Had I known that he was going to join me on the Pontoon, I would have set up on the left hand side and done battle with the four fast tapers which were menacingly pointing like machine guns through the bushes round Spud Alley. However, I like to have one bait tight behind the lilies off the old fallen tree pitch, so I'd set up on the right, which meant that I was likely to get an earful of protein every time Pat cast.

He returned, dry and comfortable. Well, he almost returned dry and comfortable. I'm sure he'd have been alright if he hadn't tried to speak and cross the walkway at the same time, but when he was half way across he tried to tell me that Bob still hadn't arrived. I half turned round out of politeness and watched in amazement as he stood on one leg and flailed the air like a frantic windmill. He almost looked as if he was trying to fly across. I helped him onto the Pontoon amid complaints from Spud Alley. I told him to get some dry clothes out of my brolly camp in the car park and rigged a handrail alongside the walkway with rod rests and guy ropes while he was gone. He came back ready to fish. The breeze was freshening from our right and conditions looked good.

Unfortunately, Pat had a further problem. Bob was bringing the baits and hadn't arrived. I could have let him have some of mine, but how could I? They weren't working, but they would if I gave him some. Full marks to him, he didn't ask; he ferreted in his box of tricks and pulled out a ball of bait. Well, I think it was a ball of bait. You don't need me to tell you what a two week old ball of protein looks like in a hot spell. He wanted to peel the fungus off but I though it was his best chance and persuaded him to leave it on.

"Do you want me to cast for you?" I asked hopefully.

"No, I've been practising. I'll be all right".

I could see from his back swing that his idea of alright and mine differed somewhat. I rolled off the bed chair and flattened myself in a sudden search for a lost hook. On reflection, it was precipitate of me and it clearly unnerved him.

He swung half round and his end tackle flew in a flat trajectory across the face of Spud Alley. I thought for a horrible minute that he was going to fall in again, but he retained his balance at the expense of his hat, which was one of those snap brim creations that so many of us wear. Mine's got out of control and I can't see out from under it now.

The hat started to drift down towards the machine gun nest and Pat, having regained his composure, started to retrieve line. One of the machine guns disappeared and a voice said, "Missed it".

"Hang on, you're across my line", Pat said loudly. Attack is definitely the best means of defence.

"I'll go and get your hat", I said hurriedly and shot round to Spud Alley.

You've seen them a thousand times – steel eyed, chiselled features, smooth as aftershave adverts. I'd have sent Deeppocket round if he'd been there. I switched on the old charm.

"Please can we have our hat and tackle back?" He was disentangling Pat's end tackle from his line. He gave me a long, searching look when he saw the bait. Even I was slightly lost for words, but I had to say something. I glanced round nervously and said, "Try not to say anything. We're field testing it for Duncan".

As soon as I mentioned Duncan's name, this kid looked at me as though I were Dick Walker himself.

"D'yer know Duncan, mite?"

I gathered he was from southern climes. I wasn't quite sure how to answer. I mean, for some obscure reason people accuse me of name dropping but, in all honesty, I've never, in my whole life, met anyone the mention of whose name I would consider to be name dropping, if you know what I mean, and with due respect to the splendid Duncan. I mean, if I claimed that I had slept with Sophia Loren, well, all the previous highlights of my life would be relegated to second place and mention of the occurrence would be name dropping. (In the event of Miss Loren reading this, I should add that I am the soul of discretion and that the occasion, should it arise, would be just as memorable for her as it would be for me.) Grief, where was I? These things get sillier. I settled for an enigmatic smile and he continued.

"Is there any chance of getting hold of any of Duncan's stuff?"

I wasn't sure which stuff he meant so I smiled even more enigmatically and hurried back to the Pontoon. Pat had got both rods in the rod rests, bottle tops swinging in the freshening breeze. I reeled in and changed one of the baits. It was supposed to be instant and wasn't being.

Pat had been tidying up, which was roughly the equivalent of me spring cleaning the flat. The Barbour was back on his chair and he'd put his brolly up to the sun to dry some of his stuff on.

I'll pause a minute while I collect my thoughts. I'm not quite sure of the sequence of the events that followed, because I was busy watching a carp play water polo with a floater in the middle of the pool. I was just thinking, "Great, time for floating baits", when Pat said, "Bob's here".

At the same time, one of his Optonics started its intermittent bleep, which rapidly became continuous as his bottle top hit the second ring and the reel handle started spinning.

We leapt up in astonishment; his chair did a quick back flip into the lake;

his umbrella fell over sideways and his hat blew off. Notwithstanding all that, he joyously struck, almost severing his left thumb on the wildly spinning reel handle; he was oblivious to all pain and chaos.

"Carp on", he shouted, Jack Hilton style.

Now, with some people I might have been just a little bit envious, but in the circumstances I couldn't possibly be. I was well chuffed for him – and I was too busy. I quickly rescued his chair and coat and made a mental note of the direction in which his hat and umbrella were travelling. Towards Spud Alley, obviously, and, by a strange coincidence, the fish was some sixty yards away on the Spud Alley side of the lake. It looked to be far enough away for me to nip round and recover the errant tackle. The line was arrowing through the water towards the house and I suggested to Pat that he stop the fish and start playing it, while I started the salvage operation.

Nervously I made my way round to the machine gun nest and bombarded the whizz kids with slightly hysterical humour, part of which was totally lost on them.

"Sorry about the intrusion lads".

"Okie mite".

Duncan's name seemed to have worked wonders.

"What is it your mite's using; what is that new bite of Duncan's?"

That put me in a difficult position. I ad-libbed with a total disregard for the truth.

"Oh, it's a culture. Actually, that one's an ultra-culture".

They looked suitably impressed and I just managed to keep my face straight. We only had to reel in two of their lines to recover the umbrella. The hat sailed in up the margins anyway.

Meanwhile, back on the Pontoon, Pat was slowly winning his epic battle. The carp was among my three lines by this time, so it was obviously getting close. Pat had blood pouring down his wrist and was looking anxious, I presumed about the carp and not the fact the he was possibly bleeding to death and was certainly emptying my three spools.

I located the landing net under three soggy jumpers and Pat's Barbour. Much to my surprise, he got the fish over the net at the first time of asking. It was a good fish too – fifteen pounds four ounces, from memory.

After we'd taken the pictures, sorted out the chaos, cleared up the mess and put fresh tackle and baits out, I turned to the jubilant Pat and asked,

"What was that bait originally?"

"Red Slyme".

I made some unworthy and unprintable reply.

Next day, Pat decided to fish with Bob on the Centre Bank, the causeway between the two lakes.

I was still fishing the Pontoon under the three day rule. The previous afternoon had been almost normal after the traumas of the morning. Pat had a couple of smaller fish and I'd had a near twenty on a mix I was getting anxious about. I didn't feel that the bait was right, but I was going to persevere with the successful one, and try a new instant one.

I had a pleasant Brummy lad for company. Basic, as most carp men are: the ones you read about are from another planet. He was fishing an enormous crust on one rod and a cube of luncheon meat on the other. He was very quiet. Apart from the opening "Good morning", he more or less pretended I wasn't there for quite some time. In fact, it was an odd sort of day altogether.

It was beautiful again. I'd had a new bait out about fifteen minutes when the silver paper hit the butt ring and stuck there. It was a mirror, twelve pounds odd. Quarter of an hour off for weighing and photo. Recast. Another quarter of an hour. Same bait, butt ringer, mirror, fourteen pounds odd. Weighing, photo, recast, silver paper, leather, fourteen pounds odd. Throughout this whole performance, this kid on my left never took his eyes off his crust, except to watch me mould another ball of bait on the hook. He couldn't really miss the bait because it was a bright yellow one.

After I'd rebaited and recast the third time, he said in a gentle Brummy drawl and with a wry grin, "Do you mind if I ask you something?"

"Not at all". I was in a good mood and got ready to parry some searching questions about the bait.

"Do you never use bread?"

After the third fish, things went quiet and I had a chance to have a coffee and relax - and to watch the performance on the far bank.

Pat and Bob were in the middle of the bank, roughly in what were swims four and five, from memory. There was a tree to the right hand side of Pat's swim. Bob was also on his right, but far enough away not to be a hazard. I'd forgotten all about them until I saw this tree shaking and Pat waving his rod around. Bob joined him and they gazed seriously up into the tree for some time, then eventually freed the tackle. After that I sat and watched them. I knew that sooner or later I would have to go and knock another instant bait mix together, but I tend to lose a bit of interest in the fish once I've caught a couple. Not that I'm suggesting that my catch of that morning was earth shaking, but it was sufficient to keep me happy for a while.

If I said earlier that being on the Pontoon was like being on a stage, then I meant it, but watching Pat and Bob perform on the far bank, which is perhaps four or five feet higher than the Pontoon, was like watching two actors performing a mime from the stalls, with the difference being that it wasn't always possible to interpret all the actions.

I soon gathered that Pat's bait mix was too soft, but he apparently didn't have an alternative, or believed in that one so much that it had just got to be out there. He would cast, retrieve, rebait, cast, retrieve, rebait, one into the tree, play the tree for a while, occasionally retackle then start again. He averaged one into the tree for roughly every two or three into the water and roughly one into the water with a bait on per dozen abortive casts. It seemed to go on for ever before he settled behind his rods.

What this kid on the left must have thought I don't know. You know what it's like when something's amusing you but you're trying to suppress your mirth – like when you're reading something outrageously funny on a crowded bus and you don't want to laugh out loud. You sit there, getting red in the face, squeaking, yelping and shaking like something going demented. So I was sitting there on the Pontoon, the complete carp tiger with three doubles under my belt, snap brim pulled down onto my nose, inscrutably gazing out across the water and periodically emitting squeaks and yelps and shaking like something going demented. To his eternal credit, this kid didn't mention it; he probably thought it was some sort of attack which would pass off, a condition that was just part of the price you pay for double figure carp.

Then it got worse and the squeaks and yelps and shaking escalated to potential hysteria. The wind was getting quite strong by this time and when there is a strong wind at the Mill there is a very heavy pull on the water, so heavy that it could almost be related to the Seven Bore. (I've wrestled with that but I'm not going to make a joke out of it. Supply your own.) So when the pull is on the first thing to do is to bury the rod tips deep into the water to partially overcome it. On the middle bank, which Bob and Pat were fishing, this is a problem, let's be clear about that. It is a high bank and to really bury the rod tips, the front rod rests have to be pushed into the water at the edge of the lake itself, rather than into the swim at the top of the bank. No sooner had Pat got himself settled behind his rods than he started to have problems with the drag. I guessed that was the reason for the new pantomime, because I started to have the same problem at about the same time.

I could see that Pat's rests were positioned at the top of the bank so when he suddenly reeled in both lines I deduced that they were either going for a meal, which was a pretty frequent occurrence in their party, or that the rests were about to be repositioned at the bottom of the bank. I had just adjusted my front rests, guessed that they were about to do the same and hysterics set in with a vengeance.

Bob is taller, younger and more athletic than Pat, so he got the job. I watched him lie on his stomach and push the two rod rests, with the buzzers on, into position, which he managed quite comfortably and without mishap, so that seemed to be the end of that.

The next time I looked across though, I got a nasty jolt because Bob had got the landing net in the water; but there was no sign of a fish and no bent rod in evidence, so I couldn't understand it. The landing net bit went on for quite some time; perhaps the lad was just practising for later. However, the next manoeuvre made it clear that one of them had dropped something into the water, which hardly came as a surprise after the previous day's performance.

My suppressed giggling and latent hysteria rapidly neared the uncontrollable stage. Bob rolled his sleeves up, lay down on the concrete of the swim and gently lowered himself down to the water while Pat knelt between his legs and held them, wheelbarrow fashion. By now I sounded like a donkey with a bad attack of asthma and I could see out of the corner of my tear filled eye, that my slow smiling Brummy neighbour was casting anxious glances in my direction. He obviously didn't know my two friends across the water, so had no idea what was wrong with me, and could certainly have no concept of the humour of it. On top of the previous day, the anticipation of what seemed imminent was too much for me.

I was watching them intently by this time, not really having a clue what they were up to. Suddenly, both their heads whipped sharply to their right, towards Bob's swim. My imagination briefly took over. I lost control and emitted a half suppressed hysterical yelp. Clearly Bob had a run.

Well, do you know what I mean when I say that for a moment, time stood still? The projector stuck and the film froze.

There was Pat, kneeling on the bank with his head turned to the right, and there was Bob, upside down, head turned to his right and apparently they were stuck there, paralysed at the sight of this butt ringer. Probably that paralysis was a good thing in this instance because Bob managed to think marginally quicker than Pat, and his plaintive "Don't let go!" came clearly across the lake.

The crisis passed and Bob made it back to the vertical without what had seemed the inevitable ducking. It was a big fish too, and he had all sorts of trouble with it.

Now I think that Bob would be the first to admit that he does get over-excited when he catches a good fish, but as this was his first twenty, his leaping about and lap of honour were perhaps in order.

Gradually, sanity returned to the lake. After all the fuss had died down, I reeled in the baits and went round to talk to them. Bob had a grin like a Cheshire cat. The fish had weighed over twenty four pounds and I was delighted for him. Obviously I was curious about the performance earlier and when the pleasantries had been dispensed with, I asked about it.

"What was all the head down bit earlier?"

They exchanged startled glances.

"Oh hell", said Bob, "I'd forgotten all about my watch".

They dived to action stations. Fish break over; back on your heads.

FOOTNOTE:

Recent additions to the Mill faithfuls and recent casual visitors will think I've made that bit up about the walkway onto the Pontoon. I haven't. Until the mid-80's the water ran round the back of the swim and you made your way on and off by means of a slightly unsteady plank. I think the swim was revamped after Tony Higgins took control of the water.

The story so far. Going back some years (yawn; grief another history lesson) to the mid seventies, technical knowledge on certain aspects of carp fishing was not easy to come by. Jim Gibbinson's was a lone pen passing on information which others were presumably trying to suppress, and Terry Eustace was taking the first steps towards helping pioneer the magnificent range of carp rods that are now generally available.

Initially, when I was suddenly confronted by the very real necessity for fishing at long range, I had no one to learn from, so I swallowed my pride and picked the brains of a fifteen year old kid twenty yards down the bank at Roman Lakes. He was casting fifty yards further than I had imagined was possible.

I entered the strange and confusing world of fast tapers, heavy bombs, spools filled to the maximum, shock leaders, winds-ups, crack-offs, flattened barbs, fixed paternosters and athletic, gymnastic strikes. For long enough the fast tapers and the shock leaders were the items that gave me the most problems. This was pre-carbon and eventually my search for the ideal glass fast taper long range carp rod, and a reliable knot to connect the main line to the shock leader, took me to the original cramped premises of the emerging Terry Eustace in the middle of Birmingham. 'Middle of Birmingham' is a bit sweeping, on reflection; 'one of the twilight zones of Birmingham' would perhaps be slightly more realistic.

I had already met the great man once, at a CAA meeting in Nottingham. It was impossible not to be impressed by his careless elegance and his general air of disarray. Not to put too fine a point on it, he didn't give a damn; you could either take his seven days' growth of stubble, and clothes he'd been sleeping in for a week, or leave them. (It's one of the reassurances of this commercial, competitive age that wherever, and whenever you meet him, Terry still looks more like an angler in the middle of a long session than a businessman with a turnover of millions). And yes, you could buy a couple or rods off him on the clear understanding that he was doing you a favour, rather than the other way round.

My companion in those days was a gentle creature, or so I thought at the time, one Julie, of fond, but distant memory. We were embarrassingly inseparable in retrospect, but she was good company and got on well with men; I think that's a bit of an understatement, somehow. My friend and I would frequently call in at Terry's shop on our trips south, share a few Breakers (a corrosive, bad-tempered little lager) with him then continue on our journey to some distant lake. I think Terry had a soft spot for us, or at least one of us, in a friendly, fellow carp angler sort of way, you understand.

Somewhere around that time we called in one Friday at about ten in the morning and eventually bought a pair of long range rods (T31s) some time during the early evening. It was part business transaction, part social event, with the conversation becoming more expansive and less meaningful, with the introduction of the lager.

"What kind of knot do you use for your shock leaders?" I asked, in my endless, boring quest for knowledge and efficiency.

"The water knot".

At last, someone who knew the water knot! I had seen Dick Walker mention it in print, without further explanation, but everyone I asked either

didn't know what a shock leader was, thought that you couldn't catch carp if you had a lead on the line, or had tried to tell me about the double grinner, which I had some distrust of at that time, for reasons I cannot now recall. I asked for further enlightenment.

"Here, I'll show you."

So he did.

This will be difficult to explain. Those of you who knew Terry's original shop will have a head start; those of you who knew his second shop may have a clue; those of you who only know of his third shop, the present highly organised, impressive emporium on Chester Road, will be at a disadvantage. Terry has acquired tidiness, he was not born with it.

This would be early evening and we were halfway through a crate of Breakers. My capacity for this strongish lager was one can, Terry's one and a half, and my friend's (she was semi-alcoholic) limitless. We'd had about four cans each. Now the water knot isn't the easiest of knots to tie in the most ideal circumstances; four Breakers in on an empty stomach in a shop that resembles a claustrophobic corner of an over-filled junk yard – well, the problems are magnified.

I just wanted the principle, but our man insisted on demonstrating a six turn version with a full seven or eight yard 'pull through', which meant that there was line all over the place. Inevitably the loose length of line snagged on the first pull through, the offending object being a rather large version of one of those implements used for punching twin holes in sheets of paper so they will fit into a loose leaf folder.

"Of course, you don't come across many of these on the bank side," says himself in that engaging Brummy, wrestling manfully, and successfully with the intricate looking tangle of line and punch. He made no attempt to disentangle the offending punch, but just enlarged the loop so he could thread the whole lot through! He stuck at it heroically and eventually successfully tied a six turn water knot amid mounting hilarity and hysteria.

Now I think it's fair to say that it is virtually impossible to effectively describe the tying of a knot in print, which is a fair enough challenge, so I'll try it. The water knot is designed for connecting two lengths of line of unequal breaking strain. To make it easier to refer to what we are trying to do, let's assume that we wish to connect six pound Maxima to eleven pound Sylcast, a procedure that will be undertaken not a few times in the course of a carp season. I just threw the word 'carp' in there in case you had forgotten that this had anything to do with fishing.

I should perhaps briefly explain, for the benefit of those who catch their carp at ranges from two feet to seventy yards from the bank, that in their cases shock leaders, and therefore water knots, are optional extras. They are not an essential part of the set up in those circumstances – unless you have problems with bars or snags, in which case you may need a snag leader. For angling purposes a shock/snag leader is required when the main line is not strong enough to withstand the full force of a cast with a heavy lead, or when increased abrasion resistance is required over the last ten or twenty yards of line. In the latter circumstances, the shock leader becomes the snag leader, which is exactly the same thing, but longer, and is designed for protection during playing, rather than casting. The leader wants to be about twice the length of your rod for

casting; make it longer if you want the leader as a snag leader, shorter if every inch of the cast is vital. It would take another article or two to explain those observations in depth, so if you don't understand, write to someone, but not to me. In the case of the shock leader, the minimum length must allow for some of the leader to be on the spool when the cast is made.

Tying the knot. Take the main line in your right hand and the leader line in your left, or the other way round, depending on whether you are left or right handed. I'm right handed so I take the six pound line in my right hand, and the eleven in my left – I think. I'll check that out. Yes, that's right. Overlap the two lengths of line by about a foot (i.e. twelve inches, or twelve thirty-ninths of a metre if you've already gone metric; for those who have already turned metric substitute centimetres for inches because it's all approximate anyway). Those of you who are right handed should now have the six pound Maxima in their right hand and the eleven pound Sylcast in the other, which should be the left. Those of you who are left handed will have – I don't know though; I've always found left handers to be unpredictable in the extreme so I'll not even attempt to guess what you've got in your hands. Thus far it has been fairly straightforward, but now it might start to get confusing; in fact it definitely will if you are as thick as the majority of carp men I get letters from. (Most of these letters are so extraordinary that I just presume they are wind-ups and reply accordingly, which means there will be some pretty startled recipients of my letters if some of these wind-ups are genuine).

Form a largish loop, or circle, say about six inches across, with the overlapped lengths of line. Oh dear… look, I'd better prepare you for a major problem at this point. Because shock/snag leaders are invariably lengths of heavy line fresh off a spool, they usually have a mind of their own. They are self-willed and very difficult to tame and therein lies the great challenge of the water knot. To continue… Measure off four or five outstretched arms' lengths of shock/snag leader (depending on whether your arms are in yards or metres) and cut this springy, tangly, highly independent line off the spool. Those of you who are starting to struggle should do something to take your mind off the knot altogether at this stage. Dylan can get me through most of life's crises, but not water knots. Meatloaf, and 'Bat out of Hell' at full blast might help; it makes your brain go numb enough to stop you thinking until it's all over.

You should now have the main line to your right, the circle of lines together in your right hand, about six inches of six pound line to the left of the circle, and anything up to twenty yards of malicious, uncontrollable eleven pound Sylcast tying itself round your left foot, and anything else it can reach, on the same side of the circle as the overlap of six pound line. I think that's fairly clear.

Now you'll have to close your eyes as you read this next bit to help your concentration. The loose ends of both lines have to pass through the circle of line four times which, in the case of the eleven pound Sylcast, means pulling the whole of the leader length through the loop on each successive turn, and the six inch main line tail with it. I'll not complicate that further because I understand what I've just written, which isn't always the case. Once you have successfully passed the two lengths of line through the loop four times, thoroughly wet all the line in the loop (that is the two lines together), make sure the lines forming the loop are the same length, then gently draw the knot tight, holding both lines together between thumb and fore-finger on either side of the circle. There is a tendency to panic at this stage, which arises from an hysterical reaction to the ordeal almost being over. Keep calm; an ill-timed moment of indiscretion can abort the whole project.

Once you have achieved a successful tying of this knot for the first time, pause and reflect on the greatness of a man who can tie a six turn version, four Breakers in on an empty stomach, when a large paper punch has been seized by the unco-operative leader on the first pull through.

A word of advice to close on. Tying the water knot in test conditions in the kitchen, with only a playful cat to help you, can induce a false sense of accomplishment. Always be prepared for the problems you may face when you reach the water. When you are new to leaders, for instance, you tend to forget the importance of positioning the leader knot at the back of the spool before the cast. The result is that on the first full cast of the session you may well get an exciting bird's nest, followed by an awe-inspiring crack-off. At such a moment you discover that tying a water knot on the bank – invariably in a gale force wind during a brief, early morning feeding spell – is a new, and even more unrewarding experience. With this possible contingency in mind, it is as well to master the double grinner, which I now use all the time for leader knots with no apparent loss of tackle strength.

THE WATER KNOT – *For joining two lengths of line*

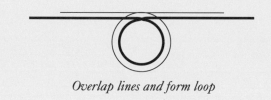

Overlap lines and form loop

Pass both lines through loop

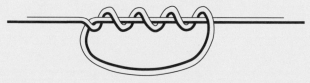

Repeat four times

Ease tight

THE STORY SO FAR. Some years ago, handsome, articulate, charming, mild-mannered Matthew Black, carp angler, met cynical, occasionally articulate, churlish to the point of viciousness, Deeppocket, fellow carp angler, under a drink laden table at a carp meeting. Our hero Matt, an occasional smoker and social drinker, was under the table for reasons involving a two pence piece dropped by Trev (20% off) Moss some hours earlier. What chain smoking, semi-alcoholic Deeppocket was doing under the table remains a mystery because even he couldn't remember when he woke up two days later, demanding whisky. But over the years, the assertive Deeppocket has dominated the impressionable Matt, and gradually elevated him to the depths of being a genuine specimen hunter. So Matt is, like Deeppocket, at the time of our true tale, a semi-alcoholic, chain smoking coffee addict who swears profusely, tells lies and does more talking than catching. Now read on:

Attitudes Campaign

I'm not really deep into explanations. To the couple of readers who may have come across us before – there's no escape is there? To the thousands who haven't you've missed nothing. Move on to the next article and come back to this when you're really bored.

If you think that the title of this piece is a bit unlikely in the context of Deeppocket and me, well I can't deny it. But Deeppocket, who is legendary in that he is able to attend three or four carp meetings simultaneously, somehow contrived to be at the first Carp Fisher magazine meeting. He reported back:

"They don't want you to write. They want it clean and honest. They're having pictures of Mike on every page."

"I'd better write then."

"That's what I thought."

"What about though? Something topical."

"How about fish nicking?"

"No, there's lots of people better equipped than I am to write about that. They could ask…" (The next four pages of the manuscript had to be edited out for censorship reasons).

"Poaching?"

"No, on the same grounds."

"Well, perhaps you could do something untypical. Write about our Attitudes Campaign."

So Deeppocket had it. Coverage of our Attitudes Campaign. I should perhaps explain that since our man listened to Yatesy at some obscure carp meeting in the frozen North, he has mellowed a bit. Or he keeps saying that he has mellowed a bit. Hearing the gospel according to St. Chris obviously had a profound impression on him, though whether it has actually changed him for the good or not – well, I've still got reservations.

I should perhaps also add, that while Yatesy's attitude to carp fishing impressed him, his fish spotting ability clearly didn't. They had a quick walk round the lake in the Conference grounds and Deeppocket was a bit taken aback when Chris proclaimed a sunken lily leaf to be a double figure wildie. Deeppocket is now wondering what on earth the so-called monsters in Redmire are.

The first actual signs that Deeppocket had thoughts of doing something about his own attitude, and that meant mine with it, came late one Sunday evening, just pre-season. We'd been East and, soon after we'd started back, he announced that he had a thirst brewing. As he was driving, ale was out, so it had to be coffee. Now, stumbling on an open coffee bar on the outskirts of Grimsby late on a Sunday evening is about as likely as catching carp at Billing. Except that we did – stumble on an open coffee bar that is, not… I'll not flog it.

It was all right as coffee bars go. Clean, and about par for the course. The first two coffees were nearly cold but we got two hot ones without Deeppocket falling out with anyone. In fact it was all pretty unremarkable. But while Deeppocket was paying (that's made me stop and think, because that must be a story in itself) the Manageress thrust a 'Comments' book under my nose – name, address, comments. Brain scrambling. You know the sort of thing; you have to sign one at the end of your holidays, so you dutifully put "A real home from home", thinking of a nagging wife, unpaid bills and endless chores, but the landlady doesn't know that so everyone's happy.

But what do you 'comment' on the strength of a couple of cold coffees, and a couple of hot ones that I could improve on one thousand per cent myself? I looked at the comments, and they were all pretty favourable – not to say glowing – so I decided to play it both ways and satisfy both our egos – the Manageress's and mine. I wrote 'Black – Nottingham – Unbelievable.' The address is perhaps slightly misleading, but this was just pre-season, and I was practising for the early season onslaught of the River Board bailiffs.

Anyway, the Manageress looked quite pleased, until Deeppocket glanced at the entry and promptly had hysterics. A quite prolonged attack. The Manageress wasn't quite sure what it was about, but she twigged that the entry wasn't all it seemed to be, so we beat a hasty retreat.

The hysteria continued for a while but once it had subsided, Deeppocket suddenly said:

"Yatesy wouldn't have done something like that. That was hurtful."

I was surprised he'd noticed. And I had a feeling that Yatesy could well have done exactly that but I kept the thought to myself. I mean, it wasn't the entry that was hurtful, it was Deeppocket's hysterical reaction to it. But he was obviously off at a tangent so I didn't pursue it. Anyway, the whole thing set him off about attitudes and not upsetting people. Quite unaided by me, he decided that we would have to reform, that it was time we improved our image and brought a bit of sweetness and light to the banks of the lakes we were going to fish.

He went on about it for the rest of the journey and he finally convinced me that that was where it was at. Be nice to people. Actually, that's how I try to be when he's not around, but he does cause a change in me. You see, the trouble is that when you're fishing with him, you are just not in a fit state to be nice to anyone. You're always short of sleep, very often suffering from a hang-over, and fishing high pressure waters, where catching is a pretty rare occurrence. This combination does not make you receptive to well intentioned intruders who have just got to tell you that you're in the wrong place, that you're using a bait that blew the season before, and that the kid round the corner, who has been carp fishing for two weeks, had a couple of twenties during the night. I've got to confess, that in those circumstances I can become less than chatty. On my good days I settle for noncommittal grunts, on my not-so-good days I openly snarl, and on bad days I get close to filling people in.

So Deeppocket waved his magic wand and made me lovable and friendly, and set about doing a full weight conversion job on himself. Well, that was the intention, but it wasn't quite that easy. My part has been made easier because Deeppocket and I have been fishing different waters this season. I've been ploughing a lone furrow, while he has been fishing with the Lounge Lizard. The Lizard is dry, which Deeppocket rates, but catches carp, which he doesn't.

My own struggles I will quickly, and quietly, draw a veil over. Being nice is all I've had to fall back on; I've certainly had no fish to show anyone. Of course, I do have an alibi in that what fishing time I've had has been largely spent on so called 'impossible' waters. I know full well that they are by no means impossible, but I've managed to keep that reputation intact for them. And as far as attitudes go, I suppose I must be objective and admit that I've done all right. It isn't that easy to keep being nice to people when you aren't catching so in answer to the many well-wishers who have accusingly informed me:

"I thought you'd have had something by now," I can only reply:

"You and me both."

But Deeppocket's attempted self conversion was far more interesting, if a little confusing. Let's be right, he did suffer some very genuine provocation, but I think I should be fair and say that he dished some out as well. Now Deeppocket is into every new expression that rears its ugly head for making reference to what he considers to be his lesser carp fishing brethren. This season, attitudes or not, it has alternated between 'keenies' and 'wallies', although I suppose that any change from the hackneyed 'noddies' is an improvement.

I've got to confess that while I may occasionally use these expressions, I'm not really into them. I mean I'm not absolutely sure what my standing is in relationship to the Hutchinson, Morisses and Mohans of this world. I could well qualify to be a keenie, or a wallie, or a noddie as far as they are concerned. (Just at the moment, car-less and typewriter bound, I'm not even a bleeding carp angler).

So Deeppocket eased himself into the new campaign fairly gently, not to say imperceptibly. He didn't get involved in any punch-ups, in fact he didn't even come close for a month or so, but neither did he instantly set about spreading the intended sweetness and light. Witness the following conversation as reported by our man:

Keenie wandering round the bank for approximately the eighth time that day:

"Any luck yet?"

Fun loving Deeppocket:

"Yes, I've had six."

Naive Keenie, leaping back in amazement:

"What, carp? Any good?"

"Hang on, I'll show you, they're on a stringer in the edge."

Same Keenie, three trips later, clearly a glutton for punishment:

"Any luck yet?"

"Couple of big bream."

Naivest keenie of all time buying it again:

"How big?"

"Have a look for yourself, they're in the bushes."

Well, let's be right. I know that Deeppocket tells me things to rev me up, and I think that was one of those tales. But no one could make up the story of the battle of Waverley Lakes.

Surprisingly, Deeppocket had not been to Waverley before his trip with the Lizard this season, and he didn't really do one of his thorough sussing out jobs before he went. Usually he likes to get the full S.P. before he goes anywhere near a water. To be honest, I think he thought that it was just a question of going there and whacking a couple of souped up boilies into the back bay on the rig, and he'd cop for the twenty six and the twenty nine.

"That was some kind of a joke," he told me. "The main lake was all stitched up. Fivers changing hands to reserve swims. But there's waters all over the place, so we decided to fish one of the lesser lakes, till the heat died off."

By the time they'd sorted themselves out, dusk was setting in and they dived into a quietish corner swim with lilies round it on 'G' Lake. A hurried tackle-up, baits in, and they set about arranging themselves for the night. Which is what they were inoffensively doing when someone cast into their swim, across Deeppocket's lines.

"I'm just getting my bedchair set up by the rods, when this end tackle touches down right in the middle of the swim. I'm quietly settling down, minding my own business, when this bleeding keenie casts over me."

"And you cracked up?"

"No, I went round and reasoned with him. Well, to start with I thought that it was accidental so I went in gentle, but this chuffing joker calmly informed me that he had been baiting the swim all week, and he intended fishing it."

"So you threw him in the lake?"

"No, I kept cool. Truth was that I would have preferred his swim, and he clearly intended to fish in ours, so I offered him an exchange."

"And he accepted?"

I was doing the old straight man bit and Deeppocket was dragging it out.

"No. Said he was happy where he was, that he and his mate had settled in for the night. Well, normally at that stage I would have just filled him in, stuffed his end tackle up his rucksack and settled down to fish undisturbed. But this kid was only about fifteen – and I was not forgetting about the Attitudes Campaign," he added as a hurried afterthought. "So I went back to our swim, carefully reeled in the keenie's line with mine, bit his end tackle off, and took it round to him."

"But that wasn't the end of it?"

"No, they put the car headlights on. Keenie retackled than recast his bait exactly where it had been."

"He was a good caster then."

Deeppocket gave me an old-fashioned look.

"My patience was fraying."

I assured him that I thought Yatesy's would have been. I was gleefully awaiting the mayhem of the inevitable climax.

"I reeled in his line, bit the end tackle off, and threw it in the bushes, then I told him what I'd done. Well, I think it must just be part of the early season scene down there, because he and his mate came round with torches, crashed round in the bushes for ten minutes, found the tackle and went back to their

swim."

"And Keenie retackled, and recast into exactly the same place?"

"Yeh. He was a good caster," said Deeppocket with a tired smile.

"Well, come on, what did you finish up doing to this evil Keenie?"

"Nothing. I'd had enough. the Lizard and I packed up and moved on to another lake."

"You're joking."

"No. What with the Attitudes Campaign, and this kid being a bit too young to crack anyway…"

I wouldn't have believed it if I'd heard it from anyone else. In fact, the truth is, that this bleeding attitudes thing has ballsed us up altogether. Things just aren't the same, without the thought of the odd bit of good, cleansing, aggro looming. I mean, it's all right Yatesy going on about attitudes, but let's be fair, he doesn't catch any big fish. And he spends most of his time fishing on his own at these secret wildie pools, and a deserted Redmire, so he doesn't even run into anyone he can get involved in any aggro with.

And I must, with some reluctance, point out that in certain areas Yatesy's attitude leaves a bit to be desired. It can be less than exemplary when he loses a fish, for instance. I mean, all that howling and rod throwing. The kids notice these things. There's this Paul, from York, who's a mate of Deeppocket's. Apparently he's into howling and rod throwing in a big way, and Deeppocket, in his fun-loving way, says he has plenty to howl and throw rods about.

Well, I don't want to labour the point too far, but on a busy day at Kettle Mill there can be anything from say, fifteen to thirty carp lost. Supposing everyone got into the habit of howling and rod throwing. The whole scene would look more like an African tribal dance than a carp lake.

But I suppose there's a balance somewhere. I've heard it said that Rod has suggested a Code of Conduct for the Carp Society. That might not be a bad thing, even if it's only to keep Rod under control. But perhaps Yatesy's attitude will win the day, provided we all wear crash helmets and ear-muffs and carry shields.

I'm not totally convinced though. It seems I can either snarl and catch fish, or spread sweetness and light and not catch fish. And I'm that confused, that I'm not even sure that I don't prefer the latter. Or we could all be like Bob and snarl and still not catch fish…

Basically I'm a romantic at heart. I love to wallow in nostalgia and tradition and I'm a soft touch for solitude and seclusion and peace. Currently, none of my waters start to satisfy all of these needs. Inflation has forced me to fish locally, added to which I'm on a hitherto unknown big fish kick (totally unfulfilled at the time of writing) so I'm grinding away at busy waters, trying to convince myself that what I'm doing is carp fishing. In fact, what I'm actually doing is trying to catch carp. The difference was forcibly and beautifully brought home to me in the middle of August.

For reasons obscured by the mists and shifts of time I was thinking over an invite to go down to re-acquaint myself with one Bob Davis from Middlesex, carp man and organiser of the Savay Syndicate. I mulled it over during a week of twelve hour nights. They're fun, twelve hour night shifts in the middle of the carp season. You start work at six in the evening and finish at six in the morning. Then you go and fish and try to fit the odd domestic chore into the chaos. By the end of the week the cat and I are just not on speaking terms and I'm out on my feet. The week in question I managed six hours in bed from Sunday night to Sunday night, and even then the sleep I had wasn't in bed. I must slow down, my mind is ahead of my pen.

I finished work at six on Saturday morning and was due down in Middlesex about twelve hours later. But in the meantime I'd got to go across to Lancashire. I should have had some sleep, but I'd got some correspondence to deal with so I didn't bother. Endless cigarettes (the season has got me back on them) and the inevitable endless coffees had to substitute.

Three o' clock Saturday afternoon I pulled onto the M6 near St. Helens and headed south. Incredibly it was two years since I had been south of Birmingham so I was strangely excited, but the unwelcome presence of sleep was close at hand and that didn't fit into the scheme of things at all. I pulled into the first services and bought a large bag of sweets. Very large. The blurb informed me that I was buying a mixture of boiled sweets and toffees. Strictly speaking, that was true, but as there were about a hundred boiled sweets and only two toffees the balance wasn't quite what I'd been anticipating. But a steady flow of boiled sweets doing battle with my back teeth conquered the invading sleep. Down the straights, through the constantly recurring coned-off chicanes: by the Daventry turn off I'd done it for motorways and turned off onto the A5.

The road was quieter and the countryside familiar and loved. Nostalgia started to set in. Two years since I was at that beautiful water at Little Brickhill: two years of memories that were best unremembered. But the pull was too strong; I had to go back and face it alone. The Bletchley by-pass confused me and I thought I'd missed it, but then there was the signpost to the village and I thankfully pulled into the car park of the Green Man. I walked down the aggregate farm track to the lake in the scorching hot, late afternoon sun and long buried memories came flooding back.

I'd hoped that there would be at least one familiar face there to bridge the years, but there wasn't. It was exactly as it had always been; the same massive, ancient trees; the same wild and overgrown island; the same dark shapes hanging just below the surface in the self-same places they had always been. But the lake didn't look fished. Swims that had been occupied by Nigel, Ken, the Johns and others, looked overgrown and unused – and no Paul. Paul who

Nostalgia
and
Atmosphere

had helped me when I most needed someone and whom I hadn't seen since. I hope he reads this because I have not forgotten. I smoked a couple of cigarettes and reflected, then turned my back on the place and walked slowly back up the track. I had come down to see Bob Davis and look into the future, and had sidetracked myself into a treasured past.

I thought then that I would have to go back, but the next few hours were to change my mind totally. Few things in life have impressed me as much as my talk to Bob and the time I spent at his water.

Bob's directions to the water were quite explicit and totally misleading. The final stages took three quarters of an hour instead of five minutes, and I eventually approached the lakes from the wrong direction altogether. Just when the car was beginning to gently tell me that three hundred miles for one day was quite enough, I pulled into the parking area, climbed out on stiffening legs and breathed an atmosphere of carp.

I shall not dwell on the whereabouts or names of the lakes. They are numerous and many of you will know the name of at least one of them, some of you all of them, but they are not my waters so I make no apology for not being more specific. I know that the lads who fish them know, and appreciate, just what they've got. They are privileged to have so much water and so many big fish at their disposal and many of them are good enough to take full advantage of that privilege.

I walked up the track between two beautiful lakes. It was late evening and a handful of carp men were settling in for the night. The pleasant and unmistakable Lloyd Bent introduced himself and pointed me in the direction of Bob's swim. He was fishing in splendid isolation under the trees of the West bank, not another angler within three hundred yards of him. There was a brief awkwardness between us, but it quickly passed. I was drinking the place in. The contrast between hours of noisy car engine and the quiet of a carp lake is always stunning, and on this occasion it was heightened by the near presence of carp beyond my experience.

Bob is anxious that I put his standing as a carp man into perspective in case his colleagues feel that he is being singled out from their number. Down there he is one of a number of very capable carp men. He does not ram his big fish down your throat, although when he starts to unwind privately it is obvious that he is no stranger to big twenties – but then nor are any of the other carp anglers who fish these waters. Many are better than just capable and some are better than that. There is the odd brilliant technician, particularly the revered Lenny Middleton, whose inventiveness and understanding of the carp has lead to tackle arrangements and baiting situations which give a whole new dimension to carp fishing. Understandably, these lads are guarded and jealous of the edge their creativity and hard work has given them and I gained the impression, though it was never put into words, that they disapprove of the minority cashing in on, and seeking glory from, the long hours of effort that a few of them have put in. That they all talk a different language to the one I know is immaterial; we all have that vital element of a love of carp and carp fishing in common.

I know that newcomers to carp fishing complain about the secrecy within the ranks of the carp fishing community, but I don't know why. Seasoned carp anglers accept the effort, thought and research, and the disappointment and disillusionment, that are all part of arriving at a new solution to lowering the

carp's defences. We have all had to spend years hacking our way through the wilderness on our way to catching carp with any sort or regularity. You serve an apprenticeship and the longer you are around, the more you are accepted and the more you are told, the easier it becomes to think for yourself. But a good carp man has got to be able to solve his own problems and I have always accepted secrecy as being a totally acceptable part of the carp world. I digress.

In deference to the occasion, I had taken plenty of cigarettes with me, which was just as well. Bob and I somehow contrived to dispose of a hundred and twenty of our own, and a fair number of anyone else's who chanced to stop by over the next twenty four hours. We talked right through Saturday night and well into Sunday, drank endless coffees, ran Bob out of coffee, milk, sugar and, ultimately, gas, then started into everyone else's coffee, milk, sugar and gas. I went down to record a conversation but in the event it was unimportant. It was carp men's talk, repeated all over the country a thousand times right through the carp season and beyond. Ours was no different; it was alternatively intense, technical and highly amusing.

Mike Wilson, an accomplished carp man in his own right with a long list of very big fish behind him, called in at the swim on Saturday evening and joined the conversation for a few hours. He left about midnight and our talk went on through the small hours. I should have fallen asleep the minute I got there, but the talk, the coffees and cigarettes and the occasional brief messages from Bob's Optonics made sleep a non-starter.

He was apologetic about the fact that I could not fish during the night, but I had no desire to. I had not gone down expecting to, so the necessary anticipation was not there. I did fish for some time during the Sunday, but with no conviction. How can I explain? I am no interloper; I respect the privacy of others. Catching a big fish was unlikely in the circumstances, but anyone can fluke one. If some flash bastard from up North came and invaded my secluded Southern domain and caught a biggie, I would not take kindly to him, and that was the position I felt I was in. At Bob's insistence I spent a few hours on the rods around midday but, thankfully, I caught nothing. Others did though.

There were no fish caught during the hours of darkness and as the sky lightened opposite us, I had my first skirmishes with sleep. The chill of dawn brought me back to full consciousness. Shortly after, and throughout the morning, a steady stream of new faces quietly came and went from the swim. New faces to me, that is, familiar in that setting. Gary, in a lean spell, but philosophical about it: Ritchie, committed to the fish and suspicious of me, but who thawed as the morning wore on: Geoff, Lloyd, Keith – all big fish men who are matter of fact about their captures. Mike reappeared and it became obvious that he is heavily involved with photography; he started photographing everyone and everything. All this time Bob's baits were out in the lake, not touched by him, or apparently, by the carp, since some time the previous day.

The coffee and cigarettes went on and by mid-morning the situation was getting critical. Bob's gas stove had died, Geoff's had been commandeered and was showing signs of approaching terminal gaslessness, and we were well into Ritchie's. Heroically I tore myself away into the sweltering day to go in search of supplies. Perhaps I should add that my heroism was purely selfish. We had been reduced to drinking tea and I was starting to feel withdrawal symptoms through lack of coffee. I was gone three quarters of an hour and by the time I returned, the huddle in the swim had swelled to a multitude. During my absence Bob had caught his first thirty.

At first I thought they were pulling my leg, but Bob's wet shirt and air of suppressed elation spoke the truth of it. Thirty two pounds and I didn't see it because the carp have to be returned to the water straight away. Bob didn't know where to put himself; he is outwardly phlegmatic but quite clearly, at that moment, there was inner turmoil. 'Landmark' fish are personal victories, private achievements attained over years, not in minutes, and they cause that inner conflict. You want to be alone to savour the achievement, to reflect on all that has led up to it, but part of you wants to have others around to share the achievement, to join in the excited talk.

We left Bob alone to regain himself and to rebait and recast. The simple act of rebaiting and recasting is a very private occurrence in that part of the world. I walked down the bank in time to see Ritchie subdue and land a beautifully conditioned common of seventeen and a half pounds. He returned it immediately, not with any air of disdain, but with a matter of factness that he had caught a good fish and nothing more. It topped the weight of my best common by a little over a pound.

A strongish wind had blown up from the North during the early hours and had driven the fish down the lake to Bob's right. Most of the lads immediately moved round towards the tail of the wind and activity started to build up. Bob's work mate, Geoff, had a twenty eight from the opposite bank and a twenty two

August 1981. Bob Davis looks on as Geoff Rendell plays a 20lb plus fish.

after we had left. The lake was starting to fish, but Bob's family was away and he was starting to get anxious about his dog. The attainment of the thirty had brought reality back into focus. Somehow, the catching of the fish had broken the magic spell. The mystery was still there, but it was diminished by the sight of a big fish on the bank. We drove off into the heat of the Middlesex countryside and exchanged the peace of the lake for the Sunday afternoon bustle of suburbia.

The talk went on and I learned something of the others who fish the area. The other Bob, from Kent, Rod, Andy, Kev, Cliff and many more. We talked of Bob's boxing and his pigeons, but mainly about carp and carp fishing. The previous night had faded into history but the memory would always be there.

Mid-evening, Bob's mate Keith called in. Keith, who unbelievably has twice had five twenties in a session, but fails to mention the fact; who had twenty eight twenties last season, but seeks no publicity about it. Their whole attitude to big fish was refreshing to say the least.

We had eaten by this time and the long postponed sleep was becoming ever more insistent. Apologetically I flaked out on the settee at about nine o' clock, in mid conversation. I'm sorry Keith, I felt very rude but it was way beyond my control. Reality was very much at hand for me, because I had to be at work two hundred miles north by six next morning. I vaguely remember Bob telling me that he had booked an alarm call but, in the event, it wasn't needed. Incredibly I was awake at quarter past two and on the road by quarter to three.

The remains of the boiled sweets saw me through. I was in time to open up the warehouse for half five, but the magic lingered on – and still does – and I cannot adequately explain why. I had been permitted to briefly enter a world that awoke some long suppressed feelings in me. Through necessity, my finer feelings for carp fishing had been lying dormant, but my glimpse into the world of Bob and his friends re-awoke them.

The last day of May: it's of little significance to the majority of anglers. The odd birthday, or anniversary; sadly, the odd death or marriage; to the majority just another day nearer to the magic of midnight on the fifteenth of June – but to Yorkshire men the last day of May means that the close season is over. Three months of household chores and domestic stability is at an end; school is out. From midnight, the banks will be lined with a thousand anglers – nine hundred and ninety nine of them on the water I fish.

I shall not attempt to go into the logic of the White Rose county having a season starting on the first day of June. The only argument I can put forward in favour of the arrangement is that the first tends to imprint itself on the memory. It is easy to remember. In fact, it would be easier to make out a logical argument for the Yorkshire season starting later than the rest of the country, but as I'm not of Yorkshire extraction, it's NOWT WHATEVER to do with me, so I'll keep out of it.

For long enough I could not accept the idea of starting the season early. I was on waters outside Yorkshire anyway, so June 16th was my 'off'. Times change, and I've started doing a fair bit of carp fishing locally, so for the last couple of years I've made the early start. The southern lads refer to this as cheating, but that is rather ignoring the fact that we lose a potentially productive fortnight at the beginning of March.

This last season I was in two minds. I do like to start at midnight, but there is no night fishing on the water where I wanted to start, so the last day of May saw me pottering round, sharpening the tackle and thinking in terms of a dawn start the next day. I'd been unusually thorough in my preparation during the close season. Because the local rules for the water prevent you fishing where the carp actually are, I'd done a heavy baiting programme in an effort to get the carp moving about a bit during the day, concentrating on a possible feeding area. I was using a medium protein, sweetened Cinnamon flavoured boiled bait which I'd had a fair few fish on from another water.

I'd better fill you in on the water a bit, because we're going to spend at least a couple of articles there, possibly more if I ever start catching from the bleeding place. It's a reservoir of ten to twelve acres and lies between Sheffield and Barnsley. The carp are rarely seen, and even more rarely caught. They are potentially good fish, if they are still there, but having watched the fish spawn at very close quarters, I must record that I have seen nothing over mid-doubles. That doesn't mean the big fish aren't there, it just means that I haven't seen them.

There have been some good carp out – or there has been a good carp out on a number of occasions, possibly the same fish. Certainly the first two well documented carp were the same fish; a mirror which weighed 22lb when Ray Allen caught it while pleasure fishing in 1972 and went 24lb 12oz when an overjoyed Pete Evans had it two years later while carp fishing. Pete and the Hallamshire lads put a fair bit of time in on the water over two seasons. They hooked one other fish which was lost near the net, and Pete considers this fish to have been a big common. As he is one of the biggest sceptics I've ever met, I give total credence to everything he says on fish weights, captures etc.

Bankside rumour has it that there have been at least two other captures of lowish twenties and at least a couple of deaths of 'big' fish. The captures, or the deaths, I have no reason to doubt, but the actual sizes I have got to doubt after

the estimates of the weight of the one fish I have caught.

It's only fair to say that the water should, on paper, be a great deal easier now than it was when the Hallam lads were on it. Modern tackle has made waters smaller, the rigs have made catching the big, wary fish easier, and there is no longer the weed problem that confronted Pete and the lads. The fact that the weed has been largely wiped out means that it should be easier to get the carp onto baits, because there isn't the enormous supply of natural feed that was present in the mid to late seventies.

An unusually mild and settled May meant that the fish should have been on the move and well on the baits by the end of the month. I felt more than confident; I was sure that I was going to catch. Monday midnight was openers, Monday being Bank Holiday. At teatime I was still pottering, thinking in terms of an early bed, up at half two, at the water for half three. During the evening I had a break from whatever I was doing to the tackle and wandered out into the back garden. Grief, what a sensational evening. Clear sky but very warm. No sign of a dew and not a breath of wind. The smells from the emerging garden were magnified threefold and the air felt gentle against my skin. It was overpowering and I lived through one of those brief moments of total euphoria, which rapidly gave way to a massive restlessness because I wasn't already pitched in at Snowberry, or Fox Pool, or some other tree fringed carp fishing social centre.

I started to revise the planning. There is another little carp water about a mile from the main water, where night fishing is allowed. It's a floater water. It would be chaotic but I could possibly get a bait out for a couple of hours before moving on to the serious business. Good thinking. At nine o' clock I threw a floater together and chucked it in the oven.

Better still, I could call in at the main water at around midnight, get some baits out into the prebaited area, carry on to the other little water... I was as excited as a three year old on Christmas Eve.

The floater was ready by about eleven and I was away by half past. I was on cloud nine; the atmosphere was suffocating. Everything was absolutely right for the opening night. Last season was just the dress rehearsal.

I pottered the twelve miles to the main lake, drove down the back lanes in the pitch black and pulled onto the small, car-made layby under the oak tree. I took a bag of baits and a couple of sling shots and carefully climbed the stile, sniffing the air. No signs of anyone around. Good. I didn't want to start the season by being banned, although, with hindsight, it could have been doing me a favour.

It's about a quarter of a mile, or a bit more, along the track through the fields. Halfway along I heard voices from the direction of the road which runs along one side of the water. Steady. Had the Club got the watch dogs out to keep the gun jumpers at bay? If so, they'd be sure to hear the twang of the sling shot in the still night air. I went on cautiously.

I needn't have bothered. As I came round the corner of the fields in sight of the water I stopped, with a smile. Clearly I had misjudged the significance of the early start; the numbers present made it clear that it was an event of some magnitude. There were bonfires, torches, tilley lamps, transistors and a cacophony of voices, but not a soul on the stretch of bank I had been baiting up from. It should have been jarring, but somehow it wasn't. It's a mining area and you just have to take the rough with the smooth. As I started firing baits out, someone started breaking a fence up away to my left to stoke up their ailing fire...

It was noisy and there was little regard shown for what was to come at dawn, but there was a feel to it all, a friendliness that the eerie silence of a carp water could not have conveyed. I went back to the car and got the rest of the tackle. As I set up, bodies appeared out of the gloom and stopped for a chat. Automatically, we talked in hushed tones, then they'd bellow something across to their mates as soon as they'd left me.

Through the dark hours the noise built up to a crescendo. The bonfires burned brighter and brighter as trees, fences and anything else that would provide some light and heat was annexed and consigned to the flames. I lay back, fascinated, drinking it all in and listening to four or five conversations at once, carried clear across the water in the stillness. More and more car headlights pulled up on the road, each new arrival spilling out onto the bank, ready to play his small part in the dawn ritual which crept gradually, very gradually, closer.

I'd put about fifty baits out at midnight and I resisted the temptation to add to them. The odd visit from the carp was as much as I dared hope for after the sacrificial bonfires and war dances the noisy congregation of worshippers saw fit to offer to the great God of Angling throughout the night. I half wished that Deeppocket and the Lizard had been there to wallow in the rarified atmosphere, but I'd been offered an enigmatic smile when I'd asked where they were starting the season. The smile could have meant anything from "In the disco" to "A secret water". It was a passing thought: in truth I am happy to have the water to myself until I have come to terms with it, although it can make it a much longer job.

What time is that half light we accept as dawn? I don't know, half three, perhaps, or possibly later. It came at last and with it, a heavy mist. The bank I was on started to increase in popularity, which suggested that the road bank was full, but the mist completely shut out the main body of the water.

I've mentioned before that I'm often struck by the contrast between the mystery of the black hours and the mundane reality of daylight; that struck me again as the mist finally started to give best to a big red orb of a sun already well above the dam wall. There was no apparent signs of the mayhem of the previous night on the road bank; just a long line of anglers spaced at five yard intervals, all intent on catching that first magical fish of the new season. The sounds penetrating the dark had suggested at lease one hapless soul crucified upside down, or sacrificed in some equally imaginative manner.

The odd roach started to come out, and the occasional skimmer bream, but nothing bigger. Tench were rolling all along the bank I was fishing, about twenty to thirty yards out, but I didn't see a single one caught. The level of impatience was quite staggering. Two very well equipped, competent looking anglers were fishing feeder rigs about thirty yards to my left. For an hour the feeders were reloaded and recast and the tench activity started to build up over the area they were baiting. They just had to start catching if they stuck at it but next thing they were float fishing five yards out and the chance was gone.

Mind you, I was impatient too. Impatient a few hours into the new season – barmy; but it wasn't so much impatience to catch, I just wanted the reassurance of some sign to say that I was getting it right, that the carp were having the bait. Flannel weed on the bottom gives a presentation problem there and I was starting out on bolt rigs. The baits were at fifty yards and seventy yards. I tried shutting off and concentrated on the efforts of others and the tench, busy performing their silent porpoise-like roll thirty yards out.

Quite unexpectedly a carp, a very black one of mid doubles, possibly slightly bigger, performed a similar roll among the tench. I reeled in the right hand bait and recast in the area where the fish had rolled. Free offerings or not? I dithered, then settled for half a dozen fed tight to the hook bait.

Beep-beep-beep. A six inch lift. It stopped but it didn't drop back - no liner. Mental crisis, decisions, decisions. Reel in and recast? More loose feed to hold the fish there and pull it back onto the hook bait? I left it, but I have never had a fish return to a bait it had already 'tested' on that water, and this was no exception to the rule.

It was nearly seven o' clock. There was a vault of blue sky above the lingering remains of the mist, but it was still cold. I poured another coffee and lit another in a long chain of cigarettes. Ten past seven and I started to get line bites on the fifty yard rod. I lit another fag and tried to pretend it wasn't happening. Quarter past seven and I was away! The indicator whacked to the top of the spear, line poured off the spool and the Optonic howled. Calmness has increased with the rigs, the old panic at the sight of a flier having almost gone. I shut the bail arm, watched the line lift up quickly through the shallow water and pulled firmly back up the line. I expected the twelve footer to come alive in my hands but it hit fresh air. I felt weak and the old heart was pounding something alarming, so I had another fag. That was my fourth butt ringer at the water, all with the same result. Presentation was still the problem.

The morning action was over and the day turned into a real scorcher. There was no breeze and little prospect of bottom feeding so I switched to floating baits fished just off the bottom. I had one line out of the clip during the afternoon, but I wasn't happy with the way I was presenting the bait, and neither were the carp. A mate from the local club, Brian, called down late afternoon and promptly commandeered the rod of the matchman to my left. The lad had been catching throughout the day, on and off, but only roach. He was almost good, but he wasn't getting it quite right. Brian thought the way I'd been thinking and altered the presentation. He drew an hour's blank and went off in disgust. Clearly the lad had been getting it right.

Throughout the afternoon the sky behind me and to my left grew ever darker and thunder growled and rumbled in the distance. What little breeze there was quartered round during the afternoon and I thought that the distant storm would pass by, but slowly the day's dry heat became oppressive and the thunder rolled threateningly closer. By five o' clock the two hundred plus anglers had dwindled to about a dozen, mostly on the road side. The sky had darkened to a near purple colour, and a steady rain started to fall. The rain never got worse than steady, but the storm, which drew in closer and closer and apparently totally surrounded the Reservoir and the local village, sat right on top of us and was frighteningly spectacular.

I am uneasy about lightning. I'm never quite sure what to do for the best when I am out in it. I suppose it's a classic case of if your number's on it, you'll get it. If it was my turn I was a sitting duck, but thoughts of the apparent

relationship between storms, and the big fish occasionally being stirred into indiscretion by them, guaranteed me staying right where I was.

For an hour the sky overhead was low and threatening. The thunder growled and snarled and crashed continuously, frightening in its intensity and irritating in its regularity.

The lightning was majestic and repeatedly split the sky above the dam wall in two as it struck, and struck again at the local pit village. The danger of the lightning was brought home to me by the fact that the Optonics bleeped each time the livid sky was breached. It had not occurred to me at that time that carbons are excellent conductors of electricity, but they are, which explained the rather unsettling Optonic activity.

The fear of being instantly electrocuted apart, the storm was magnificent and elemental, but it was over by soon after seven and left a coolish, gentle evening in its wake. I had expected activity during the storm but it came soon after. Beep, beep, beep. The indicator started to climb, then slowly beep-beep-beeped its way back to its original position. A liner. Followed by another, then another. I nervously lit my nth fag of the day, which just served to fuel a raging headache. Nothing for ten minutes; was that it? Then an exact repeat of the morning episode. An absolute flier, bail arm in, a steady pull back up the line – nothing. My knees turned to jelly and I felt sick. I reeled in and recast but that was it. End of action.

I fished on till dark, hoping for a pre-dusk flat calm to aid possible fish sighting, but a breeze got up and put paid to that. I packed up slowly, analysing, planning and wondering. The euphoria of the close season anticipation had

Twenty
Four
Hours

materialised into the usual reality of the actual problems. I draped tackle all over me and trudged the quarter of a mile to the car. I don't know where I'd be without the problems. I'm one of those people who like two and two to make 3.9 recurring. The minute they add up to four, anti-climax sets in and I start wrestling with three and three.

I heaped the wet gear in the back of the estate and drove the twelve miles back to the flat. Back into the season, three or four months of being penniless and nackered; the land of the permanent red and no sleep. The cat materialised the moment the car stopped, as it always does, and played hell with me for the unexplained absence. It demolished a tin of Whiskas as I carried the tackle in. It was just after half eleven. Twenty four hours on and not a carp caught.

"Stop right where you are!" I looked up in alarm. A fierce looking bearded face with a blowpipe sticking out of it loomed overhead. The whole scene was unreal. I was a stranger lost in the depths of darkest Surrey. The rain and mist of a miserable October evening swirled through the huge, gloomy trees. I was frozen from a near two hundred mile journey in a car with a deceased heater and now I was about to suffer the indignity of having sweetcorn or paprika flavoured racing beans splattered all over me from a great height. If this was Yatesy's idea of hospitality, the sooner I dived back in the freezing car and headed North, the better.

I mean, I presumed it was a joke, but I had heard rumours of Chris's 'eccentricities'. The thought did cross my mind that this could be part of some sort of initiation rite inflicted on anyone about to be accorded the hospitality of Vale Cottage. I cast a glance over my shoulder, wondering if the blowpipe attack was to be reinforced by the lumbering charge of a tame badger.

Funny how things strike you. That's just how it felt at the time. Vale Cottage after dark, nestling among the massive trees and with no road lights, is one of the darkest spots I have ever come across. I'd been travelling for ages, and I'd been lost for the previous half hour. Plus I wasn't even certain that I was at the right house – it just looked like Vale Cottage somehow. On top of all this, the unexpected emergence of Yatesy's disembodied head made me jump.

"We were getting worried about you. I was going to ring and see if you'd left. I'll come down and let you in."

Reality took over. The blowpipe disappeared and the head with it. I was stammering some explanation to the empty window when the front door opened. I'd forgotten how tall he is.

What was I doing outside Yatesy's front door anyway, apart from feeling a bloody fool, apprehensive and cold? Well, people interest me, carp men in particular. Exceptional people intrigue me, and Chris Yates is exceptional, both as a carp man and a person. In the context of this article I must lean towards the carp fishing side of his life, but not to the exclusion of the man himself. If I can bend a quotation from 'Confessions' – 'The two are indivisible, the background and the man'.

I make no apology for asserting that, as a carp man, Chris is exceptional. I sense from what he himself says that he is perhaps viewed with suspicion by some of his contemporaries, carp men with whom he has fished. He does not conform to any carp fishing pattern. He cannot be categorised, and perhaps the fact that he is so different somehow clouds their assessment of his ability. It's too easy to be over objective from afar, but I will try and explain.

He doesn't believe in buzzers, and rarely uses paste baits (laboratory specials as he refers to them). He has used glass rods but prefers his old cane Mk. IV built by Dick Walker. His baits are simple and his tackle just as basic. And it is fair to say that over the last few years he has not been over successful when compared to some of his colleagues at the 'Mire' in terms of quantities of big fish.

But for all his 'unorthodoxy', his shunning of rigs and many of the modern bait additives, and his disregard for modern set-ups, he has caught the two biggest carp to be landed in this country during the last thirty years. The two biggest carp since Dick Walker's '44' in 1952, and three of the current 'Top Twenty' reported big fish. As a carp angler, that makes him very exceptional,

Yatesy

and perhaps it is because he is 'unorthodox' that he does get the chances for the very big fish (beyond the obvious condition of fishing a water that contained them). Perhaps a feeding situation which will account for three twenties in a day will be avoided by the very fish that the angler most wants to catch.

It could even be that there is more to it than just the practical side of it; that there is more involved than just putting a bait to a carp. Chris's reverence for the carp has been cultivated to almost cult level. He wants to catch carp the traditional way, and not the modern way. I know this will cause some smiles, but it is just possible that he is, in some strange way, rewarded for his traditionalism; for his old fashioned approach; that the guardian angels which watch over the really big fish occasionally relax their vigilance to increase the purist's chances. Reflect on the capture of the '43' and the '51'.

First the 'Pot of Gold' in 1972. The carp were bubbling in front of Chris and he saw a big patch of bubbles that he wanted to cast to, and this is what happened – taken from Chris's account at the time.

"I spotted a huge cloud of them, halfway across the lake and directly between Rod and myself. I was using only a three swan link and I was just going to change to a five swan when a gust of wind blew up behind me. I cast immediately and the tackle went sailing out, to land nicely just beyond the bubble cloud." Providential old gust of wind; lucky old Chris.

Yes, the fish had been caught previously: and it must be said that the fish was not a natural '43', for it was spawn-bound. But no one else caught it at over forty pounds and that was the last time it was caught. It died some time later.

A year later, Chris caught the '38'. To catch a thirty eight pound carp would be exceptional in any circumstances, but somehow, at that time, it was not. That's badly put. In retrospect it was less exceptional than it might have been, because the '38' was in a bad spell. There were some first class carp men in Redmire, stock levels were high, and the heavy eater kept falling for the bait traps. When Chris caught it, it was its fifth time out of the water in two years.

But then the stock levels were reduced, the summers of 74 and 75 pushed the food levels up and the '38' was able to go back to nature and eat its fill of the natural food supply. In addition, the fish apparently started to accumulate spawn. Somehow it evaded capture for seven years, narrowly at times because it was hooked and lost more than once. And by 1980 the '38' had made '50's' and Yatesy got lucky again. Fate, or destiny, or whatever was sitting on Chris's shoulder when he encountered the fish feeding on the shallows. He cast his bait to a group of feeding fish, and a twenty pounder sucked it in – and ejected it before Chris could strike. How can you be lucky not to catch a twenty pounder? The result of the next cast is history.

Leney said that the '51' would not be caught again. Tom Mintram is reported to have said that the fish would not live two years (hearsay). They were both right. I have spent just one day at Yatesy's cottage, but half an hour after I walked through the door, Tom rang Chris to tell him that the '51' had died. There was some strange irony in the timing of that phone call, some sardonic twist to the tale, because I was about to innocently and quite unwittingly attract the wrath of Tom and the Syndicate Committee over that fish, and the whole sorry chapter was at least partly responsible for Yatesy deciding to turn his back on the Redmire he loves.

We talked about Redmire. He was going to fish it the next week and had

high hopes for one of the 'monsters'. There is considerable scepticism in carp circles about the big fish of Redmire, but Chris insists that there are four fish in the water bigger than the unofficial record. He will, if pressed, conjecture that the big common must be in the 80-90lb range. He has seen it just twice in seven years on the water, the second time at quite close quarters from the punt last season.

He feels that the other three 'biggies' are around the sixty pound mark, and thinks that he hooked one of these, the leather, which, like the '51' took a bait cast in front of its nose, on the last of October in 1977. He described the all-too-brief battle with that carp in his 'Memorable Blanks' article in Coarse Fishing Monthly, although he did not specify the fish or the water in that account. For all his 'good fortune' at the Mire with the two big fish, he had a terrible run of luck there, and had a long run of losing good fish. I've had the good fortune to read Chris's Redmire diary and just to put the '51' into perspective, it was one of only three fish over twenty pounds that Chris landed in his last four years on the water. And anyone interpreting that sentence as a denigration of Chris's ability is misinterpreting me.

Chris suffers from the conflict that rages in many of the big fish carp men who have been around a long time. He talks about his wildie waters and of fishing for pleasure. He writes about peace and seclusion, and can no longer involve himself with the pressures of the known Southern big fish waters, but big fish are in his blood and he has that irresistible urge to pursue them, much as he dislikes, and tries to suppress, that part of his approach to it all.

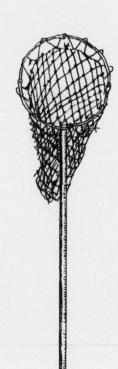

In his latter years at the Mire, the conflict grew ever greater. He loved the place but his mind was filled more and more with thoughts of catching one of the really big fish. The conflict eventually resolved itself as Chris himself outlines in his 'Twenty Years On' article in the summer edition of the Carp Society's magazine, Carp Fisher 2.

Much of his carp fishing life has emerged in his articles. He is a brilliant descriptive writer and philosopher, a vivid portrayer of mood and atmosphere, though if I dare say it, slightly less at home with the technical pieces he occasionally writes. It's a sad fact that only time can set an artist in true context, that greatness always has to be retrospective, because to me Chris is the greatest descriptive angling writer of all. He feels what he is doing very strongly, and where those feelings are for carp fishing, the full perception of it all comes over in depth and in quite beautiful natural English. His chapter in George Sharman's book, and the letter he sent Hutcho after the capture of the '51', which appears in Rod's book, are carp fishing classics. More than that, they are literary classics. *(Clearly written before the publication of 'Casting at the Sun' and 'The Deepening Pool'.)*

He is currently writing three books. One is to do with carp fishing, and one is about the night, about darkness. Chris has had a fascination with the dark since an early age. As a boy he used to force himself to sit for hours on end in a pitch black conifer wood and fight the panic of his fear so he could enjoy the beauty of the dark. On one occasion, when he had forced himself to the limit before fleeing in terror, he had just emerged from the blackness when he remembered that he had left his gloves behind. He went back for them. "The night is man's oldest enemy, but making peace with it, and conquering the natural fear of it, can lead you to some memorable and beautiful moments." – C. Yates, 1982.

Chris is also a dreamer. Not in the sense that most of us dream of winning the pools, or catching a fifty pound carp, but dreams fascinate him and he has dream diaries going back 20 years. He has this favourite dream about a carp pool, a dream he has had from time to time over the last six years. The pool is the most perfect, beautiful carp pool imaginable – 'The Hole in the Air Lake' it's called. In every dream he is allowed a glimpse of this water, as a vivid memory of it while he is fishing elsewhere. But so far he has not been given the honour of putting in a line. He spent his last 'Hole in the Air Lake' dream wandering through a green landscape of woods and streams, knowing the lake was nearby, but not being able to find it.

Chris did ask me to make special mention of that dream, if I touched on that subject at all. Having mentioned it, I cannot resist quoting from another letter on the subject of dreams, (this is a strange world to me as I have very little recall of dreams myself).

"…the detail of each dream is always vivid and no different at all from the memory of an actual event. It's only the label 'dream' that makes it seem a non-event. Take away the label and you are living a new life. And who is to say that your dreams did not happen on some other level of reality!"

In addition to being an artist with a pen, Chris is a superb artist with a camera, and many of the images for his photographic work come from his world of dreams. He actually does photographic work for a living and I suppose the blunt description of his occupation would be 'commercial photographer', which rather conjures up pictures of him on Brighton front taking snaps of couples in 'Kiss Me Quick' hats. Which is very much what he doesn't do. Technically, even understanding his work is way beyond me, but it may make some sense to the photographers amongst you. He composes record and book covers within his camera, putting his final shot together piece by piece on the one transparency. Again, he has illustrated some of his articles with his specialist shots. (The covers of "The Carp Strikes Back" and "Ritchie on Carp" were designed by Chris.)

He is a freelance, which explains why he is able to devote much of his summer to what he loves doing best, carp fishing. He tends to complain bitterly if he is landed with a photographic commission he can't avoid during the carp months, choosing to line the larder during the winter and close season. He is as traditional in his view of the carp season as he is in most aspects of carp fishing and turns to river fishing with the first frosts of autumn. As a rule, his Redmire season always finished at the end of October.

Although he lives in a fashionable area, he lives a simple life and does not seek any of the standard luxurious trappings demanded by modern society. Vale Cottage is simply furnished, and for transport he cycles, motorcycles and goes from one old Renault to another, proud of the fact that his cars, or vans, are able to get by without any attention until they decease and are towed away by the corporation. I didn't like to pursue the logical argument that perhaps if they had some attention their eventual demise could be delayed indefinitely: he has obviously found that his present system works well.

Chris is an artist who has achieved a workable compromise. He has managed to commercialise his talents – without prostituting them – to finance the time he needs to find inspiration for creation, and the time to create. But this love of the traditional is not limited to his carp fishing, it extends into another area of his life, the Golden Scale Club. Reading his slightly silly Coarse Fishing Monthly articles on this subject could give the less perceptive reader the impression that the GSC is composed of 'not quite grown-ups' with a fetish for dressing up in Victorian costumes, punting for gudgeon at Henley, and a perfectly healthy obsession with diamond smugglers. The Goons live on in darkest Surrey, mine Eccles (to be read in a Neddy Seagoon type voice, laddy).

But the Golden Scale Club is also a guardian of the unprotected environment, a watchdog on behalf of an unsuspecting society which, unknowingly, is about to have its countryside raped, motorways driven through its beauty spots, and its rivers polluted. If we are threatened by it and it is illegal, unethical or undesirable, Yatesy and the GSC will try and fight it. Chris is the spokesman at Public Enquiries, and preparing a brief for these is time consuming and requires considerable expertise and confidence to be undertaken by amateurs.

I actually went down to do a wildie pool piece, but sharp frosts through the previous week and heavy rain on the Saturday killed thoughts of that. On the Sunday we had breakfast gazing out at the Surrey woods, and the birds gathered on the window sill for their share. We talked on through the morning, went for a pub lunch out in the wilds, dropped Clare back at the Cottage, then went on to look at a couple of the waters Chris fishes – quite beautiful places, even on a soggy, late autumn day.

The rain had stopped some time during the morning and there was the

odd fish moving at the lake where Chris had his big common last season. We moved on to a smaller lake where Chris does some of his writing in the summer months.

We didn't really have thoughts of fishing, but the afternoon had taken a turn for the better and standing on this stage among the dying reed beds you could just feel the fish in front of you. We trekked the half mile back to the car and threw some tackle together. In deference to the occasion, I'd only taken soft rods and some strawberry flavoured sweetcorn (a quaint combination of traditional and modern). We used floats – although Chris seemed surprised that I carried them – and I fished with some feeling of anticipation.

I cast out just over the reeds into three feet of water, but Chris obviously knew of a spot and cast out ten yards beyond. His first two casts landed in my swim, but I protested and he settled for almost in my swim. There must have been something there but I couldn't see it. Ten minutes in, Chris had a twitch, a stirring of the float, but there was no follow up. There was an hour of daylight left and we had been due back at the cottage half an hour previously. We fished on till dark.

Twenty minutes in, my float suddenly disappeared, but I was so surprised I didn't strike. I made the excuse that the buzzer hadn't sounded but I could tell that Chris wasn't impressed. I settled for blaming the previous week's night shift, coupled with a basic incompetence.

Half an hour in, my float disappeared again, but as this disappearance followed a succession of twitches, and the float suddenly lying flat, my reactions coped and the rod bent over. Slightly. It was a half pound roach and I played it skilfully on the six pound line by striking it straight over the weed bed and into Chris's lap. I think he thought that that was intentional because he unhooked it for me and put it back. He was clearly jealous.

Daylight gave way to twilight, twilight to heavy gloom, and heavy gloom to Stygian blackness. I was frozen. A piece of silver paper furtively materialised to my left and was surreptitiously folded over the line near the butt ring. I strained my eyes, half-imagining that I could see my float just over the reeds, but I couldn't. I tried watching the rod tip, but I couldn't see that either. Chris suddenly picked up his rod (my heart sank: I thought he'd sensed a take) and announced, "You've won". I'd never actually 'counted' a roach before but I was quite willing to in those circumstances! We packed up and went home for tea.

Clare served a meal in front of the log fire. Chris showed me some of his photographic work, carp and commercial, and I looked at his stunning collection of old angling books. They were all there and I could have browsed indefinitely. Reluctantly I finally dragged myself away about eleven, hoping that there was a garage within about half a gallon's range. There was, exactly where Chris said it would be. I was surprised; it seemed a bit practical for him.

Journeys back are usually easier than journeys there. Three and a half hours does not seem long when your thoughts are full. I was stunned by the news of the '51'. No details of the death were available then and my reaction was a selfish, rather obvious one. 'For the Record' was due out the following month and nothing could stop it. What if the great fish had had dropsy and that was the reason for its death? The thought soon passed; that could not be, and of course it wasn't.

It upsets me now that the well intentioned 'For the Record' article could have been so terribly misconstrued and could have played a part in Yatesy's decision to resign from the Mire. He is a great man and he loved the place, but he is independent and there is a limit to how far you can go in swallowing your principles and your pride, however great the prize.

Yatesy the carp angler, and Chris Yates the person. For some of you I will have overdone it. I know that but I can only write it as I see it, in the hope that that is how the majority would see it. In 'Twenty Years On' Chris describes himself thus – *'an individual who has moved a long way from the common practise'*. I won't attempt to enlarge further on that, other than to say that he is the nicest man you could hope to meet.

The Middle Swim at Roman Lakes on a quiet mid-week day.

Deeppocket can be one hundred per cent impossible at times. At other times his degree of impossibility ranges from ninety five to ninety seven per cent, while it must be said that on his really good days he does a passable imitation of a human being. Unfortunately, those days are never when he's on the bank.

My mind's been driven back twelve months by some mind-blowing conversation which I'll come to later. We'd been giving the close season water some hammer, and the fish were having it good style. Like many ultra tackle conscious carp, these were totally floored by the hair and the boiled baits, and everyone who was quick onto the rig was catching carp. Deeppocket was in a spell of temporary retirement and making frequent trips across with Razzbaz, the Lizard and anyone else who had transport and could stand being snarled at if they displeased.

When fishing, most of Deeppocket's utterances start: "For naff's sake…"

It was late Friday night, early Saturday morning and I was on night shift. I'd been across to Roman Lakes on the Friday, straight from work; an hour's drive, fish the daylight hours through, straight back and somehow get through the night shift like a slow motion zombie. I was in the back of a trailer about one in the morning when the phone in the warehouse rang. I was nackered headless, starting to get the red mists, and all I could think of was the next cup of coffee and crashing out at half-six in the morning. Phone calls at one in the morning are usually a portent of disaster for someone; we don't get many social calls at that time.

It was Deeppocket – like I said, a portent of disaster. I told him I'd ring back when I'd finished the load.

Actually, I think it was probably the last load we were doing that night – it being Friday and the lads being a bit good about carrying me when I've had a day on the water. So, by the time we'd shut the trailer doors and I'd made a coffee and lit a fag, I was feeling marginally more human.

I rang him back. He was obviously smashed out of his skull, and it sounded as though he'd got female company. I'd better not enlarge on that except to say that the phone is by the bed.

"How did you go on?" he slurred down the phone, referring to the previous day's fishing.

How the hell could he have his mind on fishing at a time like that? She must have been rough. As it happens, I'd had a good day, and I broke the news as gently as possible. On reflection, I had had a really good day, which meant that at any one time throughout the day, at least one indicator was at the top of the needle, beating hell out of the rod butt. It's a 'Beep-crack' water (Deeppocket's description). You never actually see the indicator move from the bottom of the needle to the top; it momentarily vanishes, then reappears doing an imitation of a humming bird's wings, with the spool rapidly emptying.

Deeppocket gave a graphic unprintable reply, which involved the intricate juxtaposition of a number of four letter words, and which gave some insight into the kind of company he was keeping, then followed through with:

"Are we going today then?"

The question was as unexpected as it was unwelcome. It took me completely off guard. Incoherence must have set in long before because a voice that I vaguely recognised as mine answered "Better try it."

My mind was quite adamantly asserting "No way" while my

Beep-Crack, Wait There!

uncontrollable mouth was busy sentencing me to a further eighteen hours of semi-conscious walking sleep.

I tend to give the impression in print that I'm a male chauvinist pig, which may or may not be true, but if I am then it is but as a pale imitation of Deeppocket, whose audacity can be breathtaking when needs must. Apparently, at that moment there was much musting of the needs going on (and you can read that how you want as long as you don't expect to make English out of it).

"I'll get the baits ready and I'll be away in an hour to get a place in the queue."

There was a female cry of disbelief from the background, which mirrored pretty accurately what was going through my mind. I felt like offering to go across and take over where he was leaving off, but the phone had gone dead and he was presumably already giving the disbeliever the kiss of death and ringing for a taxi for his now redundant companion.

I survived the rest of the night on willpower (and possibly nodded off for five minutes in the chair, accidentally) then reluctantly followed the previous day's route across the hills to Cheshire.

Deeppocket was already standing astride the prime spot like a colossus when I got there. The place was crawling with carp men and the general atmosphere on the lake wavered between simmering hostility and open warfare. Our man seems to have that effect on people and revels in it. Two days with virtually no sleep hadn't really left me in the mood, or in a fit state, to try and ease the tension, so I just let it all wash over me. Deeppocket had three rods out and had the producing area well stitched up so I settled meekly for my pre-ordained role of understudy.

Fortunately it was an uneventful day in as much as Deeppocket didn't actually come to blows with anyone. He came close though on at least three occasions, almost sparked a major international incident and alternately slept and snarled while I struggled to catch the odd small carp, and reflected silently on the glories and comparative peace of the previous day. Why we insist on breaking our own rule that we'll never fish the water at the weekend in the close season I don't know; I mean Deeppocket can be relied on to handle so much, i.e. me and/or one other known and similarly thick-skinned companion. Beyond that, his capacities for civilised communication on the bank are strained to the limit – his temperament is not exactly geared to withstanding strain. In fact, I'm almost tempted to reflect that my calming influence (an illusion born of the fact that I'm rarely more than half awake) has slightly tempered his volatile personality over the years.

The first, and major, ingredient for disaster was a real keenie. An absolute cracker. Possibly in his first year of carp fishing, freshly graduated from Kev's book, in there with a good going bait and the rig, and clearly getting the whole thing bang right from the word go. Good luck to the kid. We go fishing to catch carp and that's what he was doing. But it can be dangerous to keep coming round and stuffing your successes up Deeppocket's nose, talking as though twenty pounds is the minimum weight for the fish in the water, and failing to notice the molten lava on the verge of erupting from the crater of the Deeppocket volcano. Mercifully, the volcano suppressed its eruptions until the kid was out of earshot, and his mounting frustration was reserved for shutting me off from as much of the water as possible. If he couldn't stuff this kid he was going to make me suffer for my previous day's efforts.

Our main trouble was that the baits going in at each end of the lake seemed to be good enough to hold the carp just where they were. The fish tend to move to the ends of the water overnight and then drift into the middle as the day wears on. Not always, but that is often the general pattern. The area we were fishing is usually good for the odd carp up to midday, after which time the beep-cracks start in earnest. On the day, our anticipated bonanza never materialised. The majority of the 'beep-cracks' came to the keenie, who kept insisting on regaling us with a full break-down of his season's successes, and a couple of mates of ours who had been pushed down by the angling pressure into a no hope area at the far end of the water. As no hope areas go, it produced a fair number of fish that day.

Now I've got this philosophy, born of bitter experience, that when you get stuffed on a water you just have to grin and bear it. On the day someone has got it more right than you and it bloody hurts, however uncompetitive you may consider yourself to be and however much you like seeing other people catch carp. No excuses; learn from it, suffer it; go home, break a few plates and snarl at the cat/dog/wife and kids, whichever is foolish enough to show first, but no excuses. Anyway, we'd run out of excuses by mid-afternoon so we had to settle for the grin and bear it routine. Deeppocket, whose grin wasn't exactly splitting his face in half, improved on that though, and contrived to take most of the credit for the carp that others caught, a stroke of genius that took my breath away.

"I see everyone's fishing the same rig as us now."

As our rig was a pretty basic hair rig as publicised by Lenny and Kev, I wasn't totally convinced that we could really claim much credit for its widespread use on waters all over the country. And, as neither of us had had the undoubted good fortune to meet the superstar keenie fishing the first peg in before, I doubted if Deeppocket's influence on him was that profound. The simple fact is that the water breeds good carp anglers, and always has done. I silently replied to his outrageous remark:

"It's a bloody shame we're not fishing his bait on our rig then," but discretion is always the safer course with Deeppocket, whose sense of humour tends to be geared to his status in his own eyes at any particular moment.

We did manage a couple of fish apiece though, which would be a good day's carp fishing in any other circumstances, and they were the cause of the strain on international relations. Now I don't know why it should be so, but it can be difficult writing about our foreign brethren. Readers are either over-zealous in their defence (as I tend to be), or somewhat disdainful of them (an attitude I cannot tolerate). So I hope this is taken in perspective because it is not told for effect, unlikely as it may sound, or read, if you read quietly. There was a party of Orientals fishing just down the bank to our left, about ten of them taking turns to fish for roach, or whatever came along, with two rods between them, and clearly intrigued by the events in the carp swims to their right.

Mid-morning, Deeppocket's right hand rod was subjected to a 'beep-crack' and the Optonic howled in fury at the abuse it suffered at the hands of the nylon being stripped from the spool at a rate of knots. Our man was in a coma, suffering withdrawal symptoms from life, occasioned by the day's

Wait there time!

bankside activities and the excesses of the previous night. The magic words, "You're away" produced some reaction: the sounds of Optonics howling can start to form part of the commonplace background noises on days of heavy activity at that water, producing no immediate reaction in unconscious minds.

Deeppocket had his right hand bait out at about ninety yards, so by the time he hit surface and made it to the rod, the fish would be at about one hundred and thirty, and flying. His actions followed the slow motion processes of his mind. The bail arm went in and he let the line tighten, and tighten, and carry on tightening. I thought he'd gone back to sleep on his feet and looked on in amazement, hoping that he was going to lift gently into the fish after all that. Thereabouts his mind must have suddenly made it back to reality because he struck the take an almighty crack. Mercifully the tackle withstood the abuse and he determinedly reeled in the surrendering carp.

Some time ago, Jim Gibbinson described the hazards of trying to land a carp on very busy waters, a description masterfully and graphically executed I'm told (this was well before my time) and one with which I shall not attempt to compete. Once someone's done something definitive, you steer clear of it, which is a good enough reason for not reading any of the current writers because what you've not read, you don't know about.

It was busy and there were bodies everywhere. Deeppocket was heavily surrounded by a multi-racial gallery, and he snarled at it in his own multi-racial language, giving them colourful, detailed, and possibly physically impossible instructions as to just what they should do. One of the Orientals made a dignified and diplomatic translation for one of his friends who was late on the scene:

"We must wait here." 'Here' being at best two feet from the raging Deeppocket's left shoulder. They clearly enjoyed the excitement of it all but had little understanding of the strange British custom of returning very large (to them), very edible looking fish to the water. Carp Chow Mein would clearly have made a lot more sense.

As the day wore on, their fascination with what we were doing grew and they inscrutably scrutinised our every move as closely as they dared. At one stage I was tying a few baits in an attempt to keep mind and body together when I had that feeling – not a carp feeling, but the being watched one. There was an inscrutable Oriental face peering over my shoulder. I carried on with what I was doing, smiling to myself at the thought of the problems such blatant spying might have caused on the banks of Brooklands or Darenth. They recognised that Deeppocket was in charge though and 'waited there' whenever they dashed up to watch a fish being landed.

Even by the standards of that extraordinary water, where distraction invariably piles on distraction, and the Lizard usually finishes up high as a kite and reeling with excitement at the outrageousness of it all, it was an unusual day. People, bulldozers, crack-offs, Optonics, 'I'm in', 'barsteward', the cacophony of sound from the endless territorial squabbles of the Canada geese, and the background sound over-riding everything (the noise that the Canadas are possibly copying) of the owner and son biting lumps out of each other over at the cafe.

The afternoon drifted into evening and the ultra keenie in the first peg kept making us have it with a succession of fish. Deeppocket almost gave him both barrels when he came round to tell us about the twenty he'd just had, but fortunately he was lost for words for just long enough for the kid to move on and stuff the kipper up someone else's nostrils.

I got the brunt of the raging character assassination, as usual. We tend to argue that one, I must admit. Deeppocket's attitude is that if he's not catching twenties from a water there's none in there, while my philosophy is slightly different; if I'm not catching the bigger fish and someone else is, then I'm getting something wrong, as usual. You can only plead bad luck or other people's exaggerations for so long.

Days quickly fade into history. You go there, you fish, and most of what happens is filed in the back of the mind or becomes a confused memory, a mosaic of other days and other events. The memory has a strange filing system. Things that felt significant at the time are beyond recapture, and other events, which appeared far less notable, are elevated to a position of some importance. I was tired and my mind was tuned in to carp, so my thoughts were centred on the carp fishing, and that made the greatest impression on my mind. But not on my memory, which considered it another in a long line of wasted days and focused its attention on the unusual permutation of events and people, rather than my fishing. But then, life with Deeppocket around is a bit like that.

That was a sequitur to that day though. Almost a year to the day later I was peacefully installed in the middle swim, with the water more or less to myself, when Deeppocket's favourite carp man from the previous year rolled up. He fished to my right, and we had a pleasant day's carping, although whether we caught or not escapes my memory. In fact I'd hardly have recalled the day at all if the lad hadn't chosen to unburden his soul about his previous year's results.

"I made a bit of a fool of myself last year I'm afraid. My scales were a couple of pounds out and those twenties I caught weren't twenties at all."

Surprise, surprise! But I couldn't help but like him for the admission, and I couldn't help wishing Deeppocket had been there to hear it. On second thoughts, perhaps not. For someone who breathes human frailty through every pore Deeppocket doesn't show much tolerance of anything less than perfection in others.

It feels like a hundred years ago now. The Carp Society was ten months old; ten months of travelling, meetings and making new friends. I first met Ritchie on the banks of the Con Club in the summer of 1981. He impressed me then – and he still does: his is a friendship I value because he possesses a loyalty to principles and beliefs that transcends the shallow demands of expediency. If he is occasionally 'out of order' that is because he has in him something that most carp men have - an extreme streak that stands apart from the common practise and which can't always be subdued.

At the time of the week's fishing described in the pages that follow, Ritchie was friendly with Clive and Malc, which explains the (now) unlikely cast list. The chapter is just my version of the events of the week in the life of… a carp water. I've called it Fox Pool because I can't mention its real name, but the name I've given it will make the water instantly recognisable to those who fish it.

I would also add that while the original version of this account appeared in Carp Fisher 2, I have made alterations to the text in the course of transcribing it. The original was written in a hurry, and to me it showed: on the other hand, a great many people have said that this is their favourite piece of mine – which is nice, but as it's strictly comparative, pleasantly meaningless.

I offered the piece to Ritchie for his book because the events of the week seemed to centre round him, and had a strong influence on my approach to carp fishing in the years that followed.

People often ask who Deeppocket is: he's no more real than I am.

Blank at Fox Pool

The end of a long, hard winter was in sight and Deeppocket and I were due down south for some meeting or other, which just happened to fall about a week before the end of the season. Somehow we came up with the bright idea of staying down south after the meeting and fishing the season out. I rang Malc and asked him if he could get us onto a water for the last week. I didn't actually say so, but what we had in mind was one of those easy southern waters where the indicators are never still, you have to reel the baits in to get any sleep and you finish up with one of Mike's Billingsgate shots every other day – twenties scattered all over the swim.

Malc rang back and said that Ritchie could get us on Fox Pool for the week. Ah well, there you go; there would be other times for easy southern waters; if they exist other than in the minds of northern carp men Fox Pool certainly ain't one of them.

There was some kind of aggro at this meeting on the Saturday, which was about par for the course. I can't remember the details now but the third world war seemed imminent at the time. Somehow the trouble seemed to drag over into the Sunday, although that's immaterial and it was nothing to do with me, or Deeppocket, surprisingly. In fact, we seem to have got a bit of our depth in the aggro stakes down south. I mean, Deeppocket can start an argument in the proverbial empty room, but these southern lads… Anyway, there was still a bit of tension in the air on the Sunday, not to mention a bitterly cold southerly wind blowing straight down the lake.

We'd seen the water before, briefly, but knew very little about it other than that some very big fish had come out of it… So what was I doing there? You may well ask. The lake covers about six acres, is an oblong shape and has trees most of the way round. We were to fish the only open part of the banks, two swims close together on what is roughly the east bank. Clive and Malc were

fishing the north bank, and Ritchie was on the west. Deeppocket was to fish a swim that was occupied by one of the biggest names in carp fishing when we arrived: he was just packing up and as he's not yet caught a fish from the water, the whole thing was quickly put in perspective for me. The lads kept making reassuring noises like "You've got as good a chance as anyone else," to boost our confidence, but I couldn't quite see it like that. I was looking forward to it though; I was ready for a week away from the paperwork and the warehouse. At the risk of repeating myself there is far more to carp fishing than catching carp as far as I'm concerned – which is perhaps as well after the season I've just had.

It's nice getting to a lake with a full week in front of you. There's no rush to set up; you can wander round looking at the water, and have a chat here and there. And you can put off the chore of pack-horsing a week's equipment from the car park and the rest of the chores that attend setting up.

We were given guidance as to how to fish the water so we set up pitch and made our plans accordingly. I followed the advice given but for some reason I was very strongly drawn towards fishing the bottom bank. I can't explain it, I just knew the fish were there but, not knowing the water, I didn't have, the confidence to follow my instincts. It's too easy to be wise after the event, and indications were that I did have fish in front of me for at least some of the time, but I should have followed my gut reaction for at least a day or two.

We set up pitch, which caused no end of mirth for starters! My ancient bivvy, which I bought in 1975 and which still does the job quite adequately - rat holes and all – was christened 'The Dog Kennel', and Deeppocket's… well, I'd better explain this one. For some strange reason, and just for that week, my friend was into guy ropes in a really big way; immaculate, white guy ropes – and miles of them at that. His bivvy is one of the Dave Barnes' type and has eyelets for guy ropes on two levels, about a foot off the ground and three feet up. So there were two guy ropes running down to each tent peg, and the bivvy was instantly dubbed 'The Sputnik'.

I didn't fully understand the mirth caused by our set-ups until I'd had another wander round and examined the resident bivvies more closely. I couldn't believe it. Now, there is a feeling up north that these southern lads have it a bit easy; lots of big fish, hundreds of lakes, very little travelling… you've heard it all before. But even the most biased northern carp man couldn't have dreamed up the reality of carpeted swims: er, not swims any more – 'lots'. I tend to refer to the area of bank that a carp man is occupying as a pitch, or swim. That's old hat; it's now a lot, a name taken from the in-vogue wrap-round bivvies which I think Ritchie designed. Some of these are marketed as Waterlots, hence the name lot. Not that I'm knocking them; they are convenient and functional, and, as used by these lads, luxurious. Clive's and Ritchie's lots were impressive but it is only fair to say that Malc's was something special and would not have been out of place at the Ideal Home Exhibition: It was immaculate; carpet under the rods, carpet all round the pitch, carpeted lot – and the whole lot stayed immaculate because just inside the entrance was a small, much used handbrush…

The first day was uneventful. We saw one of the half tame foxes which are addicted to Ritchie's slippers. Yeh, slippers… are you getting the picture? We tackled up, put out some baits, had something to eat, tightened a few guy ropes every ten minutes, talked, looked at the water, and froze. It was bloody cold on the east bank, but if it meant catching carp it was a small price to pay. Clive and Malc were a bit restless; they felt it was too cold for the carp to feed; and it's only fair to say that Clive had been on the water since the previous Tuesday without any sign of action.

Ritchie stayed put till after dark then came round for a few hours' rabbit. This turned out to be the pattern: he was glued to his lot during the day but didn't rate his chances after dark. The fox came round a couple of times while we were yakking, but we couldn't hold it long enough to get a picture.

We settled in about half eleven and I had a terrible night. There was a vicious frost and I couldn't get warm, or comfortable, plus I ran out of cigarettes – which was a major disaster. It was one of those nights that go on for ever, and I thought I'd been awake right through it, but I couldn't have been because I didn't know until the following morning that Deeppocket had had a troubled night. The fox had taken a liking to his bivvy and had caused chaos. It would take too long to explain how it was responsible for the demise of Deeppocket's bedchair, and how it tangled forty yards of line from each rod through the bushes, but that's what happened. Deeppocket wasn't at his best on the Monday morning.

Deeppocket and I were in different frames of mind that week. He's closer to Clive and Malc than I am so possibly their pessimism gradually saturated him, but he never really settled to what we were doing. Perhaps he's just more of a realist than I am, because I'm the eternal dreamer, and hoper. Because of that I felt really optimistic about catching all week: no, it was stronger than that – I knew that I was going to catch. I'd gone down knowing that, at best, one take in seven days was what I was waiting for, but I felt certain that one take would come. For hours on end I would sit behind the rods, just waiting for the indicator to bounce up and down. It never did though: in Deeppocket's picturesque parlance the indicators were superglued to the needles all week – but my feeling that I was about to have a take never wavered. Persistence was all I could claim credit for though. In retrospect I fished badly because I didn't follow my instincts to fish a quiet spot in the margins. It's easy after, but catching carp is about getting it right in advance, and while you are on the water, not while you are driving home after.

Ritchie found fish three days in after he'd moved into the Duck Pond swim. He had two fish in twelve hours over Wednesday night after he'd lost a fish on the Wednesday afternoon: they were both commons which looked about lowish doubles; beautiful fish. One was a really rich, golden colour.

I took a couple of hours off from the fishing that afternoon to talk to one or two of the other carp men who were on the water; they were mostly on Ritchie's bank: Booker the Hooker from Kent, and his loyal friend, gentle Jon Holt; Steve in the pram, an amazing self-contained portable bivvy; Steve had no carpets – but he did have television: Dennis Davies from Kent was there, rumoured to be Ritchie's comrade in arms in that notorious trip to the Welsh border – and on the verge of packing in carp fishing. While talking to one of these lads I discovered that the area Deeppocket and I were fishing is known as the Noddy Bank. Any good that? A couple of dumb northerners come down and get stuck in the most exposed, muddiest, most uncomfortable part of the lake – and why? Because there are no trees there so they will be able to cast out all right!

Thursday there was some movement; not from the fish, but the anglers.

Ian, who had caught a 31½ on the Friday before we arrived, and Jon, who had doubled up with him in the same swim, moved from the swim opposite me to a couple of pitches on the end bank. Ritchie couldn't believe his luck and was out of the Duck Pond swim and into the vacated pitch like a ferret down a rabbit hole. Clive, Malc and Deeppocket gave it best and moved down into Surrey in search of some action. Big Kev arrived and after a tactical blunder which we shall not go into (Ritchie straightened him) moved into the Duck Pond swim which Ritchie had just vacated. Kev is not one of *the* Kevs; he's just another nutter like the rest of us. He's referred to as big because he bleeding well is – and he's got hands like bunches of bananas.

Meanwhile, I lived on in hope on the windswept Noddy Bank, and I really mean in hope. I hardly dared leave the swim, partly because the 'Dog Kennel' was likely to blow away at any moment, and partly because I'd still got 'that feeling' five days in.

There is a timelessness to seven days on a hard lake. You're waiting for something to happen, but you don't know when it's going to happen, if at all. But when there is action it doesn't come as a surprise, however long you've waited. One minute the days are drifting along, minute by minute: your mind is wandering heaven knows where, and there are six or seven of you round the lake doing much the same thing. Next minute, an Optonic howls and all minds and eyes are focussed on one swim and one angler. That's what happened just after three o'clock on the Friday afternoon. Automatically I looked across at Ritchie's swim: right first time, he was in. The action-starved carp men gathered during the ten minute fight and watched an artist at work.

The fish was in front of him by the time I got round but it was by no means beaten: repeatedly it went for the branches either side of the swim, but he was ahead of it every time. Ritchie'd got it pegged at doubles; he said it was too lively for a big fish, but the fish Steve put the net under went way over doubles. It was the leather and it went thirty four. The weight was checked, the pictures were taken, the talk went on for a while, then the lake drifted back to normal. It was the first thirty I'd seen, and it was a beautiful fish; but no more beautiful than it would have been at fourteen, or twenty four, or forty four. If fact, the sight of it on the bank didn't have anything like the impact I thought it should have had.

But when I had the pictures developed, I couldn't believe it. The fish was unbelievably beautiful; big and golden in the late afternoon sunlight: what a glorious fish. I suppose I have some sort of hope that I will catch a fish that big, one day, but it is a hope rather than an ambition or desire.

I don't think any of us envied Ritchie that fish. He has earned every reward he gets from the water because over the years he has spent a lifetime there, and has suffered all the frustrations and heartbreaks of blank seasons and making no apparent progress. I thought of that capture a great deal in the weeks and months that followed because the whole circumstances surrounding the event somehow swept away the mystique of fishing for the big, hard fish. Dick Walker was the first to spell out the fact that you catch big fish by fishing for them, but until you see someone making it work, it is hard to accept that it can work for you. Ritchie got the fish feeding on a bait, then grafted, then waited. It is not the only formula for catching the biggies, but it is certainly a formula, and one that has since worked very successfully for me – as it will for anyone.

Friday and the big fish became history. Saturday was just a day. I talked to Kev late on and the whole thing was starting to get to him: he had that haunted look around the eyes. I often wonder just what Arthur Ransome had in mind when he said, "a man who fishes habitually for carp has a strange look in is eyes… He looked as though he had been in heaven and hell." Carp men do have a strange look about the eyes when they are blowing out, when it's really getting to them: not just on the water, but away from it as well, but I'm not at all sure that was what Ransome was referring to.

But he must have written those words in the twenties, or thirties; fifty, sixty years ago. Slow down lads, slow down: it's been around a long time; let it live on.

In retrospect, Saturday wasn't just a day; it was a comparatively warm and sunny day. I stretched out on the Noddy Bank and let the wind and sun start to spread their make up over my winter pallor. And somewhere in all this I stopped off to help a young, over-excited lad land a twenty plus pike; it takes all sorts… His uninhibited pleasure as he gazed at the fish and weighed it (landing net and all), was moving. He left me in charge of the fish while he charged off to find his dad. By the time dad arrived, the landing net seemed to have become part of the weight, but I didn't disillusion them.

I slept during Saturday evening, which was a rarity for me. I'm not a great sleeper when I'm at the water, but I was weary and didn't wake up until well after nine o'clock. I made some coffee and smoked a couple of cigarettes – and, for the first time, it got to me: the indicators weren't going to move. I hadn't given up hope but suddenly knew that my season was as good as over. I eventually got my act together and went round to Ritchie's lot, complete with tape recorder to put a deferred interview together. We talked a great deal during the week, and in previous encounters over the months, but would it work on tape? It came out just the same (Carp Fisher 2), sitting there drinking Ritchie's lousy tea and watching a full moon come up over the Noddy Bank and start its climb over the water that Ritchie knows like the back of his hand – but which is still a total stranger to me.

I went back to bed about three, and got up again soon after six. The optimism was back; it could still happen. I made a big breakfast, had a couple of coffees and waited for the sun to breathe some life into me. I was sorting out the bivvy when an Optonic sounded, then stopped, then started again. I looked across, but it wasn't Ritchie: down at the Duck Pond, Kev was in! We gathered and he coped well, if a little anxiously, with a heavy fish which gave him plenty of hairy moments before Ritchie could slip the net under it. The carp was Kev's personal best at 25$\frac{1}{4}$lb and was a fish that Ritchie didn't recognise. The water was starting to fish.

I thought that would be it, but there was one more result. Ritchie had to have the last say and he had a fish of just over twenty pounds soon after eleven that morning. I was round in time to take a couple of pictures of him landing it from the high bank behind the swim. Ritchie had been going to fish on into the evening but I think the last fish achieved a personal landmark for him (I guessed it was his thirtieth twenty plus fish of the season, but I didn't ask, and he didn't volunteer the significance of the capture). Enough is sufficient…

That was more or less it; the week just faded out after that. The season was gone and, temporarily, it was back to the land of hot baths and warm beds;

the comfort of the armchair – and knowing what day it is; the exchange of the freedom of seven days where the last minute is as meaningful, or as meaningless, as the next, for the urgent imprisonment of the eight hour shift and the loads to get out.

The timeless week is my week but I can't shake off the shackles of every day life: I haven't got the guts to just kick it all aside, and get out there and just fish. Perhaps it's age; perhaps I didn't come to carp fishing quite early enough to let my wild streak take over completely, although it's come close enough a couple of times. What the hell: there'll be other weeks; perhaps even weeks with my fish in them; currently they seem to be everyone else's. I love it either way.

Space permitting I'll add a footnote to that. When I saw the last paragraph in print it looked gutless and it disturbed me. Some time later I did an interview with Roger Smith in which he had this to say (about Jack Hilton): *"He believed that anybody could do anything if they wanted to badly enough and in many ways he left me with the same absolute belief, because I still think the same. Anyone can do anything if they really want to. They might have to sacrifice a lot to do it, but if they really want to, they can."*

I later went for that and I think that between them, and carp fishing, Ritchie and Roger have helped change my life rather dramatically.

Waveney again. I promised myself a late season trip down after the week with the Six in August, then promptly did nothing about it. The Lizard triggered a trip by unexpectedly announcing that he fancied a few days there. I pounced on the holiday chart, spent two days getting ready and vanished into the darkness of a back end of October Saturday morning. When I made the run in August I managed to cover 220 miles for a 180 mile journey. This time I did better and covered 260 miles, taking in the outskirts of Great Yarmouth and most of the villages on the Norfolk/Suffolk border. I must treat myself to a map book for Christmas.

I drove purposefully past 'D' lake and joined the Lizard and a close friend on an otherwise deserted 'G'. He was installed in the Slabs swim, fishing the stream bed, and seemed a bit peeved that he'd had no action (he'd been there three hours). I dropped in two swims to his right, to fish the tree line, and started making baits. I was using HNV's and intended fishing fresh baits every day. A couple of hours and I was set up and the baits were out. Quite by accident I went long with one rod, shutting the Lizard off from the tree line. Bloody shame that. The fact that he knew in advance that I wanted to fish the Slabs had nothing to do with it.

A long, hard appraisal of the water was not encouraging. It was covered with leaves and there wasn't a breath of wind hitting the surface. Local information had it that the water wasn't fishing, so we spent thirty six hours proving the reliability of the local information service. As blank weekends go, it was unremarkable. The highlight was the Lizard's battle with Deeppocket's Waterlot. The Lot had replaced the Sputnik immediately after the Fox Pool week and the Lizard spent a frustrating Saturday afternoon and evening wrestling with it. The Lot won hands down, despite six separate prolonged attacks on it with the mallet. I rated that.

The Crafty Cockney appeared on the Sunday and confirmed that 'G' wasn't fishing. I was glad of the chance of a chat because although I was happy enough with the base I was using, I was worried about the flavour. I can't remember exactly why, but I felt that I got a strong, unspoken reaction to the fourth one I mentioned (Maplecreme). Thanks Derek, a nod's as good as a wink...

In fact, the only event of any consequence over the weekend was the Leather coming out of 'D' for the third time in a month. 'D' had not been fishing for two weeks because of heavy rain and falling temperatures, but apparently the Leather was still on the move. The news was too much for the Lizard who upped roots Sunday teatime and jumped into swim one as soon as it was vacated. I'd gone down for a quiet session on 'G' but the thought of the Lizard getting lucky unsettled me. Better get in there son; may as well blank 'D' as 'G'.

It was very mild, and a strongish wind had blown up from the South. I moved into swim two. We were the only ones on the water, apart from having the female company of the Lizard's close friend. (I felt I should make the sex of the close friend clear because Hutchie, deep in his cups and at his most outrageous one night, asked the Lizard if he was gay. As this was immediately after complimenting me on the Grecian 2000 look, and immediately before assuring Deeppocket that his eyes were just made for make up, the man had obviously got something on his mind that night.)

We had no action Sunday night, which is not an unusual occurrence for 'D' lake at the best of times. Monday was the Lizard's last day; I was staying until Wednesday night. I gambled and put a fair amount of bait out. I had to get the fish eating it because I was using a chain reaction base. The first bait would help them convert the rest, presuming there is much converting going on in the low forties.

Mid morning and pandemonium broke out in swim one. The Lizard was into a fish. That was the good news; then the bad news; his line was over a branch hanging out from the hedge near the oak. I did as I was told and got the boat out while the usually 'cool' Lizard made like a mother coot shepherding her chicks across a pike infested water. I rowed out to the tethered carp and released the line. The Lizard skimmed it in, landed it and weighed it while I turned the boat round. He claimed that it went thirteen two, though I doubt if Deeppocket would have given him doubles for it. I rowed back and was instructed to take a couple of hook baits and some free samples back out to the spot the fish had come from. I dropped the terminal tackle at the foot of the hedge and spread a few free offerings around them. They floated, much to the delight of the coots which were getting exhausted from having to dive down in eight to ten feet of water. I didn't tell the Lizard that the free offerings had floated until a month or two later. I didn't want him to know that I knew that he was fishing with buoyant baits, and the thought did cross my mind that, of the two of us, I might be the only one to know that he *was* using buoyant baits. The sublety of it all didn't strike me till later. The only reason for using free offerings that float is if you are fishing single hook baits, but want other people to think you are fishing over a bed of bait...

I rowed my own baits out to the rushes and dropped them tight against the stems. The coots appreciated me positioning them in the shallow water. I spent the rest of the daylight hours making up a fresh batch of baits while the Lizard alternated between going home and not going home. In the end, he definitely went, reversing an earlier decision to definitely stay, which amended an even earlier half-decision to possibly stay, which was later modified by an in between half decision to possibly stay 'if'. We all knew that he was going all along, but then, that's the Lizard, totally predictable in his unpredictability – and always marvellous company.

The last day of October and I'd been at the water long enough for my brain to start functioning. I've got to confess that I'm hampered in my carp fishing by still having an inner feeling that carp are uncatchable. I know they're not, from photographs. On occasions I catch enough to prove conclusively to myself that they're not, but at heart I'm the eternal beginner. Every carp I land is likely to be the last and every new movement of the indicators is a joyous event. Having said which, I suddenly became very confident that I was going to catch, such was my belief in the bait.

The long night was setting in and I wanted the reassurance of a fish. I wanted to get on the oak, but I needed to know that the fish were picking up the bait. I had to get somewhere where I would have a good chance of action during the night. Martin Lanegan had put me into the Rushes swim at the end of the lake for night action when I'd been down in August, and he'd been right. The mild winter wind was pushing in there now so I moved round and settled in behind the brolly at about half past ten. I hoped for action from midnight onwards, and in November there is a lot of midnight onwards to first light. I eased the dark hours away in my usual restless habit, smoking and drinking coffee.

The first vague suggestion of the approaching day was softening the darkness when I had a single 'beep' from the Optonics. I was heavily foamed and presumed a line bite. It relaxed me and I promptly fell asleep. The Optonic woke me to a flier. On the end of the line it was anything from twenty five upwards. In the net it shrank to mid doubles. It was a start. They were *'aving it*, Clive's immortal words as oft quoted by Deeppocket, right hand emphasising. I'd had my action and I promptly pulled out into swim one. It was time to renew my frustrating acquaintanceship with the oak.

The baits went out at first light. It's a difficult cast but I had them in position at the first time of asking. The rowing boat helped. *"There are times when you have to work hard and there are times when you've got to sit a long time without the actual indicators moving,"* said Ritchie in his remarkable Carp Fisher 2 interview. I had two days in which to sit and wait. Two days for a big carp to make a mistake.

I set up pitch, spread the bed chair, tuned in to the cheerful banality of Wogan and immersed myself in a book about the unlikely relationship between Mary Pickford and Douglas Fairbanks. The conditions were staggering. At about nine o' clock Martin Symonds paid his daily visit. He was relieved that I'd had a fish – and a bit surprised?

"It's the first of November."

"Oh yes." Pretty sparking conversation.

"You can fish from wherever you want once the caravan season's over." (The caravan season finished at the end of October).

"Oh."

Oh! I didn't know whether to laugh or cry. I'd just moved for the third time in three days; I certainly wasn't moving again. I looked across to the point and my eyes travelled across to the oak. The hell I wasn't moving again!

I was installed under the corner bush on the point by eleven. There was no one else fishing the lake, or it wouldn't have been on, but the marks from the rod rests showed that I had moved into an area that was being fished. The oak was a different proposition from that angle. Casting to it from Swim One is much easier at the back end when the leaves have died, but from the point it is easier still. It's about fifty five yards to the back bank, and there are two quite pronounced gaps each side of a central branch which drops down to the water line. The gaps are about four or five feet wide – but look much wider from a distance – and about six feet apart. They are so inviting that you can almost imagine signs saying 'Left hand bait' and 'Right hand bait'.

A new cast though; a new range to find. I decided to creep up on it rather than start half way up the oak and work down. On the third creep I hit the back fence through the left hand gap. Retackle kid, patiently does it. The right hand bait went in about two feet from the edge. Close enough? Maybe not, but I left it and retackled the second rod. Within the hour I'd sussed it. As tight casts go, this was an easy one, because the end tackle was going the distance it looked to be going. I know what that means, if you don't. It wasn't 'further than it looks', or 'closer than it looks'; it was as far as it looked.

I was edgy now; I had a feeling about the afternoon. Not *that* feeling, just a vague notion that afternoon should be the best bet. The coots rated the afternoon feeding spell and exaggerated the edginess to the verge of paranoia, but it's an ill wind that dries no one's washing and a coot managed to show me that I was making a major tactical mistake, albeit with disastrous consequences to the ill-fated bird. Two of them came nodding up the outside of the branch line and started diving. Beep. They'd hit the line? Beep-beep-beep. Wrong, one of the dumb creatures had swallowed a bait.

I landed the protesting nerve stretcher and found that the hook was right down. All I could do was cut the line as far down as possible and release it. It had happened in the past with no apparent ill effects, but on this occasion the coot didn't dive away to resurface well beyond the reach of the terrifying bankside apparition; it just sat in front of me and very slowly died. I will not willingly take the life of anything and the demise of the coot upset me. Its body was just out of reach and lay there until drift took it gradually away from the swim. Its death was a painful indictment of my intrusion into what is, after all, the birds' kingdom. They'll have to start sorting out some of the terminal arrangements, though, or the expression will start to have an awful significance.

Mid-afternoon and the fates were conspiring to prevent me even having two baits in the water at the same time. The coot had died heroically though, because it had pointed out that the baits I was going to so much trouble to cast against the back bank were, in fact, finishing up well short of there. There must be a shelf up to the gravel under the oak and I was obviously pulling the end tackle off as I tightened up, or foamed. I put a back stop in about a foot from the bomb and just used the foam as a clip on a slackish line. It was the left hand bait that the coot had picked up and when I'd retackled I fired it back into the left hand gap. It went straight in the middle and dropped two feet from the back, about a foot from the hawthorn bush to the left. It was near perfect.

At that moment, the unseen powers that had appeared, to my jaundiced eye, to be leaning over backwards to hinder me, relented and took over the operations. The cast wasn't good enough. Eh? Come on kid, the cast is spot on. But the voice in my ear (yeh, I'm starting to get the twitches as well) insisted that it was *not* good enough, so I reluctantly reeled in and recast. I almost stopped it in the air: it was too tight, but I let it go and waited for it to clip the middle branch. It didn't, it went in over the middle branch and hit the water six inches from the back. I flicked the dropping line left to clear the branch, but didn't quite make it. It caught the very end of the branch at water level.

I stood and considered. The position of the bait was perfect, if fortuitous, but what would happen if I had a take? The line would pull off the branch: better leave it. I gently tightened down and received unexpected help from an unseen underwater assistant. Here we go – walloooop. I swept the twelve footer up and hung on, and at the other end of the line a demented sandbag tried to relandscape the lake by pulling the great oak into the water.

What the fish did to that sturdy branch in the first two or three minutes after it obligingly hooked itself, was laughable. It was trying to go right, which I'd anticipated because if it had gone left, the line would definitely have come clear, and with each plunge the end of the branch – the last four or five feet – disappeared right into the water. All I could do was hang on hard until the oak tree stood still for a while, and hope that the tackle would withstand the mauling it was getting from the invisible fish and the occasionally visible

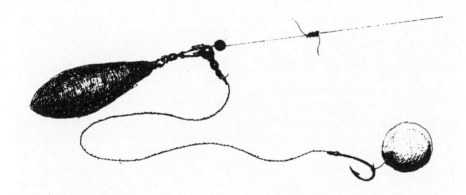

branch. At that stage I was obviously thinking in terms of the usual maximum for fish that I get connected to – the odd big double with much rarer excursions over that figure – and even that prospect was pretty frightening in view of what was happening at the other side of the lake.

The eight pound Sylcast and the glorious Drennan size six withstood the hammering, and the storm subsided. A brief stalemate. In retrospect, the stress that I then subjected the tackle to was frightening. Somehow I'd got to clear the snag and from where I was standing it didn't look too difficult. I swept the rod as far left and as high as possible, and *heaved*. It should have cleared the line, but all it did was encourage a renewal of hostilities and lead to the branch getting another soaking. We both took time out and an uneasy peace was restored to 'D' lake, but I was still connected to an unseen fish and until some unwanted alternative was thrust on it, the fish was going to remain unseen, thank you very much.

So I was standing there, like a lemon, with my rod pointing at the sky in a gentle curve, feeling very much in need of a coffee and a cigarette with not a clue as to what I should do next. I needed help but there didn't seem to be a soul on the entire complex.

Enter a tall dark stranger.

A romantic looking figure, dressed all in black, appeared walking across the lawn on the other side of the lake to my right. I opened my mouth to say something intelligent and out came a classic, a plaintive:

"Can anyone give me a hand?"

Anyone? I think that a quick census of the area would have revealed that every resident of the district within a twenty mile radius had evacuated the area for the afternoon, just in case I got snarled up in the big oak and needed help. Clearly this lone man in black was not a party to that conspiracy, had not been informed. And if my pathetic plea for help was a nonsense, his reply did not immediately inspire confidence:

"You'll need a boat then," he said, in those gentle, unhurried local tones that are as attractive as they are soothing, and always make me nostalgic for my countryside roots. He carried on walking away from the boat towards the end of the lake. I watched anxiously, but it wasn't a sick joke; he was coming round. A U.S. cavalry bugle sounded faintly in the distance.

"I don't fancy the boat but I'll hold your rod for you."

He had joined me on the point.

"Oh thanks" was my nervous rejoinder. He wasn't fishing 'D' or 'E'. For

Big Scale. How can anyone dismiss a magnificent fish like this as being unworthy?

all I knew he had never held a carp rod in his life. I hesitated. Should I explain what to do? I settled for making a hasty departure for the boat.

The line was hooked up as lightly as I thought it must be and came free with a gentle pull. The tall dark stranger didn't indulge in any heroics but just kept a light pressure on till I rowed back and took the rod off him.

The first time we saw the fish my companion, who was by now holding the landing net in a way that suggested he'd been born with one in his hand, assured me that it looked a big twenty. The fish set off to look for the branch again.

The second time we saw it, when it looked to be ready for the net but wasn't, he advised me to be careful because the fish might be bigger than I thought. Than I thought? I was more than happy to go along with the big twenty theory. The carp had given up on the oak and was apparently willing to settle for the big bush to my left. I eased the rod into a half circle under water and it remembered the oak again.

The third time it came it was ready for the net and my anxious friend showed that he was as capable of handling it as he looked as though he would be.

"This'll be your thirty," he said, grasping the mesh and heaving. "Last time I had her she went 31.5."

I was slightly lost for words and was glad that I hadn't told him how to hold a carp rod. The *last* time he had it; the inference wasn't lost on me. He staggered through to the grass with the dripping bundle and gently laid it down. While I dug out the scales and the weighing sling, we finally got round to the introductions, although I'd guessed who he was the moment he mentioned that he'd had the fish. Pete Hallam, local boy made very good, six thirties from the lakes in two seasons. I was going to add, and likable with it, but that would only embarrass him. The tall, dark stranger who materialised in my hour of need. Cometh the hour cometh *The Man*.

In all honesty, the actual weight of the fish seemed unimportant, but it would probably frustrate some of you if I didn't mention it. I left the weighing to Pete and I was obviously fortunate to catch it when I did, because it came out at 32lb.

This was 'Big Scale', as well known and recognisable as the lake it lives in and a far more significant part of the capture than the angler.

Until that moment, catching thirties was something other people did, which had made it mysterious and significant. With that capture the mystery went, although I won't belittle the magnificent 'Big Scale' by suggesting it is insignificant. It is a magnificent fish, and the capture touched me, in a strange way. It took me back to the individual identity thing I felt with the first carp I ever caught – and it humbled me. What right have we got to categorise these magnificent creatures? What right has anyone got to dismiss 'known' fish as being unworthy.

Briefly, I understood about big carp. They are awesome. The fish are mysterious and significant, whatever meaningless status we try to give them in our mindless egotistical squabbling. A carp's a carp, and bless 'em all for the pleasure they give us.

On the first day of Christmas I went to Waveney… Unlikely as it sounds, it's true. I'm no great lover… Sorry, I lost my train of though there… I'm no great lover of Christmas so I tend to run away from it. At the end of '82 I'd got some holidays left and had to tack them onto the statutories, which meant I was off work for the best part of two weeks. Some kind of joke. I tried to think of something really dumb to do and settled for having a crack at getting a winter twenty out of Waveney 'D' lake. How dumb can you get?

But it was more than going somewhere to try and catch carp. I was ready for away and Waveney offers the pleasant combination of big fish and a sociable, friendly atmosphere. Why the place offends the sensitivities of some people defeats me. Having wished the kids 'Happy Christmas', I hit the road for Norfolk at about an hour before midnight on Christmas Eve.

Do you know that even when arriving at a lake in the early hours of a freezing cold, foggy Christmas morning, you are convinced that the swim you want to fish will be occupied? As it turned out, there wasn't a single swim occupied on the whole complex, so I took my pick. Deep down I think I'd gone for a week in One on 'D', and that's where I settled. I was torn though. I'd asked Hutchie about the place in winter and he'd pinpointed a spot off Swim Three that produced in the cold months and, in retrospect, it may have been a better bet.

Christmas Day was spent settling in. It was cold, but not unpleasantly so. I think that I was possibly hoping for something really unpleasant. It's a funny thing about experiences at the water. Because I sometimes write about actual sessions, I now get questions as I leave a lake after a longish stay. What will I be writing about, if anything? The honest answer is that I haven't a clue, I really haven't. Why some sessions make a deep impression while others don't, I can't even explain to myself. I leave a water and the only thought in my mind is that I've got to face the wretched drag of going back to the real world; what has actually happened at the lake is far from my thoughts at that moment. Occasionally, a piece of writing will emerge from the stay at the water within a few days, or a few weeks. Sometimes it takes a year. More often than not there is no indelible memory, no focal point to trigger recall of the whole thing.

I write, about real situations, and real people, rightly or wrongly. Something has to stand out from a session for me to focus on and it may be the silliest little thing that acts as the catalyst in my mind to lift a series of very ordinary events and people onto a level where the whole thing becomes that bit larger than life. It is easier to write about something than nothing, but what is nothing to others may be part of the whole recollection to me. So while the trigger for an article or chapter may be on the seventh day at the water, my mind then relives the whole thing, from the cat sulking in the kitchen beforehand, to my thoughts on leaving the lake after.

Therefore, while I did not go down to 'D' lake looking for anything out of the ordinary, beyond a 'D' lake winter twenty, I would perhaps have welcomed a blizzard confining me to my bivvy for three days just for the difference of the experience. Whether or not that would have sparked a piece of writing or just merited the sentence 'It snowed and I was confined to my bivvy for three days' I don't know.

People tell me that they would love to write but that they don't seem to be able to do it. I'm not sure what they mean by that. Because I edit Carp Fisher,

On the 10th Day of Christmas

and have lots of friends who write in the carp world, I do know a little about the mechanics of other people's writing, as well as my own. We are all very different in the way we go about it and work towards an end result. In terms of putting words on paper I now find writing easy, because at some stage when it wasn't easy, I spent a lot of time forcing myself to write; but putting words on paper and coming up with a finished product are, for me, two very different propositions. The reader sees something in print and obviously measures it in terms of what he wants to read, and in terms of the writer's previous efforts. We all open a magazine and think 'Oh good, an article by so-and-so', but the writer knows that he can't possibly please all the readers every time; there is too great a diversity of tastes, and it isn't always his best pieces of writing that are the most popular. Someone will say to me, "I enjoyed your piece about whatever," and I will thank him for his kind words, but it doesn't alter my own assessment of the article.

I have written something in the region of thirty or forty articles I suppose, at the time of writing this. I've been totally happy with about two of them. I write, and alter, and rewrite, and occasionally, when I'm handling a difficult theme that I really want to put across, it may take me seven or eight rewritings to get it half right. A technical article that involves that much effort will get better with each rewrite. The 'life' sort often won't and may never work out absolutely right. Two examples.

One of my favourite articles was 'Listen Girls' in Coarse Angler. It was a sod to write and was predictably of appeal to a limited audience, but it was something I really wanted to say without getting over-serious and, as a piece of writing, I rated it about nine out of ten. As an entertainment, I am not in a position to judge. 'Blank at Fox Pool', which I've included here, was the other way round. It was a very easy piece to write, but I was under pressure for time, and there was very little alteration to the first effort. Many people have been kind enough to comment on the piece and say how much they enjoyed it, so, because it was such a good subject, it finished up as good entertainment, but I know that in terms of writing, it was about six out of ten. The week made such an impression that it deserved better than the article as it came out.

I think that writing can be an effort for Yatesy. Like me he has this need to get the words exactly right and it often takes him some time to decide just what the right words are. Hutchie is totally different and the most natural writer possible. Having worked fairly closely with him on his second book, 'The Carp Strikes Back', I envy him the facility with which he puts words on paper. He very rarely goes back over anything and his writing is obviously the product of a clear, uncluttered mind. That is not to say that every time he sits down to write the words come pouring out, because I don't think they do, but once his pen does start functioning the words come out as he wants them at the first attempt. I saw all the manuscript for 'Strikes Back' and, apart from a couple of inserts in the technical chapters, there was barely an alteration from the first untidy scrawl of the hand written material to the finished product.

But I must ask if those of you who do want to write but feel you can't, work at it hard enough? My writing cannot compete with any distraction. I don't have TV, phone, a woman and even the cat had to be banished to next door because there were times when it screwed me up. To write you have got to want to do it enough to get down to doing it, and to get down to doing it you have got to find the circumstances in which you will be able to create, because that is what you are doing when you set pen to paper.

I've had periods when I have actually been writing three hours before the words start to make the shape I want them to make; three wasted hours of words. I used to virtually chain smoke when I was writing, but I think I've kicked that. Which is great, except that it was four months before I could write a word without cigarettes. Now I drink coffee after coffee, eat biscuits, sweets, anything that helps keep my concentration intact, and I usually have Bob Dylan tapes playing all the time. I'm not making any big deal about the writing, but people do ask, and this may help some of them. If you really want to do it, you will, but it's got to be in your head, or your mind, before you can start to put it on paper: even then you've got to accept that what you put down on paper may only be a stepping stone towards the end product.

Those would-be writers who have a typist among their close friends, wives, girl friends and mistresses, should recognise what an asset such a creature is and nurture the relationship. Having said which, I've got to confess that my first wife was a typist, or, more accurately, my wife that was is a typist, so I can't claim to set any sort of example. While I now number the odd typist among my friends, none of these friendships are close enough for me to get a book typed out for nothing. I either have to type it out myself, or pay for it to be typed out. I type reasonably quickly but…

Most of my writing is done in long hand, although it is not instantly recognisable as long hand and can be fairly described as illegible. Or even more fairly as indecipherable. I did briefly have use of a typist who was able to decipher my writing, which was great, except that… Well, decipher is perhaps too strong a word. Through her ability to unscramble two words out of a sentence of ten she was actually able to put an interpretation on that sentence and make it meaningful. The end result was two versions of each article, hers and mine. I stopped using her because her version was invariably far superior to mine.

I now go through at least four versions of each piece of writing, which is a lot of trouble to go to for something I'm never particularly happy with anyway at the end of it all. I write it in long hand, then make some sense of the written version with a typed 'improvement'. Ostensibly this typed version is the finished product, but it invariably gets changed so much that I have to type it out again to make sense of the sweeping alterations, deletions and amendments. This polished, definitely final version is then joyfully reread, which infuriatingly reveals innumerable flaws which cannot possibly form part of the finished product, so the final set of alterations are made. At this stage, the thought of retyping it yet again bores me to tears, so I farm it out. I tend to be as decisive as that in everything I do.

But once someone else has typed it out for me that is it. Besides, I usually manage a few quick changes at galley proof and page proof level, and sure as hell there will be plenty in the finished article or chapter of the book that I'm less than happy with. So don't think that you are alone if the conversion of thoughts in your head to words on paper is a protracted nightmare. I was reassured to read Graham Greene's description of the way he writes, and that more or less follows the description I've just given of my own struggles, or vice versa, as he was doing it much earlier than I was, and far better. (Yes, that last

bit is false modesty). John O'Hara, quite one of my favourite writers, described the waste paper basket as the 'Hell Box' (sic) because of the amount of unsatisfactory material that finished up in it on the tortuous route to a finished product.

I don't know whether or not I thought all that on Christmas Day, but I may well have because there was no sign of fish action, and I didn't catch anything and didn't see anyone.

On the second day of Christmas, some real festive spirit rolled up in the guise of Norman collecting money. No, I hadn't caught anything. During the afternoon two notorious lunatics rolled up to fish 'C' lake, which is supposed to be the best bet in winter. ('D' is a no-hoper, which is why I was on it; I don't like getting my hands cold on wet fish at that time of year.) Pete, the Tall Dark Stranger, and his mate John, who is also tall, and dark, and even stranger. They were fishing from the caravan lawn across to the far bank bushes.

Somewhere during this weekend John arrived – another John – to fish 'G' lake, but I didn't know he was there till later. You're about to get some graphic detail hereabouts so it's only fair to warn you that it is the prelude to the capture of a fish.

When you go and fish a lake that does not produce in winter, and you are going to give it a week, you've got to be mentally prepared for what is about to happen. So I was mentally accepting that there was a better than even chance that the indicators would not move once, all week. I was also aware that there was a problem over the length of the nights. It was dark from 4.00 p.m. till 8.00 a.m., which is a great deal of highly boring darkness. Hutchie wrote a good piece on this once, and one of the things he recommended was to have a production number of a dinner some time during the evening. This can fill in anything from an hour to an hour and a half.

I use a single screw in ring on a big gas bottle and about half nine I started the preparation of some concoction for which Egon Ronay would have had no hesitation in awarding five stars. There were tins and pans all over the bivvy. The car was parked at the top of the bank and I'd got a lead running from the battery to a camping light. This light illuminated the bivvy and threw a bright beam out onto the rods. Lights while carp fishing? You've got it. The baits were eighty and ninety nine yards away respectively, and the lake was the colour of oxtail soup. Yeh, lights, radio, telly, anything to get you through a week where the indicators are not going to move.

I was foamed up tight with monkey climbers and was fishing a bottle top indicator for drop backs. I'd just finished heating the steak, and switched to the potato pan. It was ten o' clock. Two days in and resigned. Beep. A single note from the Optonic. It doesn't register for a second, that single note. The first reaction is 'What's that?' I looked out and in the light from the bivvy the left hand bottle top was inching downwards. Drop back!

I was out and reeling frantically. Somewhere out there a carp was running from against the rushes at the back towards the middle of the lake, in my direction. I caught up with it on the third strike, by which time there was mist curling round the bank. It was steam from the potatoes in the bivvy. That's handy. The fish went about sixteen pounds, a typical, lightly scaled, 'D' lake mirror.

I sacked it but didn't like the thought of keeping it till morning, but I did want a picture of it. Pete and John would be awake; I went round to 'C' lake. There was a lot of sleeping going on. I finally managed to wake Pete by playing with his Optonics, and explained to him. He said "Sack it," and went back to sleep.

I must have done a good psyching up job on myself about how hard it was going to be because I really was euphoric over that fish, and did a bit of leaping about and air punching as I walked back across the lawn.

On the third day of Christmas we took some pictures of the fish. Swims two, three and four were suddenly occupied by carp men. I think my fish caused that. Keith Kant was in two, John from 'C' in three. Somewhere in all this, an amazing young man moved into four, but we'll pretend he didn't happen, because he seems to have stopped happening.

On the fourth day of Christmas, the ever welcome Bill called to see me. Lovely Bill. He produced his hip flask and we drank to Christmas and then he went on his way to 'F' lake. The weather was cold but OK. Someone informed me that the water temperature in 'D' was 38 degrees. It mattered? I wasn't blanking and I was going to stick it out for the twenty, so a few degrees here or there didn't matter a deal.

I've missed something. In the early hours of the fourth day I stayed awake to listen to England just win a Test match in Australia. We almost threw it away, and lost the series pretty comprehensively anyway. Our efforts against the nice Aussies made a reasonable winter utterly depressing. I can't give my real opinion of Aussie cricketers because the Race Relations Act might apply. I don't know any, anyway, so I'm not really in a position to give an opinion. I think that's called blind prejudice, but it's not against the Aussie race. Clive James is one of my favourite men.

On the fifth day of Christmas, which was Wednesday, I had a game of table tennis in the games room. It was a mistake to play table tennis in Boom 80's and my feet suffered for it later. Keith departed from swim two, and we had the following conversation:

"Ah well, I'll just have to put it down to experience."

"What, haven't you fished 'D' lake in winter before?" That's me; Keith's a local.

"Yeh. I fished it every weekend from November through to the end of the season last year, with a couple of slightly longer sessions thrown in."

"Did you have much joy?"

"Not a flicker all winter. I thought it might be different this time."

He departed, leaving me bemused and hanging on grimly. Motionless indicators and silent Optonics get to you after a while. There comes a crisis point and mine came on the Wednesday afternoon, prior to the conversation with Keith, and I had all on not to pack in and throw the lot in the back of the motor. I had a hard talk to myself. You pathetic sod. You soft, gutless quitter. Heart like a pea; it was never going to be easy but the only place you will catch a 'D' lake winter twenty is on 'D' lake. Good solid logic. The crisis passed; I'd last the week. Why fish on when you're not enjoying it? There's a lot of times when you are not actually enjoying carp fishing, but you would not enjoy being anywhere else instead. And you always know that the whole thing could change in a split second; at the very moment that you are mentally fighting it out, a carp could be picking up the bait.

Some time during the evening John Bromilow from 'G' lake called round for a chat.

"Do you mind if I stop and talk for a bit?"

"Feel free."

"I'm struggling, I'm only just hanging on."

"Join the club."

He was going through the crisis I'd resolved that afternoon. His will power and motivation were hitting rock bottom. We talked of carp and the mental problems of long session winter fishing, trying to lift each other. Dave Preston refers to this as refuelling the confidence tanks. We talked for an hour and it lifted us both. He went back to the inky stillness of 'G' lake and his own silent buzzers and stationary indicators.

On the sixth day of Christmas my patience was tried to the limit. There are times when it is difficult to be a private person in a public place. Hell's teeth. On a long session there is an automatic crisis of confidence first thing in the morning. After another sixteen hour night without so much as a bleep it is inevitable. It is an every morning thing, and not just in the winter either, so I do not welcome company at first light. First light is for thought collecting, coffees, re-appraising, telling yourself that it could happen at any minute, and is likely to, and regaining full consciousness. This is not the mental crisis John and I had separately gone through the previous day, but part of waking up, a temporary carp morning sickness, a daily crisis.

But that week I suffered first light intrusion, which I would not dream of inflicting on anyone else and worse... This is a difficult one to write about because some will inevitably misconstrue it. I am one of the lads, no more, no less. I have friends all over the country and wherever I go there are people I look forward to meeting and enjoy the company of. Waveney is a particularly friendly place and I like to think that I've made some good friends there, but it makes my life a bloody misery if I get the vibes that someone is looking on me as anything other than just one of the lads.

I think some people who don't know me have the feeling that I'm some kind of ego merchant. Nothing could be further from the truth. If I can write, then I am grateful for that minor talent, but it doesn't make me 'different', because we've all got a talent of some sort, somewhere. Grief, it took me long enough to find that I'd got one, if I've got one. Ego? Wow. When some crazy woman gives you a working over the likes of the one I had, you finish up looking about a quarter of an inch tall in your own eyes. For ever more you look in the mirror and remind yourself of the fact. Pride comes before a fall. Avoid pride and you'll never fall because in your own eyes, you're already down there.

Having said which, when you are tall, good build, attractive, talented and charming, it is difficult to be too humble. But then again, with fan clubs like Hutchinson's around, you've got to have the thought at the back of your mind that someone, somewhere, sees you as a boring, overweight, scruffy Dulux dog in glasses, and as Hutchie is right about so many things...

Later on, on the sixth day, I went out in the boat. There was a snag causing problems up the right hand side of the lake. It was cutting down the area I could fish and was costing me my end tackle every time I cast short of the big fish bramble. After much patient dragging, I located it and after a further hour's effort I managed to get it up into the boat, almost capsizing in the process. It was a real life Christmas tree. Not literally, but as good as. A huge branch, absolutely festooned with end tackles of all sorts of creeds and denominations. Bombs, hooks, swivels, rigs, rigs and more rigs. Black braided with stainless steel hooks. Had to be one of Hutchie's – or two or three of Hutchie's to be absolutely accurate. Now why was that like that? I'd better ask him about that one. That should be good for a cracking blind. (It was; I got an amazing reply when I asked him about it. I think it was a variation of Roger's rig.)

I felt better after I'd dragged the branch in but I can't remember why, and I still didn't get any action.

On the seventh day of Christmas the lakes cleared as everyone went off to celebrate New Year. During the afternoon Bill called in again and we drank to New Year out of his hip flask. New Year. Out with the old, in with the new. I tried to think of some reason why I should be nostalgic about the departing year. There was none, so I didn't mourn its passing. On the other hand, nothing horrendous had occurred in my life during the year, which made it noteworthy, if not memorable. I'm a nostalgic sort of person so I probably worked myself up into a state of sadness sitting in the dark on a cold, still, remote, deserted, carpless 'D' lake.

Bill called in again and we drank to New Year.

It was only my second New Year actually on the water and the other one had been memorable. I'd had a fish almost on the stroke of midnight. Mark will tell you, five past. That was in Buckinghamshire, at Snowberry, and midnight had been marked by all hell letting loose in the surrounding countryside. Car horns blowing, railway engines wailing, church bells chiming, dogs howling, carp feeding. In Norfolk – nothing. I wondered if I'd got the right night and put the radio on to check. Andy Stewart. I switched it off again and thanked Norfolk for the silence.

On the eighth day of Christmas a pike man came to fish. He'd had a row with the wife and came to the lakes to get out of the way. He'd no pike baits so he dropped into the caravan swim under the bush, using three month old carp baits that he'd happened to find in his tackle box. He caught a carp weighing nearly seventeen pounds. I'd tell you his name if I could bear to type it. That night it froze cruelly.

On the ninth day of Christmas the lake was frozen half across. It was the only lake on the complex to have any ice, which was picturesque for me. At least the pike man didn't come back, which was a shame because his swim was covered with ice, so he could have really covered himself with glory.

This was Saturday and they'd all started to look alike by this time (the days). Another Bill (Giles) called in for a chat, a friend of Col. Dyson's, which surprised me, because I didn't know he'd got any. Dave Johnson from Stockport came for a confidence boosting chat; he was fishing Homersfield and had been there almost as long as I'd been on 'D', also without a flicker. I gave him some braided line, showed him the Dacron rig and he caught a fish that night.

Brian Nunn, John again, Brian's mate, whose name escapes me, the Burroughs, Becketts, Graham, Colin Pitelen (the terrible pike man), Pete, John, Keith. You can just hang on to sanity with all that coming and going, and the weekend is very social.

I fished it through but the heavy freeze slowed the action down (that is a joke) and I departed on the Monday. I had to, I'd got to be at work for ten that night. A long, hard session, but I'd gone down to recharge the batteries and I'd certainly done that. It was a relief to get back for a change.

On the tenth day of Christmas I went home. The indicators hadn't moved for the last eight days, and on reflection I fished the water badly, but as I could have had just the same result fishing it well I didn't get too uptight about it.

I don't suppose I would ever have been moved to write about the first twenty pound plus fish that I caught had it not been for the fact that the capture eventually became part of a remarkable coincidence. And if you're not sure what a coincidence is, it's when the little known pub that no one knows about, way out in the country, which is frequented by you and the girl friend turns out to be the favourite drinking place of your wife's best friend.

Coincidence

I thought it was 1977, but on reflection it must have been 1978. 1977 was the season that started cold and wet and I had one four pound fish in a first four days session. The 1978 season started on a Wednesday night, in the Green Man at Little Brickhill on the A5. I wish I'd kept a diary because I'm not sure who was there exactly, but I know that John was, and a friend, and a few of the lads, and my friend Julie. The apres pub part of the night is a hazy kaleidoscope swirling in and out of the mists of time. I was fishing the Planks under the weeping willow and vaguely recollect landing a brace of double figure commons some time during the small hours. It was a moonlit night, magical, and the feel of it is still overpowering, though the finer details are lost. There was an evocative combination of alcohol, grass and carp to heighten the already rarified atmosphere of a first night of the season at Snowberry. Never was that freedom from the storm more urgently needed than it was in those bitter sweet days.

We pulled off and chugged up the aggregate track to the farmyard on Sunday afternoon, Cuttle Mill bound. It was my first trip to Cuttle. Bob Sellars had motivated me into going and I was glad he did. Dear Pat was there, and Martin, and we had a few laughs and caught a few fish, as they say.

I still carry a disproportionate number of memories from that week, although some of them may well be from another Cuttle week; it's that sort of place. One is of meeting the outwardly misleadingly serious Baz for the first time, on the lawn, which was a lovely place to fish.

On the Monday, the first day, I did not draw a particularly good swim. It was the little corner swim at the house end of the field side, and the wind was blowing from that corner towards the island. It was an awkward swim to cast out of, and I didn't see a fish within a hundred yards all day. As I'd gone to Cuttle to catch fish, I didn't take the long, blank day particularly philosophically. Next year will do now, but in those days, if it wasn't happening that minute I got jumpy.

Dusk drew in on a long day and just as Mrs. Brewer appeared on the lawn to blow the whistle, the left hand indicator drew my attention to a slow run. Now, rightly or wrongly, I get more excited about slow runs than I do about fast ones. I've always had this theory that big fish set off slower than small fish, a theory which has been disproved so often by small fish taking slowly that my faith in the idea should have been dented long ago. It hasn't; whenever I get a slow run I mutter 'Biggie' to myself as I pick up the rod.

By my standards this was a biggie. It was my first twenty and, at twenty one pounds eight ounces, it remained my biggest fish for four years. I caught it on Bacon Grill, a bait suggested to me the previous close season by George Sharman and which helped me catch a number of good fish that season. For all that the fish came from the Mill, it was a lucky capture. I took it on my first day there and although I have fished a total of something in excess of three weeks at the Mill over the years, that was my only twenty plus fish from the water. In common with many other waters, the Mill has started to produce more twenties since the use of the rigs and boiled baits became general, but in the time I have known it, it has never been an easy twenties water - not for me anyway!

The last night of that week is an indelibly pleasant memory. The car park at the Mill does not sound the most romantic of settings for a drinking session, but it is an atmospheric spot. The car park is the old farm yard, and the waters are just up the slope past the old barns. Beyond the tree lined hedge, the fields stretch away into the distance, so despite the discreet proximity of the Brewer household, the spot has a feeling of remoteness that frees spirits and loosens tongues. Bob, Martin and Pat had returned to civilisation. Julie and I still had it to come and the prospect was as unwelcome as ever.

Does time elevate the odd occasion beyond its actual true station in the scheme of things? Was that whisky coloured night in the company of Gorgeous George Whitaker, Ken Selvey and Terry Eustace really as special as it feels from five years on? Yes, I think it felt as magical then as it does with the hindsight of change. It was probably childish, and a bit silly, like the days of late youth when the perception of all the rare moments is magnified by the suppressed knowledge that nothing that good can last. Where are they now, George and

Tim with his first twenty from the Mill in 1978.

Ken? Mill fixtures at that time but soon to turn their backs on it for life, or whatever else it was that got in the way. One of the reassurances of a changing scene is that the Eustace man never changes. Next time I walk through the shop door, that slow, sly grin will crack his face from ear to ear, and it will be just like I'd never been away – as it is with everyone he knows. A marvellous man.

The evening of alcohol and banter faded into memory; Eustace chugged off up the Mill lane to domesticity, George and Ken bedded down under the barn in anticipation of their weekend's carping, and my friend and I mourned the passing of a special week, and a memorable evening. Another treasured memory fading into the mists of time…

In 1982 the season started mid-week. On the first Sunday my friend, Greg Fletcher, in company with the amazing Jim Fielding, went and set up camp in the car park at the Mill. They were booked in to fish the water from Monday to Friday of the first full week, as I had been four years earlier.

The majority of Greg's fishing had been local till then and he had not had the good fortune to bank a twenty pounder. (You don't think I'm going to stop telling it *now* do you, however far you are ahead of me.) He went down to the Mill armed with a million boilies flavoured with some evil smell that Hutchie had worked up him. The smell was so obnoxious that the bottle containing it was kept locked in the garage at the back of Greg's flat, which immediately became a gathering ground for all the dogs in the neighbourhood.

Jim and Greg started fishing on the Monday, and though Jim had the odd fish during the day, Greg had no action at all until some time during the evening when he had one solitary run. The fish weighed in at twenty one pounds six and was the same first twenty that I'd had on the same Monday in the season, four years earlier.

That's an inconsequential little story, but I like coincidences and that's a happy one.

Fletch with the same fish, same first twenty, on the same first Monday of the season in 1982.

Coincidence

Dave Preston, he of the spidery scrawl.

A letter from Dave Preston, which did not come as a surprise as we have a pretty regular exchange of correspondence. I get three types of letters; those I don't open, as they are obviously begging letters from councils, providers of household services and the County Court; those I put on one side to be read when I've made a cup of coffee; and those I can't wait to read and open immediately. Dave's letters fall between categories one and two. I chuck 'em towards file thirteen and if they miss, I read them when I've nothing better to do.

This was March. The writing was the familiar spidery scrawl, the contents slightly more riveting than the usual instant cure for insomnia. He droned on about this fifteen acre water with just two swims and a boat. What was I doing at the start of the season and would I like to fish the water? It was a lake he had had an indecent number of commons from in twelve days the previous season. Now, it must be said that as far as personal correspondence goes, I am a slightly unpredictable letter writer. It can take me up to three or four months to reply, regardless of the urgency involved. This letter I made an exception for and replied by return, having by then clearly marked the first ten days of the season on the holiday chart at work.

This last close season was chaotic, included no fishing whatever, and passed very, very quickly. The weather was less than inspiring and I made no attempt to start with the Yorkshire season. I'm not good at getting ready for that first session of the season, I don't quite know why. My mind is invariably trying to handle two or three problems at once and the practical problem of getting all the tackle, sleeping gear, food, bait, clothes and so on sorted out for a lengthy stay at the water is a bloody chore. It should be a labour of love, but by mid-June I've forgotten what the hell it's all about anyway. There is just this lemming like instinct to shut society out and go and get bedded down on the bank of some lake for as long as possible.

The apathy abated on, or about, the fourteenth of June when the rain stopped, the weather turned warmer and the world started to feel carpy again. The reality of it suddenly got hold of me and swept through me. Tomorrow I was off to some unspoilt, remote, unexploited little-fished carp paradise. Overnight I became nice to know again. The cat looked at me through new eyes, which gradually became suspicious when it remembered what my highs usually lead up to. As the mountain of gear in the kitchen grows, the cat settles into a depression which manifests itself as a pointed sulk. It knows when I am going away, is as temperamental about it as any woman could be and has me feeling guilty as hell by the time I drive off. At the time of writing I'm in the process of having it adopted by the next door neighbours, an arrangement the cat is having problems coming to term with, or, more probably, is being one hundred per cent bloody minded about.

In my planning, the journey took an hour and a half. In reality, three hours was about par for the course and, after four years, he of the spidery hand writing became an actual person. I almost said 'real person', but I'm not in the habit of lashing out lavish praise. I had a brief relax and a sort of coffee while he gathered his tackle together.

I've paused there, recalling the first sighting of his tackle. Heath Robinson home made buzzers, rods painstakingly as far from being matched as possible – different colours, lengths, materials and handles. I never saw Hutchie in action

in the days when his gear was reputed to look like the remnants of a jumble sale clearance, but it really must have looked immaculate compared to the assortment of bits and bats that he of the spidery hand assembled in the middle of the kitchen floor.

"Follow me," he said, and blasted off up the narrow country roads with all the bravado and quick reflexes of comparative youth, not to mention the local knowledge of a native. I followed him with growing excitement and a head full of disjointed thoughts. I hadn't asked him if he smoked. I'd been off them for a month and my survival depended on him being a non-smoker, and even then it wasn't guaranteed. As it happened he didn't smoke and I survived. He soon twigged that he would have to moderate his rally driver's elan. I wanted to savour this bit and take in the unfamiliar countryside – undulating, wooded patchwork quilts of fields, reminiscent of some of the Fylde countryside of my childhood and youth. My kind of country, far divorced from the harshness of the Yorkshire hills and dales which have formed the backcloth to my existence for over twenty years now. Aren't we creatures of habit? Six months of turmoil and I could be installed in some rural area of Norfolk, Buckinghamshire or…
wherever, but I shun that turmoil for the 'safeness' of an existence I understand, unexciting and uninspiring as it is. Better the devil, my mind says, but my spirit denies it.

First time journeys take for ever, particularly when an understandable impatience to arrive takes the place of the patient appraisal of the surroundings. I can recall a silly anxiety that everything was not going to be as my friend had suggested it would be. I don't mean that I was worried that we wouldn't catch, but that we wouldn't be able to fish, that the whole thing would go horribly wrong.

Eventually, the journey ended in a rural paradise. A big, old mansion in a rolling, wooded estate and an office which obviously controlled some kind of farm business. Brief, pleasant, idle chatter with Graham in the office and I proffered a ten pound note for the ten days' fishing. No problems, it was all very matter of fact; beyond my ken, but familiar to them. Where is the justice? What on earth had I done to suddenly have this privilege heaped on me? I was only too well aware of what a large proportion of the carp world would be going through on June fifteenth and we just rolled up at teatime and were given the keys to the kingdom.

We drove down through the fields – no track, just fields – but by this time the water had been plucked from my imagination to become an actual reality, there at the foot of the slope. Three months of conjecture, totally false images and wild guesswork were at an end and the water was there, in all its glory, and nothing like the water of my close season planning.

The whereabouts of the water will have to remain suitably vague, which is a shame. I mean, you know what I'm like about waters; route maps supplied, depths and weed beds charted, going baits detailed – but not this time. It is more than my life's worth to give any clues. The fact of the matter is that the local Mafioso wasn't exactly over-enchanted to discover that I was visiting the area, so there you go, we'll never know where it was.

Incredibly, looking back, my initial mental reaction was one of slight disappointment. Not with the water, which was all any water ever could be, in that it was remote, wild, overgrown and startlingly deserted, with the exception of the presence of two slightly subdued carp men. It must have been my carp fishing mind that was registering the minor disappointment. There was no way that the carp in the water could be readily catchable, particularly as I was supposed to dump myself down in the first swim I encountered and fish from there, which was what was supposed to happen.

Dave indicated the few square yards of grass we were standing on.

"That's your swim; I'm fishing from a little swim fifty yards down the bank."

All my life I've suffered from little swims fifty yards down the bank. Was it really on to fish from the first swim we encountered? The water looked to be a reasonably rich one, the wind was blowing over our heads to the far bank, and the opposite half of the water was completely fringed by lily and reed beds of some density. All this was observable at a glance.

"There are only two swims on the water," my companion assured me, sensing my unease.

I'd got ten days; the swim was undoubtedly a very comfortable one; I was well tired as I'd made the run more or less straight off night shift, and I was anxious to get some bait in the water. The latter particularly, because I was using boilies and I didn't know if the fish in the water would even recognise them as food. We started unloading the cars. The close season had about six hours to run and it ran them within the hour. By seven in the evening, the baits

were out, the stall set up and the camera in action.

I slept well, disturbed occasionally by line bites causing the odd brief flurry on the Optonics. Half light was about four o' clock. Half light on the first morning of the new season is utterly special, whether you've scored or not. The half filled kettle was already standing on the stove. I brewed a coffee, still lying in the sleeping bag, and watched the water emerge from the gloom of a misty dawn.

The first morning coffee of the season was just a toast to whatever was to come. I relaxed and enjoyed it. How often in the coming months would it be an utter necessity, a perspective regainer to clear away the mental clouds brought on by blank hours, or days, or weeks? At such times it's for confidence repairing or restoring; I was still easing in and savouring.

I crept down the bank to the little swim fifty yards away. Dave is a Maddocks man. Bed chair by the rods. Umbrella, no bivvy. Feet installed in a massive plastic bag (bright orange) and a six inch drop on the indicators, fishing churn.

"How're you doing?"

"Couple of seventeens, mirror and a common. How many have you had?"

"Well, nothing."

"But your buzzers have been howling all night."

A slight over-exaggeration for a couple of line bites. Two seventeens, the common a pound heavier than my best common. I slunk back to base and put the kettle on again.

My major memory of that first day of the season is that it went on for ever. My watch had packed up on the way down and I wasn't feeling the need for the radio by then, so it was just a question of waiting for the indicators to move and performing the few chores that were necessary.

My first Mangrove fish about to go back.

I sat on the bed chair gazing at the water, trying to think my way into it to some extent, but feeling pretty helpless. The fish were moving fairly generally but were concentrated in an area straight across from me, about two hundred and fifty yards away, and around the lily pads to my left, beyond Dave's swim. I felt optimistic about picking up the odd fish, but I didn't feel as if I was on fish. I'd switched the Optonics off, as I always do when I'm wide awake and fishing for runs, and Dave had just come round to my swim for a chat, just before seven o' clock, when I was away. A run's a run, except that they are all very welcome, and that first one of the new season is as welcome as any. The bait was out in open water and I'd all the time in the world to set the hook, then had to backwind frantically as the beastie made a long, strong run away from me. Thereafter, it behaved as the first fish of the season should and came to the net without much further ado. It was a common, a little over twelve pounds.

We had a photographic session and the day drifted gently, and ever so slowly, along. Some time later I was away on a suspended bait and landed a common of thirteen pounds nine ounces. I put it straight back and went to check on the time with Dave. I was convinced that it was early afternoon; in fact, it was mid-morning. Thirteen pounds nine ounces. It's a little sad how time changes our attitude to fish of similar sizes. Six years before, at Snowberry, I'd had a lovely golden common of exactly the same weight, my best common at that time, as it was for three years. I'd taken the fish at dusk, at the tail end of a three day session. We'd taken pictures but the flash hadn't synchronised with the shutter and they hadn't come out; I was sick about it at the time. Now an equally beautiful fish of the same weight had been put back, unphotographed and unremarked – but no, I don't think I was being blasé: I don't take a lot of photographs of fish and the common was not unappreciated.

Morning drifted into afternoon and the sun swung from left to right across a sky that was taking on an unfamiliar clear blue look, a sky which was to become all too familiar over the first couple of months of the season. I reeled in and went walkabout. It took me three hours to give the margins of the water even a cursory examination. It felt like a very old water and was as wild and unkempt at close quarters as it looked from afar. Only two fishable swims was a slight exaggeration, but only slight.

I landed back in the swim early evening, dying of thirst and starving. I recast and made a meal, which was interrupted by a common, which was brother chip to the first fish of the day. The sun started to slide down the sky towards the great house at the top of the fields and the comfort of the cool of the evening felt gentle on the skin. The light started to fade, but it was a gradual fade out. Officially, the longest day was a week away, but unofficially, that first day of the season was the longest. The good days are usually over in a flash, while the bad ones are interminable. This was a good interminable one.

One abiding memory of that swim and those first couple of days of the season was a reed warbler that obviously had its nest in the tall reed bed to my right. The water was an absolute sanctuary for reed warblers but this one little bird sang its heart out deep into the night, and the combination of the beautiful cool dusk closing down over the water and this lovely, delicate little bird, singing fit to bust, made me feel utterly nostalgic for something I couldn't put my finger on. Some long buried memory? Julie and the Snowberry days?

No, that wasn't it. It suddenly occurred to me that the nostalgia was for then, for that moment. It wasn't nostalgia at all, but that rare commodity peace of mind, happiness, such an uncommon visitor that I'd had a struggle to recognise it. It had never been better, and it never could be.

It was so special that I sat on the bed chair looking out at the water, listening to the over exuberant reed warbler until well after the light had left the sky behind me. I felt cold and put the kettle on for just one more coffee before turning in, then had a couple more, afraid that I was going to lose the feel of the suffocating atmosphere the combination of time and place had let me feel. Dave's Mangrove Swamp, Bill's Mere, jealously coveted by the locals who don't fish it anyway. Surely it's not just about the fish for them too?

Eventually, I turned in, emotional and weary. I slept the darkness through, totally undisturbed, and was woken at first light by that most welcome of all alarm calls, a howling Optonic.

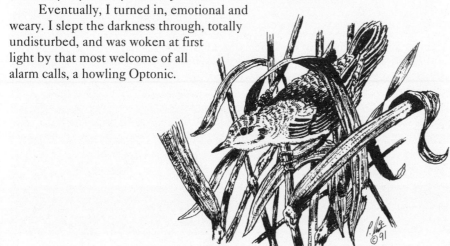

8.00a.m. 17th June 1983. First Mangrove twenty.

Somewhere in the many thousands of fascinating words Rod Hutchinson has written about carp fishing, there is reference to the capture of a twenty six pound carp which didn't give him a great deal of satisfaction, because he didn't know why he'd caught it! At the time I read that I found it (a) unbelievable that a twenty six pound carp could be less than satisfying in any circumstances, and, (b) extraordinary that one so knowledgeable could catch a carp and not know why he had caught it. The second day of the season left me understanding exactly what he meant, although my dissatisfaction was tempered by an overwhelming gratitude to the fates for their unexpected and inexplicable generosity.

The howl of the Optonics had me scrambling from the sleeping bag and diving for the rods in my stocking feet. There is a school of thought which says that a fish that takes while you are sleeping is a slightly unfair capture, it is undeserved. Possibly so, but... I've only just started to sleep on the rods over the last couple of seasons and the experience of being blasted back to consciousness by a running carp in the dark hours is quite one of the most exciting carp fishing experiences I have had. For me, the biggest problem is to hold my half awake mind together and fight a slight feeling of panic, induced, I think, by the urgency of the Optonic. When you are awake, you see the indicator start to move, or hear the start of the alarm signal, and know how long the run has been going when you pick up the rod. I'm never absolutely certain that the Optonic has woken me as the run develops – the fish could have been on the move for quite some time for all I know – hence the urgency.

The four o' clock alarm that morning was a fourteen pound mirror. First light. I put the fish back, made the inevitable coffee and had a think. I'd got a problem of the nicest kind. I'd baited up sparingly the night before because I still had no idea what sort of overall reaction I was likely to get to the maple flavoured boiled baits. I'd chosen maple because it is a natural flavour that carp will react to from the off, without education; but reacting to a flavour and actually eating the baits are two different things, as I was to learn later in the sessions on the water.

If there were fish in the swim, which was a reasonable deduction seeing I'd just caught one, there wasn't enough bait out there to hold them for long if they were eating it. On the other hand I didn't know whether this was a water where you could fire baits in over the fish's heads or not. Gut reaction said I would have to risk it and build up, so I fired another hundred baits out. I was still far from convinced that I was fishing the water anything like right but I felt that the next few hours would clarify the situation, which they didn't.

There was no further immediate activity and I thought I'd ballsed it up. Four o' clock to seven o' clock is a long time when you are in the main feeding period, and I passed the time listening to the radio, drinking coffee and aching for a nerve soothing cigarette. Even while I was thinking it, I knew that nerve soothing was a fallacy. Cigarettes used to make me jumpier when I was jumpy and calmer when I was calm. The only time they really did help was when I was writing, when I would chain smoke and drink coffees back to back. I could have done with a fag though.

What's the point of sitting there worrying about it? They either do or they don't once you've done all you can do. This time they did. Just after seven o' clock the left hand rod was away to a real flier and I found myself back-winding

Richly
Undeserved
Success

129

8.30a.m. 17th June 1983. First recorded Mangrove capture of a fish known as Scaley.

on a powerful feeling fish. "Common," I said to myself, and started to win back line. In fact, it was a near leather of twenty one and a half pounds. I summoned Dave.

I didn't realise how competitive Dave was until much later in the season, so I put his lack of enthusiasm down to morning sickness. I sacked the fish to let the light improve slightly but I'm not happy about retaining carp at all and we took the pictures at about eight o' clock. I didn't think there would be any further action and was well content with what was then probably my best brace of fish at fourteen pounds and twenty one and a half.

Bacon buttie time. Isn't it odd? I wouldn't dream of buying bacon or making any kind of cooked breakfast when I'm at home, but I automatically take bacon with me when I go on a long session. I'd just taken the first mouthful of bacon and tomato sandwich when the middle rod was away. I vaulted the barbed wire fence, set the hook and again went through the back-winding bit. Dave had warned me that these fish were fighters and it was noticeable that they would scrap absolutely to the point of total exhaustion. A few of them took some protracted nursing when they were returned to the water.

The scrap was fireworks and the carp was undoubtedly one of the most beautiful I will ever catch. Dave was still in the swim, trying to recover from the previous fish, when I hooked this one. I had it on a short line within five minutes or so and he waded out with the landing net and crouched down in front of me to my left. And there he remained for the best part of ten minutes – the fish just wasn't having it and wouldn't come in. We'd seen it a number of times before it was actually landed and we were both anxious because we knew that it was something special.

My first reaction when I saw it, was that it was a fully scaled, big double. By the time I'd seen the fish four or five times I was convinced it was twenty five plus, which was a little optimistic. Eventually it gave up, and the reality was a near fully scaled mirror of exceptionally beautiful colouring and weighing twenty three pounds exactly.

For two days I'd baited a spot seventy yards out, taken six fish of increasing weight and was finally convinced that I was on the right track; that by chance, the method of fishing the water that I'd more or less had thrust on me was the right one. Or was I? No, I don't think I was fully convinced at any time that I was getting it right, and I wasn't. The brace of twenties was almost the last fish I took from the baited area. Sometimes luck is the residue of careful planning, and sometimes it's just plain luck. Those two fish were the latter but I can't go as far as Hutchie and say that I got no satisfaction from them for that reason. We all get our share of bad luck. If it turns out good, just shrug your shoulders, smile and balance it against the next disaster, which, sure as tonight's dusk, will be just around the corner in carp fishing…

You get those weeks don't you? Or nine days, or ten days, or what the hell ever. The season was three weeks old and I was counting the hours to a renewed acquaintance with the Mangrove Swamp when one of my many admirers, who must have been short of something to do, pulled a wax effigy of me off the shelf and started sticking Lion d'Ors in it. The result was a funny couple of weeks. Not funny ha-ha to me, but possibly to the wax effigy artist.

I was all revved up for away on the Friday morning. I'd already had one ten day session on the water and things had gone O.K. More importantly, I'd fallen in love with the place. It had been marginally harder than the Black Adder had suggested, with signs that it could get really difficult, but the lake had an undoubted edge over many of my waters in that there were carp in it.

I should perhaps explain that I'd given up smoking in May (again) and made it through the first session because the Black Adder didn't smoke, and there was no one else on the fifteen acre water. In addition, I'd been dieting, doing exercises, running and generally making a fool of myself, as usual. The result was that I was feeling pretty fit and well able to handle everything that the Gas Board and the bailiffs could throw at me – until the Tuesday before I was due to go away again, when I was struck down with back-ache. I'm not good at suffering pain stoically and on this occasion it was as well that I live on my own because I was unlivable with. Back-ache was a new, unwanted experience.

I waited for it to go away but it didn't, it got worse. I couldn't sleep, it didn't help over much at work and, more worryingly, it took the edge off my anticipation for the coming session. It was an effort to mix baits, assemble all the paraphernalia, re-spool reels, get the dry mixes ready… Friday morning I gave up the unequal contest and went to the doctor's. We'd met once, five years previously, and I'd forgotten that he is one of the nicest people I've ever met. He listened sympathetically, sent me for an X-ray and gave me a prescription for pain killers. The X-rays I could well have done without, but the pain killers I was totally in favour of, except that I should perhaps have listened a bit more closely when the Doc asked me if I was all right with antibiotics. I just said "Yes" and smiled. Anything that got rid of the pain.

I went for the X-ray, was amazed at the speed and efficiency that had been injected into the Health Service, picked up the prescription (£1.40? When did that happen?) and crawled back to the flat to die. There was no way I was going to load the mountain of gear into the motor and attempt a hundred mile journey in my condition. I swallowed two capsules and stretched out on the bed, convinced that I was unlikely to make it to the vertical ever again.

I surfaced an hour and a half later. Glory of glories, the pain had gone. An hour and a half later still I had, too. Get yourself down there son, and keep taking the tablets. The heatwave was still making its considerable presence felt. There were three mixes of frozen baits in the cool box, and I wondered just how long they would stay frozen. I drove suspiciously waiting for the pain to return, but we were doing all right. Half way there I stopped for petrol and ice cool drinks. Another hour or so and I'd be there. Whistle, whistle, life was looking marginally better by the minute. I restarted, or went through the motions of starting. She wasn't having it; as it turned out because the battery was flat, the long term significance of which was somewhat lost on me. Minor crises are an hourly interjection into my motoring life and I bought some jump leads, hi-jacked a commuter who clearly objected to having his weekend delayed by five minutes,

Hooked in Reed Warblers

133

and made it to the water without further incident.

There are at least four really special moments in carp fishing for me. The best is, without any doubt whatever, the movement of an indicator. I live for that moment, that upsurge of excitement and anticipation, that materialisation of all the hopes and planning; the moment that says you've got it right. The other high spots are much of a muchness, but special for all that: arriving at the water, settling in behind the rods when all the graft of tackling up and setting up pitch is done, and banking a good fish. Having said which, there's settling in behind the rods for the night…hell, it's all magic. But actually getting there is always that bit special, particularly with nine or ten days in front of you.

This time it wasn't. I felt like death, but at least it wasn't down to that pernicious back-ache. As I didn't know what it was, I put it down to the ice cold drinks I'd consumed on the run down. I dropped into the nearest swim and started firing baits out. There was a lovely light breeze running into the corner to my left and I couldn't help but feel hopeful about catching, despite the obvious terminal nature of my illness. I just wanted to set up, crawl into the pit and start again next day. I started the camp pitching process and found I'd arrived without the storm sides for the brolly. Well, there you go, that should cap it; ten days unbivvied under a brolly at my advanced age and in my tender condition. I felt grubby from the journey and had a wash and a teeth clean. I rinsed my mouth and found a filling swimming round in there. The back pains started up again with the onset of self pity so I had a coffee and a couple of the magic capsules and died.

My recollections of the night are hazy. I didn't catch, but if I had felt on top of the job I might well have thought my way into the fish; but as it was, the brain was moribund, coming up with zero by way of deduction or determination. Night is usually for sleeping on that water, but that night wasn't. From midnight onwards I was getting liners, half runs, the constant sounds of fish heaving around over the baits. I couldn't believe it. I had three hookbaits in a tightly baited area seventy yards out and the fish were clearly on the baits. Or were the 'liners' twitches from eels, which were supposed to be a nuisance on the water? I wasn't absolutely certain that the baits were rock hard after the freezing and thawing so I reeled in each hook bait in turn – to find they were all well in order. I recast as accurately as possible, presumably missed the loose feed and got a decent night's sleep with no further interruptions.

I woke up to find that I was still alive, just, if you could call that living. The fact that the main feeding time of four till eight didn't produce fish wasn't a great help. By the time the Black Adder arrived, late morning, I was desperately in need of someone to moan at. He hadn't had anything big from the water since the last time I'd been down, and he listened to my long list of complaints with relish, interjecting the odd unsympathetic snigger. By midday I'd just about got the whole thing back in perspective. Fortunately, the back-ache didn't recur. I'd recalled the doc's warning words about the antibiotics, and stopped taking the capsules. By Sunday I was feeling myself again. On a long session it's Hobson's choice.

I rowed the Adder across to his maize fed swim on the other side of the lake, rowed back and set about trying to make some sense of the carp. It was a problem. A water that had started the season with the easy tag was in the process of rapidly re-classifying itself. The carp were learning fast, but surely they weren't sorting the rigs out? Not that I was using anything complicated; I've used the braided rig for a season and a half now. As it turned out what seemed to have happened was that the high water temperatures had caused a blow out on all the artificial flavours.

By Sunday I felt well enough to move camp and set up stall in Reed Warblers. I'd arrived Friday evening and by Monday morning Dave and I were still fishless. I was spending half my time up the viewing tree, trying to work out what the hell was going on, watching fish over some baits. I was fishing two different versions of the same bait, one going flavour and one flavourless, relying on the taste enhancer. The flavour now seemed to have blown and the unflavoured bait wasn't getting through to them. Or had they just blown out on boiled baits altogether? No, that couldn't be the case, and watching half a dozen carp moving over a dozen boiled baits directly under the viewing tree in three feet of water was fascinating. The carp seemed to be playing chess with the baits.

I should explain that the viewing tree swim was an agreed no-go area as far as fishing went because it was too valuable as an observation point. Watching those fish on the Monday morning I was quite convinced that four of the six fish below me would have been caught, or hooked in a fishing situation, and yet in an hour and a half not a single bait was actually eaten. Two of the fish didn't touch the baits. The other four were sucking them in and apparently testing them or 'tasting' them, to find out whether they were food or not. Some of the time the bait was just sucked up and rejected at leisure almost immediately. At other times the bait would be sucked in and the fish would move slowly round the swim, obviously chewing at the bait with its throat teeth. I can't explain how I knew that was happening but it is apparent when you see it occur. But every time the bait was eventually ejected, sometimes three or four yards from where it was sucked in. Had I been fishing a hook bait in among the free offerings, I would undoubtedly have hooked carp that morning, and yet not a single bait was eaten in an hour and half's grazing. Very thought-provoking. I went back to the reed warblers and they serenaded my troubled mind.

I was fishing three rods, rightly or wrongly, and it was late morning, well past feeding time, if such a thing still occurred on the water. I'd cut down the loose feed to just half a dozen baits by this time, and I cast out the hook baits to the baited area while I thought. The third rod was fishing three grains of corn on a standard hair rig tight under some lily pads thirty yards to my right. Two days and three nights without a fish. The mental battle was starting and I was in danger of starting to mess about with the bait. The right hand rod interrupted my thoughts with a howler. I dived on it, expecting the fish to be ten yards into the lilies, but it was headed for the middle of the lake and came in without any fireworks. It was a very welcome mirror of fourteen pounds.

Something was bugging me so I reeled in the other baits and went back to the tree. It's odd, but it's often the way. You start to get a feeling about something but the fact that you aren't catching obscures everything. Landing a fish cleared my brain a bit. What was bothering me was that one of the fish under the tree had rolled over the baits. Now that hadn't happened in previous observations. There had been some sort of turn on there and yet the baits hadn't been eaten. No change: the baits were still there and there were no fish around.

Dave was pulling off for a day so I rowed across the lake to collect him. We went up to the pub and had egg, sausage and chips and I bought some food. I inevitably finish each session foodless and penniless and rarely bother with a decent meal, so this one went down well.

I returned to the lake alone with my total confusion and went back to the viewing tree. Some of the baits had gone, the original version that I'd taken down with me that had attracted so much attention that first night. Now that my brain was starting to function again I related the heavy rolling, line bites etc. to too high a flavour level. A smell turn on and a taste switch off. So why were they eating them after they'd been in the water for the best part of a day? Perhaps that was taking the edge off the flavour level, or perhaps the stimulation of the other ingredients was making itself felt after so long.

Well, if they wanted the things out there the best part of a day they could have 'em. It was mid-afternoon. I went back to Reed Warblers, whacked two hookbaits out into a new area, fired six free offerings out with them and became a vegetable. There are times when I wish I hadn't got this fascination with baits. A couple of pounds of maples would soon sort these lads out – and would only teach me what I know already – that maples are a marvellous bait.

It's a good swim for night action, but not this time. I woke at first light and the indicators were doing their superglued bit. Grief, there's some pain to carp fishing at times, and it's all supposed to be for pleasure. The mental crisis was temporary. I sat drinking coffee suddenly knowing full well that one of the indicators was going to move. I was right and had two runs within the hour, a twelve common and a thirteen and a half mirror. I moved.

Confidence was increasing but I'd suddenly got that feeling about the Royal Box. I follow every gut reaction without hesitation and I didn't stop to

Superglued in Reed Warblers

136

Superglued in the Royal Box

wonder about this instinct, because it was part logic inspired anyway; all the bigger fish I'd caught had come from the Royal Box. I'd completed the move by late morning and stuck the baits out across towards the lily beds, keeping the feed to a minimum.

It's a gruesome form of carp fishing, sticking the baits out for three quarters of a day in the hope of action at feeding time next morning, but that week it wasn't as bad as it might have been. I listen to the radio a lot when I'm putting in long sessions on my own, and this summer saw plenty of activity on the sports front, what with the cricket World Cup, the Tests and Wimbledon. So by the time the commentaries had finished for the day, the cool of a beautiful evening was closing in and the anticipation of possible night action and the probable morning feeding spell was increasing.

No night action. I woke to a misty dawn, heavy with disappointment and frustrated at the lack of activity. I remember that morning particularly vividly because I just lay in the sleeping bag feeling utterly blown out, doing what we all do hour in, hour out, day in, day out in the course of a season; gazing at the inanimate rod set up. The baits had been out there seventeen hours. Were they still there or were they slowly breaking down just enough for the eels or whatever to whittle them away? Was I lying there like a dummy with three unbaited end tackles on the end of each line?

My mental crisis was resolved when the middle rod suddenly exploded. The longer you have to wait, the more exciting it is when it does eventually happen, and that run was a real gut-churner. The lily pads… I burst out of the bag (it's the type you burst out of, given me by Hutchie for services rendered –

mind your own business), grabbed the rod and shot twenty yards up the bank to my right in my stockinged feet, leaning on the fish as hard as possible. I was to have a number of such takes and scraps over the next couple of days, and trying to organise myself in anticipation became more and more complicated. The umbrella and bedchair were tight on the rods, but every time I had to go through this twenty yard stampede up the bank to keep the fish out of the pads.

Having accomplished that, the next priority depended on whether or not I was conscious when the take occurred. I sleep with the glasses under the bedchair. Sometimes. At other times they can be anywhere: this was one of those other times and I couldn't find them. The fish was beginning to feel like a good one, and was inevitably kiting behind the weedbed to my left, which meant that I would need the waders to wade out and ease it round them. Trying to put waders on with one hand, while keeping a firm hook hold with the other, could form part of a contortionist's routine. The complex permutations of glasses, footwear and landing net (I invariably had to land the fish at a part of the swim where the landing net wasn't) eventually began to feel like some fiendish mind bender from Jeux Sans Frontiers. I actually laughed out loud as I was playing one fish because I suddenly imagined an Eddie Waring commentary on the complex ritual.

"Ay, this lad 'ere, good lad this Mattie Black, ayyayy, losing a bit of time on the waders 'ere. Could go in 'ere if 'e's not careful. OOOps, steady with the net now – aayy, 'ere she comes – oopp and under," accompanied throughout by Stuart Hall's maniacal laughter.

First the good news. I landed the fish and it was a beautiful, young looking mirror of twenty pounds ten ounces. Then the bad news. I eventually found my glasses in the sleeping bag. I'd been sleeping on them, which hadn't improved them. The frame was badly distorted, but fortunately the lenses weren't broken. I took a couple of pictures of the fish with remote control gear, and was just rewinding the cable on the air release trigger when the right hand rod was away. I hit it solidly, played a powerful feeling fish for upwards of twenty minutes, then dropped it as I applied side-strain to keep it out of the rushes. That hurt; that really did hurt. I just couldn't believe what the loss of that fish did to me; I just didn't know where to put myself. Hell, we all lose fish, it's part of the game and you have to learn to handle it or go barmy. Yeah, I can rationalise it, but it hurt. I gently propped the twelve footer against the fence and howled, Yatesy style, then howled again. Ten minutes later I'd got the fish pegged as a bionic fifteen pounder and the pain had gone.

The next thirty six hour spell was extraordinary and I had another seven good fish between fifteen and eighteen pounds, with the takes coming at regular intervals. One particular fish is imprinted indelibly on my memory. It came the following night, in the early hours of the morning, if you'll excuse the lapse into Irish. (In fact, I haven't a clue what time I had it.) The Optonic was in full cry as I made the conscious, or threequarters conscious. I was standing playing the fish somewhere away in the darkness when I became aware of the incredible beauty of the night and the conditions. There was a dull, deep red moon halfway down the sky above the lake to my right and the air was still and mild. You need someone with you to share moments like that, or some satisfactory way of recording it exactly. It's too much to have it all to yourself, but perhaps it's the best way; you have to be very much in tune with someone for them to be able to see and feel what you are seeing and feeling. You can't describe it: you have to experience it yourself to know what it feels like, but such moments are too rare to be lost instantly and recalled but hazily and unsatisfactorily. You can remember what happened, but not how it felt.

It wasn't much of a scrap until the fish got near the net, when the whole thing became a bit hectic. I'm very careful about playing a carp 'out' in the dark: trying to net a fish that's still lively can be disastrous, so I first saw the fish some time before I put the net under it. And it was an eel, a very big eel.

Now I've heard Ritchie Macdonald's Redmire eel tale upwards of half a dozen times, and I'll listen to it as often as he's willing to re-tell it, and it's often struck me as bizarre that someone with Ritchie's bottle should have this fear of eels: but it's not a natural 'fear', it's an unwelcome, uncontrollable instinct. I'd never had to land a big eel in the dark before and when confronted with the prospect, I wondered what the hell I was going to do about it. In actual fact it was a mid-double common carp, so I didn't find out how I would react. But how on earth did I come to mistake it for an eel?

The fish was one of the run of good fish and all was right with the world. The session that had started with pain and discomfort and nearly three blank days was building up to a climax. I came back to earth with a bump when I dropped two good fish in succession on the Friday morning and went back to the reed warblers for consolation. They welcomed me back – then gave me a real mauling.

I was back in Reed Warblers by Friday teatime. It was a lovely spot, shut off, all water, reeds, sky, trees, reed warblers, and the occasional carp. It was only a couple of pallets perched precariously on some bales of straw among the reed beds and was an awkward pitch to organise, but the straw made it warm at night, and the reeds, and the margin trees broke up the relentless heat of the days.

I'd made out fine without the brolly sides but then, who wouldn't in those conditions? I went up to the pub with Dave at dinner time from whence he made one of his periodical onslaughts on civilisation. It's very difficult to imagine Dave being civilised, or polite, or making any sort of compromise with the artificial rituals of suburbia. Or that's how he'd see it. The reality is probably less stark. His uncompromising philosophy that "it's all a load of crap anyway" sort of epitomises his world weary cynicism.

Having eaten, drunk, re-provisioned and mentally recovered from the two lost fish of the morning, I went back to make some baits. All the fish I had caught that session had come on the one bait mix, and I was desperately trying to re-create whatever had gone right with that mix. I'd got about six of the original baits left.

Friday evening, Steve arrived for the weekend and took up residence in the Royal Box, which I'd vacated that morning. His girlfriend dropped him off, showing a totally unnecessary amount of thigh in the process, and I hooked myself up on the barbed wire fence while straddling it and trying not to notice her long, shapely legs. I spent a highly undignified couple of minutes easing the barbed wire out of my cords in the groin region, while trying to maintain some element of sang froid. I slunk back to Reed Warblers with my tail between my legs. Or perhaps I could have phrased that better.

I had two fish on suspenders Friday night, both low doubles, one a common, one a mirror. Unlike the Royal Box, Reed Warblers had possibilities

The lovely young looking 20lb+ linear from the Royal Box.

during the day, and on the Saturday I worked at it. I was rewarded with a run early afternoon, a take on a suspended bait against some pads sixty yards to my right, played a lively fish for ten minutes, then dropped it just short of the net. It wasn't a big fish, and the loss didn't gut me, but it certainly worried me. That was three lost fish out of the last five. I'm very painstaking about hooks, and have total confidence in the Drennan hooks I'm using, but I resolved to be extra careful with the sharpening.

Saturday teatime the heavens opened and there was a ferocious thunderstorm which spent a good hour camped on top of my umbrella. It turned so black, and the rain was so torrential that I dug out the camera and flash and took a picture. It was as dark as it looks, and this was about six o'clock mid-July. The thunder was undoubtedly the most extreme I've ever experienced. I pulled the storm-sideless brolly down as low as possible and weathered the storm.

I didn't know what effect torrential rain had on the water and turned in, not knowing if I was likely to be disturbed by the Optonics or not. I wondered how Steve was going on. His buzzers were shorting when he arrived and he'd had to set up with coins balanced on spools and plastic cylinders on tin cans, in addition to which I don't think he slept a wink all weekend in case he missed a take.

The rain eased off late evening but I'd turned in by then. This was to be my last night of the session, possibly for the summer, on the Mangrove because of work commitments and an early close down for duck shooting. The Optonics had me out twice, the first time for a common in the region of thirteen pounds. The second time… Oh dear, that second time.

A blistering run that had 'common' written all over it: all hell let loose: five minutes of anxiety and in she came. A beautiful looking fish of fifteen pound-ish, a common again, and in the dark it had that deep golden look to it. I'd sack it for a couple of hours and get a picture at first light. I carried the landing net to the back of the pitch and laid rod, net and fish on the damp, sweet smelling straw. The take had been on a suspended bait and the hook had gone right through the lower lip, but was held close to the mouth by the position of the anchor shot. My scissors were three yards away in the tackle box, or I would have cut the line. Or perhaps I was anxious to keep the tackle intact to get it out there again as soon as possible. Judgment on me.

Whatever the reason, I made the mistake of trying to work the hook back through the hole in the carp's lip, which the long-suffering fish didn't take kindly to at all. It set off backwards at a rate of knots and pulled the hook firmly into the top pad of the middle finger of my left hand – well in – then kept flapping round with ever increasing abandon. I dived on it, held it still and got hold of the hook with my right hand. I mean, well, we all get pricked by the hook at times, and that was what this felt like. Except that I wasn't pricked, I was hooked. And because of the position of the shot I couldn't move my finger further than an inch from the demented carp's mouth. The shot, which was on a braided hook length, wouldn't slip, so in the end I'd no alternative but to get my mouth tight up against the carp's and bite the line between the hook and the shot. Heaven knows what anyone walking into the swim would have made of that strange operation!

Thoughts of photographing the fish in the morning had flown right out the window. I managed to bite the line, carried the carp carefully back to the water and put it back, then got the torch out and inspected the damage. It wasn't good. I flatten the barbs a little bit, but not completely, and I'd had a hook sharpening purge that very day. Removal was going to entail some sort of minor operation, but the carp were feeding and daylight was only an hour away. The operation would have to be soon, and quick. For the first time in two or three weeks I felt in need of a fag.

I thought about it. I'd got some clean, wrapped razor blades. The combination of a clean blade, Steve in the Royal Box, boiling water and me looking the other way and screaming might just resolve the situation. I walked the two hundred yards to his pitch. He answered immediately from the depths of his long service weather-blanched brolly camp and emerged into the cool night air. I explained the predicament and showed him the hook. The lad was a man of action. He pulled out the Bensons and lit one, assuring me that minor operations of that nature weren't right up his street.

Bensons. What a cigarette. The smoke drifted round me and my lips started to form the well practised line "Give us a fag," words I'd uttered with machine gun like regularity on the banks of lakes all over the country. Fortunately, I recognised the incident for what it was in the nick of time. The common was the devil's disciple and this was the final ploy to pull me back on the weed. Temptation passed and I went back to Reed Warblers with my problem. I couldn't blame Steve for not having a go. I had a tentative dabble myself but that hook was well in. I wrapped some bandage round it (the mind boggles at the thought of what must have doubled as a bandage), and carried on fishing. They'd had enough; they weren't having it, which was singularly frustrating because for

A Reed Warblers common that didn't give me any grief.

the first three hours of daylight there was a lot of movement over the baits.

I was, of course, aware that the hook couldn't stay in there indefinitely, but my car wasn't starting, Steve hadn't got one with him, we were fifteen miles or so from the nearest hospital, the hook was in my left hand, it wasn't over painful, and Dave was due down late morning. I'd been depending on Dave coming to give me a jump start with the car; his presence now looked like being unusually welcome.

He arrived at lunch time, bursting with enthusiasm. I explained the situation to him, showed him the finger and the Drennan size six and waited patiently for the hysterical laughter to subside. I was actually torn between driving home and going to hospital there, or having it done straight away, but Dave insisted on running me, and displaying the finger to everyone he knew between the lake and the hospital. Actually, that part was not at all unpleasant because it consisted of Bill, the owner of the water, and his delightful wife, who was suitably impressed and insisted that I should call back for a reviving drink if I survived the hospital experience. I didn't think it likely. It was one of those prospects that escalate in the imagination with every minute's delay – like going to the dentist, or giving a slide show.

Two hospitals in nine days: definitely a new personal best.

"You're the second hook we've had today," said an intrigued receptionist as she filled in a five page form in triplicate. (The third hook arrived while I was there!) I hoped they'd cleaned the blood off the pliers from the first op. I waited nervously with the sundry broken bones, bust heads – and hooks. It's unbelievable how busy an accident ward can be on a peaceful Sunday afternoon. Dave had gone to alert the undertaker. I joined the other patient waiters.

A little nurse minced up and cast my name to the ceiling. I looked up in case they'd got a fly named after me but had to accept that it was me she was after.

"Walk this way, please," she said and swayed off down the corridor. (Has Hutchie used this one?). I tried my best but I haven't got the build for it and I'd left my high heels in the back of the car.

She was gentle and kind, but a bit blase about it.

"Another hook is it?" she asked in her sing-song border accent. She inspected it and couldn't suppress an involuntary since. "OOhh, that's the worst we've had."

"I'm a carp man," I murmured modestly, trying to look about ten feet tall while hoping that the naked fear and film of sweat on my brow weren't showing through the nine days of accumulated muck.

"That'll need a local anaesthetic."

"Only local?" I'd been hoping for a general. I'd been living with this thing for over twelve hours by this time and was quite attached to it. She laughed politely, thinking it was a joke. I did some half-hearted chatting up, and she halfheartedly responded. What these kids must have to put up with. I was not unaware of the disgraceful nature of my appearance, the probable contrast between my deodorant (Long Session '83) and the sterilised hospital, and the fact that her domestic situation was probably as stable as mine is chaotic, but these girls have a knack of making you feel wanted just when it's needed most. I haven't got a lot of bottle for operations, however minor. In the event she hadn't either.

I got the full operating theatre treatment, and two jabs in the base of the afflicted finger. The surgeon (he'd appreciate that) was as gentle as my own doctor and patiently went through a number of checks to ensure that the finger was freezing up. It took a long time, and I think he thought I was inventing feelings that weren't there. I wasn't and he wasn't wading in with those pliers until the finger was well dead. I was staring fixedly at a spot on the wall to my right, and the knuckles of my right hand were showing white against the bed-head.

"What am I doing now?" he asked, perhaps a little impatiently, five minutes after the jabs.

"Waggling the hook around." The nurse giggled.

Another couple of minutes and all feeling had gone, although I could feel that the dreaded deed was being done. There was a loud, squeamish exclamation from the nurse. Her tension eased mine.

"Thanks for that," I said laughing, proud of myself that I'd handled it and amused at her bottling it, but then I hadn't had to watch (and I was soaked in sweat). They reverently wrapped the hook in lint, and I took it away with me. For the wound I expected heavy bandaging and splints, but all I got was a little plaster.

They hadn't finished with me; the dolly nurse pulled me back from the waiting room, where Dave and I were debating whether it was a size six or an eight. She'd got to give me a tetanus jab. She confided that she was a novice (I thought that was nuns) and very inexperienced. I didn't follow through; Dave was waiting and it was time I hit the road for home.

We left the hospital. I'd got a weight off my mind, and my finger, and all I wanted to do was hit the road for home. Well, I didn't want to, but when needs must… We called in for the drink which Bill's wife had promised us and finally rolled back down to the water early in the evening. Time to be off, I kept telling myself, reluctantly no doubt.

"You'd better stop another night after all that", said Dave. I looked at him sorrowfully for being a bastard. 'Course I was stopping for another night. I rowed him across to his pitch, revelling in the freedom of being unhooked. We tipped half a ton of maize round his marker and I rowed back to unload the car again.

I'd got this bait problem, but I had got the remains of a mix that was three days old which might be starting to tell them something. I wasn't confident that I could get them on bait strength though. It might take more. My action in Reed Warblers had been on suspendeds, but I hadn't any confidence in the rig for the bigger fish. For convenience, I was setting up in the Royal Box, which was the area most of the bigger fish had come from. Think about it kid, pillock 'em. I've got this mate at work, Frank, who's a bit of a lad. Exiled southerner, living up north; Tottenham supporter, a bit wide, but smashing with it. "Pillock 'em" is his expression for conning people. He says about himself, "You can't pillock one who's pillocked thousands". I've not gone into why he's living up north.

Better go for the best of both worlds. I settled on a two hook rig on a fixed paternoster set up. Two separate hook arms, one to fish a suspended bait, the other to fish a bottom bait. Got it? The large, and extremely nervous carp swims up and encounters a bait weaving around in front of it, two inches off the bottom and smelling very desirable. No way he is falling for that one, he'll settle for the free offerings that are lying around on the bottom. Beep-beep-beep. Pillocked him. I must have believed in it because it took me two hours to set that lot up, and getting it out involved the use of at least five yards of PVA. I rigged two rods like that and settled for a straight bottom bait on the third.

I put the brolly up, assembled the bed chair, got the stove going and ate and drank, then thankfully settled to sleep at dusk. I hadn't had much sleep the previous night. The Mangrove season had almost run its course and I was about ready for away. My atmosphere buds were becoming saturated.

Another superglued dawn, indicators and eyelids to match. I crawled out at half past six and took an intravenous coffee resuscitator. All right, I didn't, I drank it, but it was needed. My guts always feel slightly uneasy on days when I've got to return to the land of the living. That's possibly hereditary from the days when I was married and expecting GBH of the eardrum, or perhaps it reflects realistic thoughts about how I'm going to get through the rest of the month on a couple of quid. On that particular dawn there was a surfeit of unwelcome reality and a confusion of thoughts concerning the impending five weeks of twelve hour shifts, a car that was sulking, a cat that wouldn't be talking and would be temperamental for the rest of the week and, no doubt, other minor troubles were magnified out of all proportion. I might be free to do as I want but that doesn't stop me feeling guilty about it.

I switched the radio on to soothe my troubled soul. Ray Moore. I'm not 100% sure about him, but then, that's true of the rest of them. I'm a radio two man, so I take what I'm given. The morning mist slowly cleared away. There was no fish movement and no signs of life across the water in Dave's swim. He's a good sleeper in the morning.

Mangrove Finale

7.30 brought Wogan, Gilbert Becaud and a 19lb+ mirror. The plaster from the previous day's hook removal is well in evidence.

Half past seven brought Wogan and three quick smiles in as many minutes. He came in with some instant inanity and I smiled. His first record was Gilbert Becaud – 'A leetle love and understanding, ho-ho-ho'. I love that and smiled again. Beep, beep, beep. The smile kept going. It was a solid mirror of nineteen and a half pounds – it had taken the bottom bait. I sacked it and then clucked round it like a mother hen for twenty minutes until I was certain it had recovered. I adorned the end tackle with another five yards of PVA and stuck it out there again. It had been worth the extra night.

I sat on the bed chair drinking coffee, listening to Wogan, reflecting, contented. This was where I came in. A figure appeared from the right. It was Dave, walking. That meant he had a tale to tell… Was it worse news than a nineteen pound mirror? Far worse; it was a twenty four pound common, for God's sake. That wasn't on. Yeh, it was. Dave had suffered not a little on that bed of maize with next to no return; he'd earned his second big common of the season from the water.

We took some pictures of my mirror then rowed across to take some shots of the common. It was yet another beautiful, very young looking fish, golden and superbly proportioned. It was a shame there was no early morning sunlight to highlight the lovely golden sheen of the carp's scales. I rowed back to fish out the last few hours.

We were well past the time I'd had any morning action in that swim – since the first morning when I'd had a common at about eleven o' clock. It was after nine by the time I got back behind the rods but I knew that I was going to have another fish. I didn't think it, I absolutely knew for certain, and I'd told Dave as much when he was across. I'd decided to fish until twelve. It would give me ten hours to pack up, resurrect the car, complete the three hour drive home, bath, have a sleep and be ready for the night shift at ten.

The morning ten came and went, and Wogan with it. JY burst out of the radio, breathing life into the world. The Optonics were switched off and I was sitting on the bed chair expectantly watching the indicators poised on the needles.

Half ten. It was getting late for action, but I knew it would come. Not only would it definitely come, but it would come in the shape of a twenty pound common! Now that thought must have been put into my head by Dave's fish, but where did the certainty that I was going to have another fish come from? At ten to eleven, and this you won't believe, just as I was thinking 'The best part of carp fishing is definitely when that indicator starts to move', the middle one started to scrape slowly up the spear. My heart leapt and the rod bent into my last fish of the Mangrove season.

A fish at the tail end of a session is not one to lose; that sours the whole thing for a day or two. It's like having a last minute goal stuffed up you and losing the cup through it: you get no chance to answer back. I didn't lose it, which I was never going to do, so certain was I of another fish, but that didn't stop the uncertainty.

Dave with his 24lb common. The first recorded capture of the big common now known as Trio.

I still had it in my mind that it was a twenty pound common, and I smiled when I first saw the fish. It was a common, and it looked a good one. I took a deep breath as I put the net under it; it had taken three attempts to get it in. I picked up the mesh and waded ashore with it; the fish felt good but it didn't look twenties - and it wasn't, but it was yet another personal best common at eighteen pounds five ounces; a beautiful, well proportioned fish. I looked at it, lying on the mesh, and remembered a picture in Jim Gibbinson's book 'Carp' of a glorious looking common similarly posed. I'd often marvelled at that picture and I had the same feeling about this fish. It had taken the bottom bait.

I had a slow, reflective pack up then rowed across the water for the boy wonder. He'd had no further action. We photographed my common, the pictures of both fish clearly showing the plaster from the emergency the day before, and decided on a pub lunch before giving the car the kiss of life. The Mangrove season was over – well, almost.

The car gave me the only bad time I've had from it in two years, and that was my own fault for ignoring the implications of the problems on the way down. She started alright on the jump leads, but died five miles up the road. I boarded her with a bemused lady who lived in a beautiful, remote country cottage and flogged it back to the lake in the scorching hot afternoon sun. All the world gets dragged into my car problems when they do occur.

Graham let me commandeer an office phone for half an hour while I tried to find a railway station enquiries office that wasn't engaged. I had to drag Dave back across the lake and scrounge a lift off him into Sh… you know where. Then borrow a fiver off him because I didn't have enough for the astronomical train fare. Magic Kid.

The two hundred mile journey involved two changes; I made it back to Sheffield at half past nine and had to ring for the van to pick me up. The car needed a battery and an alternator, which Dave sorted out for me and, of course, I had to go back down to pick the distant creature up. Well, of course, I had to combine the trip down with a final five day session, didn't I?

That was a betrayal, and the water thought so too. I blanked it, having just two takes in the whole five days, and they came within thirty seconds of each other. I lost both fish for reasons too sordid and too tedious to go into. When you've had a good finale, don't risk an encore.

"Isn't it time you came down and fished in Kent?" asked Bob Morris at some close season free for all. Is it ever time for going down to fish in Kent, I asked myself, only too well aware of my own inadequacies and quite content to give them no greater exposure than they were already receiving. On the other hand, Bob Morris was one of my boyhood heroes – he was one of my heroes when he was in his boyhood – so it did seem a bit churlish to refuse this kind invitation.

"How about Brooklands for the first week of the season?" I asked.

Bob and Peter the Eater exchanged amused glances. I couldn't convince them that I wasn't joking and they wouldn't have it. Now I'm not that dumb. I do recognise that Brooklands, otherwise known as Dartford, or Goodwood, heaves with bodies that first week, that bailiffs run riot battling hell out of the innocent carp men, that the atmosphere rivals the one out in the middle in an England-Australia test match and that any resemblance between the whole performance and carp fishing is purely emotional. But that is the sort of carp fishing I'm used to. It would be like Roman Lakes on a quiet week. I would have every excuse for not catching carp and hopefully finish up with enough material for a dozen articles.

Apparently it was out of the question; they wouldn't hear of it. I tried again. Where else would a week's fishing have all the necessary ingredients for a serialised world war three? What was this Darenth that everyone talked about? The mad axeman incident. Youngie's eight thousand doubles in a season. Or was that Sutton, or both? Darenth, the place where Lenny first cast out the hair rig and took fish. Hadn't its banks been trodden by Maddocks, Middleton, Little, Stritton, Savage, Wilton, Kemp, Davis, Davies and Davies and a host of other household names. Who hadn't fished Darenth? I'd even heard Ritchie McDonald talk of having fished it once. He laid emphasis on the once. I put it to them. Darenth.

Bob smiled. I thought I detected a hint of evil but there isn't any in him, so it must have been wind.

"Yes. I'll take you to Darenth. The Tip Lake."

The Tip Lake. Ah, there's romance for you. I could see it clearly in my mind's eye. The Tip. Not a blade of grass in sight. Trees denuded of leaves by four ounce bombs, bait droppers, fish spotters, leaf eaters. Undergrowth flattened by the queues of hopefuls waiting patiently for their turn in the going swim, or any swim, or just waiting. The Tip Lake – it sounded ideal for a massive denunciation piece on the annihilation of all carp fishing principles in the carp angling mecca. We made arrangements for September. Wouldn't that be a bit late? Would there still be the massed ranks of carp men necessary for a true impression of Kent Karping? They would guarantee that by arranging for the Cockney Poison Dwarf himself to be on the water throughout the week. And if they could include little Jimmy and Lockie in the cast list I might possibly witness some real Kent aggro.

Mid-September found me high-tailing it down to Kent. Work and other bits and pieces had kept me off the water for six weeks. I was well ready for whatever Kent had in store for me – apart from the Dartford Tunnel. The old Cortina purred her way down, behaving immaculately for reasons best known to herself. She's saving herself for an absolute cracker, I can sense it, but she owes me nothing. Ten years old and well over 80,000 miles in the last three years. But however sweetly they purr, the end of a three hour plus drag is always welcome.

Near Blank at the Tip

The Dartford Tunnel signposted the end.

Have you ever been through the tunnel? It's a doddle, and not even a long doddle. There are signs that warn you to have your fifty pence ready at the toll. You have to pay to get into Kent. Had I got fifty pence? I drove along, my face contorted and my body twisted into an alien shape, trying to extract a 50p from the strangely shaped and oddly situated pockets they have in cords. Whatever else they are designed for, it is not for extracting change from while you are driving.

By some strange chance I had a 50p and managed to extract it without colliding with anything. I'll give the southern drivers that; their efforts to evade drivers extracting change from cords' trouser pockets are to be applauded. Not that there was a great deal of traffic around. Well, that isn't quite accurate. There didn't seem to be much traffic about until word got round that I was about to make a fool of myself, then the massed hordes appeared from nowhere. This is not new and it is not a southern phenomenon. I am fairly convinced that there is a law of density of onlookers which operates for the majority of us. I mean – look, think back on your greatest triumph, the pinnacle of achievement in your life, that climax to your pathetic existence when you would happily have shared the moment with the world. What did the audience consist of? Two cows and a coot? A cleaning lady waiting for you to vacate the premises? A groundsman who just wanted to get home for his tea? Yeh, I've had it.

But the moments of disaster. Well for Heaven's sake, what is this universal ability to sniff an impending calamity? Where do the serried ranks of spectators instantly materialise from on these awful occasions? All right, traffic does tend to increase in density as impetus is lost and everything slows to a halt, but one minute you look in the mirror and there is one other car immediately behind – and he's trying to change lane so he can get in front. Next second disaster has struck and you glance sheepishly into your driving mirror to share the moment with the one impatient lunatic; there are forty eight sets of teeth grinning at your discomfiture.

I'll confess that it had not occurred to me that there was potential disaster involved in passing through the tunnel, provided there was no old bill checking tax discs. I approached the barrier, window down, fifty pence clutched in my sweaty right hand to proffer it to the man who was collecting them, all set to enter the promised land, if I wasn't already in it. The Toll Collector (there's got to be a ten year waiting list for that job) took the offering from the car in front, then vanished, dragging a large bin into position by the barrier as he disappeared. I'll allow that it was a very large bin and that it carried the clear instruction 'Throw Your Money in Here', or words to that effect.

I could make excuses to the effect that I was too far to the left. Or that the bin was positioned too far from the line of traffic. Or that the late afternoon sun dazzled me as it dropped on Dartford. Or that I'm a lousy thrower of fifty pences... Whatever the reason I missed. I did. That bloody great bin there, yawning, inviting, unmissable, barrier triggering, but 50p short of the barrier triggering material required to let me into Kent. I'd no idea where the 50p had gone and I didn't have another one. Fortunately, no one sounded their horn.

After what seemed like about three hours, but was probably only two and a half, an attendant appeared from nowhere, located my fifty pence and dropped it into the bin with a totally unnecessary air of condescension and superiority. The barrier rose and I made it to the Mecca with half a million pairs of eyes boring into the back of my head. I was within a few minutes of my destination – and inside a couple of hours I'd found it.

This was Saturday teatime. We were due on the water in about twenty four hours. When I got to Bob's he was down at the lake, sniffing the air, relaxing after a long hard week on Savay which had yielded one fish – quarter of an hour before he packed up to go home. John (Dad) ran me to find him and I had my first sight of the Tip. All trees, grass, beauty and carp men.

We went back to Bob's and had tea with John and Mrs. Morris. I mention that because prior to going down I had no idea that there was a Mrs. Morris. But there is and she is charming, makes lovely tea, and is Bob's mum in case I haven't made that clear.

I was hoping to have a chance to talk to Fred Wilton while I was down. Such chances are few and far between and I'd never talked to him at length before. We had to drag him off a lake, which came as a surprise because no one knew that he knew of any lakes, and he certainly wasn't known to be fishing one. Not just fishing, but carp fishing. Having located him – and there's over two metres of him – we talked and drank tea and coffee until somewhere in the region of first light. Bob lost his way on the journey home.

Sunday teatime Bob and I made the taxing journey from his house to Darenth, the best part of a mile. Sutton is in his back garden, and Kirby a good wind up with a three ounce lead. My mate Mark Summers was already on the water, the poison Cockney Dwarf himself, all bristling aggro and enjoying a summer of exceptional fish. Peter the Eater was on Booker's Bend. Bob set up on the Big Lake end of the Tip, in the Pallets. There was a motley collection of down and out, unemployed local celebrities on the Fence Bank between the Tip and Tree lakes. I was installed in the wide open spaces of the Dry Dock on the end of the lake opposite Bob. Mark was in the Gap.

I noticed during the Fox Pool week that down south, the minute an angler leaves the water an elaborate game of chess takes place with all the carp men making pre-arranged moves into different swims. A chain reaction. When we had called down on the Saturday all the discussion had been about who was moving off and when, and who would be able to move in to where and which swims that would leave vacant. There seems to be an indefinable pecking order in this allocation of pitches, but there is also a reassuring recognition of the fact that an angler may be putting in a great deal of time and hard work in one swim, and that swim will very often be left vacant pending the arrival of that angler, when it would otherwise have been occupied. Carp fishing maturity.

A week in the Dry Dock swim on the Tip Lake. There have got to be worse things in life. Mentally it was hardish because, rightly or wrongly, I did feel under some pressure. I have a smashing relationship with most of the Kent lads but I am not unaware that wherever I go there are going to be at least one or two uncharitables who will have the attitude – "The clever Bugger's always writing about it, let's see if he can do it." I suppose that's fair enough, except that I've never claimed to be any great shakes at catching carp. Anyway, I proved to the reception committee of Micky Sly that I could definitely live up to my writing by going through my usual pipe opener of casting into the densest vegetation in range. In this case it was a bramble a full fifteen yards away. Attempts to pull clear reassured me about the quality of the eleven pound Sylcast.

Physically it was an easy week. No long range work. A comfortable swim. The water was only fishing at night and the days were filled with coffee and visitors, as were some of the nights, come to think. Derek Stritton materialised late one evening, the time and day being etched on my memory for a reason I shall return to later. Brummer Gummer, about to be deported to his native Aussie land. Gray Cowderoy – and others just as familiar, but nameless in my appalling memory. Denis Davies was on bailiff duty and his daily visits were a high spot of the week. His is a name known and respected throughout carp fishing and he was one of the first to catch the big fish of the Tip with any consistency. Everywhere you go there are carp men like him who have seen it all and done it all, are rarely mentioned outside their own area, and never ram their successes down your throat. His attitude to the Tip was reassuringly realistic and he helped me keep what was going on in perspective. I had the feeling I would be lucky to catch a fish in a first week's fishing and he confirmed that.

I was bothered about presentation, inevitably, but his thinking on that was clear and absolutely right. If I was sure that the bait was good enough, relax and wait for it to happen and don't get too snarled up on rigs. Once the carp had total confidence in the bait they'd even take it on the hook, so give them a chance. It's advice worth remembering. Most problems of presentation are caused by a bait the carp aren't confident in, or a feeding situation that spooks them. You can only trick them into getting the hook for so long. Sooner or later you are going to have to get them feeding to catch them. Any 'success' I've had in terms of catching carp has been largely down to bait strength and thinking, having said which…

At a carp fishing meeting I was once referred to as a leading carp angler. I jumped on the person in question with both clogs flashing sparks and made an indelible impression on him. I am close enough to carp fishing to know the score, and I know that I am an above average carp angler, but by no stretch of the imagination do I consider myself 'a leading carp angler'. I've not taken enough examinations to be thought of as one of the lads. Yes, I know that given time I would catch from the majority of waters that carp are caught from. My baits, physical ability and thinking are good enough, but by the same token I would have got a degree had I gone to University, but I didn't and haven't and I haven't fished and caught carp from enough of the acknowledged hard waters. In some senses, 'D' lake and the Tip are hard, but not in terms of location, which has got to be an essential ingredient of a top carp water. I think a fair number of carp men kid themselves as to their carp world status, which is not to suggest that I think it matters.

There is far more to catching carp than knowing a water like the back of your hand, coming up with a good bait and sitting it out until the carp have it. All right, over a period of time most of us would be able to sort out most of the waters available to us; over a period of time… but how long is that? Some of the waters take too much time, or are too far away and involve too many sacrifices. Rightly or wrongly, the lads who do sort these waters out, or at least have some consistent success on them, are the ones who are single minded enough to really want to do it, and are good enough to do it. They put carp fishing before everything, and are out there, week in week out through three, six or nine months of the season. I don't even kid myself I could do that, and I'm not convinced that it is desirable, which is another story and another argument. I've seen the effect full time carp fishing has had on people and lives. "It's all right for so-and-so, he's out of work, he can spend as much time as he wants on the water." Well, if that's all right for so-and-so, it's all right for you, so get out there and do it. Chances are it will wreck you and your life and you'll finish up equating carp fishing in terms of trophy shots, which is a sad state to be in.

So in terms of all that has been said and done, and pioneered and rejected, and worked on and worked out, and succeeded or failed, I don't kid myself that there was any great significance in my spending seven days occupying the Dry Dock, other than that it was a very enjoyable seven days, in carp fishing terms. I suppose that to a great many of the Kent devotees, the word 'enjoyable' will be a joke. Well, maybe I'm a bit older and a bit wiser and want it to be an enjoyment. Busting yourself in half in pursuit of carp is an individual choice because there are two sides to cracking the hard waters, the elation of success and the despair of mind-blowing failure. We can all punch the air and grin like Cheshires when the rod is getting bent. Good winners – the world's full of them. Bad losers – there's a hundred times as many.

You've got to be a good bad loser to succeed and be lived with. We all have to bite the bullet at times when the water is being thrashed to a foam in someone else's swim and there is the equivalent of an oil slick in front of us. But be civilised about it; build yourself a padded cell at home and howl your jealousy and frustration into the confines of its privacy. Grit your teeth and congratulate whoever is making your life a misery – and keep working. If you have got what it takes, you will sort it out. If you haven't, then you are in for a permanent nightmare and you'd be best getting the hell out of it and carp fishing elsewhere.

I was confident of catching, and that is not hindsight. But confidence beforehand and the confidence of sitting through days of motionless indicators are two different things. Judging whether you are just waiting or getting it wrong is the biggest gift experience can give you, but it's an instinct you have got to believe in, and be objective about. Bob Morris caught on the first morning in circumstances that rather took the edge of the capture for him. He loves the Tip and had spent countless hours there with Cliff Webb and John (Dad) going back further than most of us can remember in carp fishing terms. He has had far more than his share of the fish but this season they were being uncooperative. When you are as close to a water as Bob is to the Tip it is hard to be totally objective about your results and Bob was having problems assessing whether or not he'd got a problem or whether he was just having one of those spells that we all suffer.

I started fishing early Sunday evening and had no action that night. In fact, there was none to any of the rods on the water, but Bob had his twenty two at about eight next morning. Just to get the Tip into perspective, that Sunday night was Bob's nineteenth of the season on the water, for that one fish. On the other hand, he was having a good season on Savay. There was no further action of any sort for anyone from Monday morning until Mark had a twenty seven pounder in the early hours of Wednesday morning.

When you know you are in for a hard week it helps to set yourself a realistic target. I was hoping that the indicators would go twice during the seven days and I was not unduly anxious by Wednesday because I felt that the longer

the week went, the more confident the fish would become in the bait; plus I might start to get an insight into exactly where the fish wanted the bait presented to get them to pick it up. I was making heavy use of PVA as usual, but using little by way of loose feed. It would have been nice to bag up, but a fish would do me.

Wednesday evening was wet, wild and windy. In fact there was a complete wind switch at tea time that wrecked the bivvy and called for a complete re-appraisal of the situation, a drenching for me, plenty of cursing as I struggled to get the brolly and the storm sides re-erected on the hard gravel bank, and superb looking conditions. Surely they would be having it now?

I was sulking after the soaking and crawled into the bag early to listen to the England-Denmark International at Wembley. That really helped; the selected team would have struggled in the Isthmian Sunday league and were one down to the Danish part timers at half time. Twenty minutes into the second half we were still one down, at which moment the Optonic sounded and the indicator to the right hand rod started bouncing. The run was to the close in bait and if the fish was running in the wrong direction I'd got problems. But what a moment! What is it you feel when the indicator finally goes after three nights and three days? Massive relief probably, mixed with some disbelief, but excitement too. On a water like the Tip chances are that it's going to be a good fish.

I dived out into the wet night and swept the rod round to my left. The run was to the bait fifteen yards from the rod tip and setting the hook presented no problem. All went solid and the rod tip followed the fish round then stopped. The carp started to come back to me, under heavy pressure, then dropped off. I didn't scream. I don't know why, but there have been far worse fish losses. Just briefly I didn't know where to put myself, but it was brief. They were picking up the bait and I didn't feel it would be my only chance of the week. I'd found a presentation, or had I? A fish hit squarely as close in as that shouldn't drop off. I changed from a size four to a size six Drennan to cut down on hook weight. Does it really make that much difference? I don't know, but anything that increases the chances of the bait being sucked well in has got to be tried.

I went round to Mark's swim for a moan. He had a visitor, a little man in a flat hat and an Essex accent, complete with cup in his hand and chair round his neck. It was schoolmaster Stritton. Aren't the shifts of time and place and fortune extraordinary when you reflect? Bob Morris and Derek Stritton, writers from my most formative carp fishing period. How many times did I read and re-read their contributions to the second BCSG Book? I was wrestling with the early frustrations of winter carping at the time and their words of wisdom were gratefully digested and acted upon. Unsuccessfully though; they always held the most important bits back; quite rightly – and of course I wasn't fishing their waters at the time

Derek came round to my swim and we chewed the fat until after midnight. He was having an exceptional season and was as full of enthusiasm as ever about his carp fishing. Bob and Derek have been pursuing carp for many years and have graduated to the big 'uns, but I've watched Derek fishing for small carp and he was just as enthusiastic about them. I've watched Hutchie feeding floating particles to single figure fish with the occasional bigger one around. He was like a kid at Christmas – "Look, look at this coming in here"… They are

The Gap Swim in 1983, Marks Summers in
and Mark with one of the big fish he landed t

carp mad, not just big fish hunters.

Derek eventually melted off into the wet, windy night, due back in the classroom in a few hours. I'd no further action during the night and there was none to any of the other rods on the lake.

Next day I changed the way I was fishing the pitch. In fact, I'd been changing it slightly each day, trying to find a couple of hot spots in what was a very heavily featured expanse of water. I don't sleep during the day and if I did, Mark would have made it impossible with his ceaseless demands for coffee and rabbit, rabbit, rabbit. There are drawbacks to making the best cup of coffee that ever graced the banks of a carp lake. I didn't want to miss any of the socialising anyway, but the end result was that I couldn't stay awake at night. I never used to sleep at all at night when I was on the banks, but now I've gone the other way, which was dumb that week, seeing I was hoping for night action in a snaggy, weedy swim.

Thursday night I fell asleep uneasily. Time was getting short but there was sod all I could do. You're either getting it right or you're not and when it's as slow as that you don't get much feedback on which to make an assessment. Instinct said I was on the right tracks, but there is a natural anxiety starting to gnaw as you go into the fifth night without a fish.

I woke suddenly, unnaturally, but couldn't find a reason. My heart sank, it was getting light. I looked at my watch and it said quarter to twelve. What a relief: it was moonlight and the possible early hours feeding time was yet to come.

I settled back down but there was a sound recording in my head. Beep-beep-beep. I peered myopically out and discovered that I'd got an isotope indicator up against the rod – the right hand rod with the bait round the corner in a veritable jungle. Was it snagged? I was lucky, it had buried itself in the nearest weed bed under pressure from the foam and was lying there sulking. Five heart-stopping minutes later it was in the net and felt good as I lifted the mesh. It was good – a beautiful, dark coloured, lightly scaled mirror, in superb condition and of lovely proportions. It gave me more satisfaction than any fish I'd caught up to that moment.

Shortly before dawn on the Saturday morning I had another run from the same spot. I think I was a bit late waking up to that one and although I could feel the fish, it was snagged solid. After light I went in for it, in water up to my neck but I think I accidentally kicked the fish while I was feeling for the line with my feet and shocked it into severing the hook length. The loss of that fish was worse than the dropped first one. I'm usually wide awake at twenty past five, when I had this run and…oh, what the hell; you've all got your share of heart breaking tales to tell, and in carp fishing just one more-might-have been is neither here nor there. But there were about twenty bodies on the water by this time and that was the only run of the night. Hell, I'm not competitive but there has to be some ego buried in there somewhere, and to go down to Kent and catch the only fish from a water on a weekend night – what an unworthy thought. Shame on me.

Big Dave 'Webbo' Walker and his mate Russ had arrived down on the lake on the Friday night and settled into different areas. Their presence provided me with one of my indelible memories of the week. I was frozen after my early morning dip on the Saturday and had a walk round the lake to warm up. Now

I've fished with Dave a couple of times and know him well enough, and it has to be said there is a great deal of him – nearer seven feet than six, and wide with it. I see him pretty regularly and while I never get used to the size of him standing up, I've got accustomed to being amazed at it, if you follow. But the sight of him stretched full length on his specially constructed bed chair is something else altogether. The length of the man!

I'd no further action after the snagged fish. Mark had a twenty six on Saturday night, or early Sunday morning, and I should record that he lost a fish at dusk one evening, a piece of action I'd almost forgotten about. Russ had a low double from his weedy swim away beyond Booker's Bend, on the Saturday afternoon and Martin Locke, one of the local stickers putting in a great deal of time on the water, had a low twenty from the Fence Back early Sunday morning. End of story. It was a nice week; lovely surroundings, big fish, a smashing bunch of carp lads – but somehow it wasn't Kent, or what we are led to believe is Kent. Perhaps they were all on their best behaviour because I was there – an agreed truce until I'd turned my nose for home and was having my passport stamped at the Dartford Tunnel on my way back north. I eagerly gave the man my 50 pence. It made more sense to pay to get out of Kent than to pay to get into it. Thanks though, Bob, Mark, Peter, Denis and the rest of the Kontingent of Kent Karpers. But for Heaven's sake, a week's a lot of fishing for one carp, even if it did weigh twenty six pounds ten ounces.

Have you noticed that nostalgia is booming? All of a sudden, yesterday rules – OK? Well, OK! I suppose we are all a bit like that, those of us who are oldies, golden or otherwise. And it isn't just about carp fishing is it? Anything that happened more than ten, fifteen or twenty years ago was laudable and to be glorified; everything current is iniquitous and to be vilified.

I am sure you don't need me to stir your memories about the way things were, which won't stop me doing it. Take the early fifties. All summers consisted of six months of clear blue skies and uninterrupted sunshine, with the occasional light rainfall at night so that the water shortage did not become a problem. In cricket, every batsman scored three thousand runs a season and even leg break bowlers took two hundred wickets at a cost of a mere eight runs apiece. All soccer matches were like an instalment from 'Roy of the Rovers', 4-3 home wins watched by eighty thousand sober, dignified fans who cheered friend and foe alike: the winning goal was inevitably scored in the dying seconds by an Adonis of a centre forward whose private life was beyond reproach. Hilary and Tensing climbed Everest, Gordon Richards won his only Derby, Stanley Matthews won his only cup final medal, Bannister ran the four minute mile, the Queen was crowned, I almost had my first sexual experience on the local playing fields (catch me naming names) and Dick Walker caught a carp of forty four pounds. The world has never quite been the same since, neither the real world, nor the angling world, which, to the majority of the readership, may well be one and the same thing anyway.

But if the world hasn't been quite the same since, I think it's equally true to say that it was never quite the same before either.

Obviously I'm too young to remember much of that, although Hutchie and Roger Smith have filled me in on the parts I didn't know, or my father didn't tell me about. I can recall some of what was apparently the golden age though. I vaguely remember the USA beating us at soccer in the World Cup – Matthews, Finney, Wright et al; the lovely Aussies comprehensively thrashing us at cricket year in, year out; one good summer in ten; no pill (which was immaterial because there was no sex either); dirty steam trains; a bus every three days; rationing; no television; no cars and the thrilling choice between the third and light programmes on the wireless. I won't go on about the inch thick frost on the windows each morning; mowing four million square yards of lawn with a hand mower and the thousand and one other inconveniences that neither made, nor marred, the good old days. They were all part of the way of life and if you knew no different, you accepted what you'd got.

I've got alternatives now, but in some senses I live what many would consider to be a spartan existence. The flat is not centrally heated, and much of it isn't carpeted. I have no television etc., etc. The etceteras represent whatever you may feel is essential to a comfortable life, but I have got a choice and I don't criticise those who choose to surround themselves with all the luxuries that life can provide. I am not materialistic, therefore I do not accumulate money and worldly goods. If I did I can envisage that I would get on very well with thick pile carpets, sophisticated stereo, video, cocktails, wall to wall women and all the other creature comforts that indifference, carp fishing and writing inhibit me from pursuing.

Possibly all that will give the impression that I am cynical in the extreme, don't believe in looking backwards and will have no truck with nostalgia,

Past Preferred

whereas nothing could be further from the truth. I love reflecting on certain periods of my life, and particularly on some special memories of my carp fishing days. I am not a realist and I am not a dreamer. I am not a romantic and I am not a modern, in that I want the best of all worlds in carp fishing terms. I love the feel and atmosphere of fishing but I do like to catch carp. And I think that the true carp fishing romantics deny themselves the pleasure of catching in an endeavour to preserve an imaginary set of rules, inflicted on them by the distortions of time. They wish to apply twenties' and thirties' technical standards to what is now an eighties' pastime. I think it is unrealistic to blame the universal, and lamentable, decline in moral and ethical standards on the technological advances within carp fishing!

If pressed, I will admit that there is a great deal of the romantic in me but in practical terms, I have got to stand alongside the modern carp men. I have read all the old books, and reread them frequently. The romantic school of carp fishing quotes the names of Sheringham, Ransome, 'B.B' and Dick Walker, cluck their tongues about what is going on today and cite these favourite authors as the true chroniclers of the spirit of carp fishing. I'm inclined to agree that they were the true reflection of what fishing was all about, so let's have a look at them.

These angling literature greats are somehow connected in many minds in the sense that their names are often bracketed together, although their writings span three-quarters of a century. Hugh Sheringham was early century, Ransome the twenties and thirties, BB and Dick Walker on from there. 'Confessions' was inspired by a line from Ransome's brilliant essay on carp fishing which was reproduced in 'Rod and Line'. 'Drop Me a Line' was dedicated to Sheringham, and Dick Walker had two chapters in 'Confessions', in addition to being a prolific author in his own right. What all these greats had in common, beyond their obvious love of fishing and writing, were words; brilliant, atmospheric, descriptive, captivating, evocative romantic words. They were able to take you to the water and keep you there. They were able to reflect your thoughts and experiences, and dreams, without you even realising you had thought, or experienced, or dreamed them. They were, and still are, marvellously readable but the fact that they wrote brilliant prose did not mean that they weren't concerned with the catching of fish and the improvement of methods. In particular, Sheringham and Walker, forty years apart, wrote similar, very progressive books pointing the way to the improvement of methods, and even the more pastoral 'Confessions' carries much material that can best be described as technical.

Dick Walker was undoubtedly one of the pioneers of carp fishing as we know it today. I will no doubt be told different, but wasn't he the first angler to advocate the use of buzzers and design some of the earlier versions? Would it be unfair to point out that a drawing of one of these designs appeared in 'Confessions'? Yes, perhaps that would be unfair because B.B.'s caption didn't exactly convey enthusiasm for the gadget! Didn't the Carpcatchers use 'bivvies' from the very start when they camped out during their long sessions? Bivvies and buzzers were pioneered in an age which even the most extreme of the romantics must look back on as the golden age of carp fishing, so I don't think it is very realistic to lay the blame for this type of fishing at the feet of the bivvy and buzzer brigade of today.

Then there's the bait scene – modern baits. The romantics don't like them. I'm not sure whether this aversion is a practical one based on scientific knowledge, or an aesthetic one based on the sentiment that if it isn't a potato or honey paste it is not traditional. If it is not traditional it is bad news before it is even tied to the hook – whoops, sorry, put on the hook. (I'd better not wander into that particular minefield. The romantics are very unenthusiastic about bare hook set ups, even though the hair itself now seems to have been traced back to some time BC.)

But just how modern is the current bait scene? Rod Hutchinson, in his first book and Chris Currie in Carp Fisher 8 both quoted carp bait recipes from bygone ages that are probably more sophisticated than many of the so-called specials that many carp anglers start their carp fishing lives with.

Sheringham on baits, in his 1912 treatise, was quite masterful. He had an enviable ability to combine the illuminating with the entertaining, and to saturate his writing with the bemused awe of a permanent beginner. He conveyed the feeling that no matter what the angler did, and however lucky he may be in terms of catching carp, the fish themselves were always in charge of the situation.

"In theory, they will take anything from a lobworm to a boiled potato, but in practice they will usually take nothing at all."

I think we all know the feeling! Slightly irreverently he goes on to suggest that you prebait with bread, bran, biscuits, peas, beans, strawberries, rice, pearl barley, aniseed cake, worms, gentles, bananas and potato. He refers to the French carp fishers' use of beans (the description suggest lima or butter beans) and adds that they boil them with a flavoursome mixture of herbs etc., giving the following examples – wheat, fennel, hemp seed, thyme and honey. He does mention honey paste but dismisses it as a small carp bait – in 1912! The fact that Sheringham's style of writing is so light rather disguises the reality that his 'Coarse Fishing' was a first class instructional angling book. I wouldn't think that it was ahead of its time, but rather of its time, that time being seventy years ago and more.

In 1930, eighteen years after Mr. Sheringham's book was first published, Albert Buckley took his incredible catch from Mapperley reservoir, using pea sized baits of brown bread and honey. Two years later, he had a nineteen pounder from the same water on the same bait. Two years between carp is hardly what one would call a going bait! But undoubtedly the Buckley catch was staggering, and still would be today for the majority of us, from any water. Sadly, for me, the edge has always been taken off the feat by the outcome – the fact that he had to gaff the fish to land them, then chucked them onto a hand barrow and wheeled them off into the setting sun. But then, this was the romantic age – all right, I'm getting naughty again – they didn't know better, which was why they were still using honey paste. And to me Albert Buckley's catch does go some way to spelling out the paradox in nostalgia.

"I caught the tram to Heanor where I got off and set forth on the two mile walk on the road by the rhododendron woodlands, climbed the road by Shipley Hall grounds and went down the other side to the anglers' paradise in the valley, Mapperley Lake."

In terms of now, that is a lot of trouble to go to for a day's fishing, although I suppose such a comment betrays the modern in me. Does a two mile plus walk heighten the anticipation? And how far is the same two miles at the end of the day? Is it all part of the pleasure? How many times did Albert go through all that and not catch? Two years between carp. Don't two years pass quickly in retrospect and isn't the same period of time for ever when it's still in prospect, especially if it measures the length of a carp blank?

While I am not what I would call a realist, I am enough of one to recognise that nostalgia is largely just a trick of the memory.

"Yesterday is just a memory,
Tomorrow's never what it's supposed to be."

That's Dylan and I suppose it goes a bit too far. It is realism turned cynicism. "Never" is too strong a word in the context of life, or carp fishing, when you are talking of tomorrow, because it is the day many of us live for. Others live in the past and prefer nostalgia to anticipation. Living in the past, or the future, is an escape from the reality of the present, which is what carp fishing tends to be anyway.

In carp fishing terms, my strongest nostalgia is for Snowberry Lake in Buckinghamshire. It is a beautiful, secluded, atmospheric place. I have some lovely memories of it, and some lousy ones, but the latter I don't wish to know about and conveniently forget, or romanticise. The lake was the setting for much of my early carp fishing and the anticipation of any trip there was always massive. It is among all my yesterdays, so it is just a memory, and the feel of what actually happened between the anticipation and the memory is possibly based on forgivable distortion rather than less memorable fact.

Nostalgia ignores doubts, discomforts and fears, but was there ever a carp session that wasn't attended by a sprinkling of all three? It is never, ever quite as simple as just going fishing and catching. Even the anticipation is contradicted by doubts. You won't get the swim you want. You don't know whether the carp will be on the bait or not, or even if you'll find fish. The car's playing up; the wife's not speaking to you and you inflict a headache on yourself by smoking far too many cigarettes on the way to the water.

And then, briefly, every care in the world vanishes when you get to the water and you find that your favourite swim is vacant. Carting a ton of gear round to the pitch is a labour of love. Lining up the rod rests, tackling up, setting up the bivvy, getting the baits out. It's all part of the anticipation and the rising excitement. You settle on the bed-chair with that first brew and that is the zenith. The moment that nostalgia is built on. Ransome's benign moment out of context. First impressions are the strongest and in the memory that is how carp fishing feels. "Better to travel in hope than to arrive" and in those first few minutes of fishing you are still in hope, still travelling. But very often, particularly on the hard waters, the moment the first cup of tea is finished, your mind starts a slow process of deterioration. First and foremost you want to go carp fishing, then you want to catch carp. But carp fishing can be very, very slow and anyone with any imagination at all must have doubts. The memories of the way it was are always better than the reality could ever possibly be.

For a year or two it has been different because we have been able to catch carp. That is probably the main difference between now and then: the anticipation is greater and more enjoyable because there is a greater chance of fulfilment. We have progressed from honey paste and potatoes and are actually using baits the carp want, as opposed to baits they will eat when they are driven to desperation by an unusual extreme of hunger. If paste baits and flavours offend the sensibilities of some, there is still a wide range of natural baits that will catch carp. But is it really so unreasonable that progress has at last started adding to the list of flavours that Sheringham published in 1912?

I don't think I am alone in mildly resenting the tone of condescension in the minority who imply that if you use carbons and HNV baits you have no feelings for carp fishing. I use carbons, HNV's, heavy leads, bare hooks, buzzers and a bivvy and fish for pleasure and because I love carp and carp fishing. I'm not part of any figures race or prestige trip (I don't think); I have no time for hooking outside the mouth; I think my carp fishing is entirely moral, whether it be on a pressured, overcrowded water or a remote, deserted one. I catch carp from time to time; they are an essential part of carp fishing - but no more so than the atmosphere that goes with it all. I catch them by hooking them and exerting a persuasive force by means of rod and line, until they are close enough for me to guide them over a landing net. Whatever your attitude to carp fishing, that is ultimately what you are trying to achieve and there is no way you can glorify that.

I can quote tracts from Sheringham, 'B.B.' and the rest and I can derive as much pleasure from some of the modern writers. John Bailey is a modern romantic and during a break from wrestling with the words to express all this, I reread one of his Coarse Fisherman offerings. It was called 'Hector and the Heroes' and it oozed nostalgia. The piece romanticised a day which must really have been ordinary beyond belief. Whether that is true or not is immaterial, because John's pen conveyed exactly what it set out to convey – that here was a day among days. A cold, frost filled, anxiety racked day in which he eventually caught a few roach and was fulfilled beyond his expectations for reasons private to himself.

Carp fishing is an individual pursuit and our nostalgia for it tends to be personal rather than collective. No one objects to people not catching carp. Some spend lifetimes not catching; for others it represents a period of learning, and we all go through spells when the indicator does not move as often as we would like it to. I suppose, logically, that if you are not going to catch you may as well do it with or without buzzers, with carbon, glass or cane, with potatoes or HNV's and with the bait on the hook or off it. But to make a cult out of not catching is unrealistic, although I suppose the more time you spend not catching, the more time you've got to wallow in nostalgia! But surely, reality must make a compromise with idealism. I'm sure Sheringham would be very flattered that carp anglers are still using his guidance three quarters of a century on, but I'm equally sure that he would have moved with the times. We live in a carp fishing age. It is right and fitting that we remember and respect our beginnings, and give due homage to our forerunners, the pioneers. But it isn't possible to halt progress on the strength of a nostalgia inspired whim. Carp fishing can only be a reflection of the activities of the majority who participate. If the minority resent what the majority is doing then the tail is trying to wag the dog. Rightly or wrongly, as far as the majority of carp anglers is concerned, these were the days.

The rain is lashing against the kitchen window; the trees that are blocking out what little afternoon light there is left are being tossed by a persistent, moaning wind, adding an extra bleakness to the scene. Deeppocket has just been round for a couple of coffees and a think tank session on end tackle and hook patterns, and he's gone back to the drawing board to think it out again. I'm left with a jumble of disconnected thoughts of an evening last September, the events of which have been trying to find their way onto paper for some time now, and the remnants of a gloomy August Bank Holiday Monday in which to find the words to give credibility to the unlikely. I mean many of the things that happen on the lakes I fish just couldn't be invented. The main difficulty with this particular tale is in bending it slightly so that it doesn't reflect too badly on one of the principal characters, namely me.

I was on the Skip Lake, but Peter the Eater's splendid tale has confused me so much that I haven't a clue which swim I was fishing. I know it as Jackson's, and for reasons I will briefly explain, I think I will adhere to that name for it. I'm all for re-writing the record books, and for taking the sharp edges off reality, but in addition I have a strong sense of tradition. If, therefore, in this highly selfish carp world there is an occasional recognition of the deeds enacted and suffered and swims fished by others, then I do think it only right that we respect that recognition. No one could dream up Lee Jackson, or Little Jimmy, and even the most vivid imagination could suffer withdrawal symptoms if exposed to the mildest possible version of Ian Booker's carp fishing history – so to me it is rather nice that these successful, and respected carp anglers have had swims named after them. In fact, we could do with more of it. So I shall make it clear to those readers who have the extreme good fortune not to know the lake where the following events took place that Booker's Bend, Lee Jackson's and Jimmy's are actual swims. Two other popular Skip Lake swims were actually named after anglers, the Gap, which refers to the space between Mark Summers' ears and the Rats' Nest, which commemorates most of the carp men who have spent time on the water.

I was fishing Jackson's and suffering. The water was fishing badly, and so was I. My confidence was still high, and I was expecting action but doubts were beginning to creep into my mind. I'd already put in one nine day session on the water without catching, to my considerable disbelief. That had been one of those wretched sessions when you never quite find out if you are getting it wrong or the fish really just don't want to know. There had been two fish out during the nine days. One of those had fallen to the Godfather's going bait, which put it out of our reckoning for valid comparison purposes, and the other to another heavily prebaited and established HNV. Three of us were using the bait and we weren't sure about the attractors. Half of me said "change," the other half said "persevere, they are starting to have it." There was some truth in that but in the mood they were in the attractor/bait package had to be that little bit better than good enough.

That nine day blank was three weeks into history and I'd made the run down with Cyclops for a week's session. Prospects were better. Phil was pulling out of Booker's when we arrived, and he had caught. He felt that there were fish in residence in the area of the Bend and Pallets. The latter was occupied, so Cyclops followed Phil into the Bend while I set up stall in Jackson's.

We had arrived on the Saturday evening. We are now at Monday teatime

To an Unknown Angler

*Ian Booker (above)
Lee Jackson. Both
have Tip Lake swims
named after them.*

and there hadn't been a fish out in the intervening period. Apart from the fact that I wasn't catching, I was enjoying it. Blanks are slightly more tolerable when no one else is scoring, the weather was pleasant without being glorious, the social scene was in full swing and the sun was being unusually co-operative in posing for its dawn portrait each morning.

I think it has to be said that there was perhaps a faint hint of tension in the air for at least some of the time. While most of the Skip Lake regulars are as affable and easy going as I am, you do encounter the odd personality clash, and the occasional merest touch of hostility. Most of this unseemly aggro seems to centre round the Sidcup Assassin, Slapper Summers, but the Godfather has been known to call a spade a spade. And in my gentleness, even I have been known to voice a mild protest when some Malcolm Winkworth clone insists on smashing a battery of banksticks two feet into the gravel ten yards down the bank, this performance usually being timed to coincide with a possible thirty second feeding spell.

Now, the weekend immediately prior to the evening in question had been a difficult one for some of the established regulars. Slapper was undoubtedly in the middle of a bad spell after a couple of years of what he might, in his competitive way, consider to have been a period of comparative supremacy. This bad spell had warped his outlook on life which had, in turn, been further soured by an unexpected, and widely broadcast result for Rockin' Ronnie. The outcome of this result was that Slapper withdrew still further into his shell, emerging from it briefly, and painfully to have a violent disagreement with an extremely physical foursome at a quiet social event – which had nothing whatever to do with carp fishing. Slapper insists that he was only trying to iron out some minor disagreement involving two other people, but there was a certain unspoken scepticism regarding this version in the minds of those who know him well.

A further outcome of Rockin' Ronnie's result was an increase in the Skip Lake cast list, the additions including the Godfather's new favourite, an Alex Higgins look alike who was about as proficient, and prolific, with a mallet as the said Alex is with a snooker cue. This is, of course, a difficult area – hammering on the banks of carp lakes. There does seem to be some acceptance of it, which mystifies me. I would make it a hanging offence. There is little a mallet can do that can't be done four times as quickly, quietly and without aggravation by the Les Bamford Ice Pick. In fact, I showed the intrepid Alex one of these indispensable implements during one of our conversations. He gazed at it for a while, then realisation dawned.

"Ah, you hammer that in" he suggested, intrigued. He wasn't joking.

Come Monday, early evening, and prospects were improving. I had fish moving in front of me, on the back of the first bar, thirty to forty yards out, and I was starting to get signs of action on the baited area against the island, seventy to eighty yards away. My mind was in neutral. Keep doing it right and wait for the mistake. They are educated fish and I knew I wasn't thinking clearly enough to come to terms with presentation, but I was trying, as was Cyclops across in Booker's Bend. That evening, that night, or whenever… it is that sort of water.

I was watching the fish behind the first bar. I'd got a bait on them but was unsure about tactics for the night, whether to fish one bait long and one short. I feel happier with islands than I do with bars, for the simple reason that I've had more experience of them, but when you've got fish swimming backwards and forwards under your nose you can't ignore them, can you? But if the sky cleared, the fish would move off the bars and the area under the trees of the island would be the better bet. I could always reposition a long bait short if I wanted to, but not vice versa.

My deliberations were interrupted by an enthusiastic "Any good?"

I glanced round at the speaker. He was young and had keenness oozing out of every pore. It's funny how you can get the full SP in one sometimes, and the vibes from this pleasant young kid were unmistakable: it was a Cuttle Mill type enthusiasm, not the easily recognisable calm, resigned acceptance of a session man coming to put in the hours towards the next fish. We all go there wanting, hoping, and probably expecting, to catch but you have to hold something back or not catching becomes a strain. There are some mornings when you wake up to a feeling akin to despair, tinged with disbelief that the indicators haven't moved again, but within a few minutes you are back in control and your thinking is centred on the next feeding time, and what that will bring, not what the last one didn't.

But this kid standing in Jackson's with me radiated enthusiasm, and it made me feel uneasy.

"My mate came down on Friday and had one."

"That's nice."

"Yeh, he fished on the end there," motioning vaguely towards the Dry Dock.

It isn't a water you go to for the day and 'have one'. Occasionally people do, usually regulars with a going bait, but not to the extent that you ever expect anyone dropping in for a night, or a day, to catch. I felt I should make some contribution to the conversation.

"How long are you down for?"

"Well, I'm supposed to be round at the girl friend's later…"

My mind relaxed and wandered back to the fish behind the first bar, and he went off to set up for his evening session. The swim to my left was free, which was a reflection of the way the water was fishing because it's a popular swim, and he set up there. I heard a swoosh of his rod some time later, and just happened to glance out to see where he was putting his bait. He cast both baits short of the first bar and catapulted a few free offerings out to the same area.

Dusk was an hour away and I would have to make a decision about the position of my baits for the night. The close in fish seemed to be staying put so I decided to fish one bait long and a stringer over the first bar. The island bait took some getting in position but eventually it was bang right. The stringer dropped in on the right spot, just over the bar at the first attempt.

I was aware that my efforts were being scrutinised from the swim to my left, which was in order, because his had been scrutinised from the swim to his right! The stringer just over the bar resulted in a bit more rod swishing activity from down the path, and I noticed that at the third or fourth attempt an end tackle dropped in just beyond the bar. I had the feeling that 'range' was a problem because he was only using very light leads. I had a coffee and went to bed. It was a still, overcast night and the bait under the island branches would certainly catch, but I was hopeful about the first bar situation too. I was overdue a Skip Lake fish.

The right hand Optonic to the island rod woke me, a trifle apologetically perhaps, with a subdued drop-back, and I jumped on the rod with heart pounding. The bream I reeled in looked a bit embarrassed, but I treated it with the kind consideration all God's creatures are entitled to, even stupid looking, slimy bream that have just negated twenty four hours of carp fishing effort. My hopes were suddenly pinned entirely on the first bar producing. You get one chance tight against the island, which is why I usually put both baits there in the first place. I rebaited the rod with a stringer and cast it out to the back of the second bar, or thereabouts. I crawled back into the bag, slightly disgruntled. The optimism just drained away from me because I had no bait against the island. I had no feel for the water and it was frustrating me at that moment.

"Are you awake, mate?"

The slightly plaintive question came from down the bank.

"I've got a problem."

The same voice from the same direction.

"O.K., I'm coming," I offered resignedly, wondering how big the problem would turn out to be. I tried not to think uncharitable thoughts but had a strong feeling that I could well do without what was about to happen.

From the bend in the rod, the problem was sizeable. The kid was hanging on with a sort of frantic determination which didn't seem to entertain any thoughts of losing whatever he was connected to, or even letting it move. He was quite chatty considering the situation.

"My landing net's the other side of my rod and I can't reach it. You can empty the other fish out. I was only going to use them as livebait in the morning."

I had a sudden surge of hope. He was playing a pike! The hope was unfounded.

"I didn't think I was going to get one. It had been twitching with it for about two hours before it went."

I'd emptied the livebait out and was crouching at the side of the water, appraising the uncompromising battle and listening to his excited chatter.

"Have you had anything yet?"

"No." I almost mentioned the bream but it felt a little inadequate somehow – in addition to which the events of the evening had put a restraint on my vocal chords.

"Your mate's had two across there."

"Has he?" The restraint was undermined by a mild hysteria which was reflected in the uncontrollable falsetto of the question. I had sensed, rather than seen, the nodding of his head towards Cyclops in Booker's.

"Yes, I've heard him have two runs."

The restraint re-asserted itself to the point of paralysis. The Rails isn't the darkest of swims and we had sufficient light for the landing of the fish, but we hadn't even seen it yet. The rod looked to be permanently set in its over-exaggerated bend and we seemed to have reached some sort of stalemate. It did strike me as an odd set of circumstances for the social chatter in which the kid seemed set on engaging.

"My girl friend isn't going to be very pleased about me not turning up."

I didn't tell him that there is a carp world full of that, but did ask him

about the fish. I began to wonder if his glass rod was up to getting the thing to the surface.

It's difficult to give advice in that situation, other than to suggest shaking it off, but eventually we sorted it out and the carp wallowed on top. I'd just put the net under it when I heard his rod hit the branches above the swim. The hook length had parted but the fish was over the mesh and all was well.

I lifted the dripping bundle onto the bank and asked him to find something for us to lie it on. He didn't hesitate and stretched his anorak out on the gravelled bank. He was so full of the fish he didn't know where to put himself.

"It's only my second carp," he rejoiced "My first was a twelve pound common from Hoo last season."

I listened in disbelief and concentrated my switched off mind on the practicalities. I *wanted* to share the kid's enthusiasm for the fish. It was a magical capture.

"Have you got any scales?"

"No."

"Weighing sling?"

"No."

I went up the bank for the necessary, and collected my torch because he hadn't got one of those either.

"Hold the torch."

I hoisted the carp up onto the scales and he shone the torch on the dial. I hadn't zeroed and was working to a six ounce deduction for the sling. The scales took the load and the needle swung round to twenty dead. He was chattering away excitedly and it briefly crossed my mind to forget the sling. I'd given the pike lad at Fox Pool the weight of the landing net but this was different, don't ask me why, and I gave him 19.12. I think he would have been just as delighted if it had weighed five pounds. We photographed it and he put it back and I reeled in and went round to release the inner tension on Cyclops' ears – and to find out how big the two he had caught were.

As it happens, the kid was right in that Cyclops had had two runs. The first had been a false one, presumably a liner, and the second had resulted in a big fish being lost in wretchedly unfortunate circumstances. We cried on each other's shoulders and drank coffee for an hour or two, both gutted by the events of the night, but for different reasons. Life came back into perspective as we talked and, in the end, we could see the funny side of it all.

"I bet the kid's on Richworths," I laughed. "I'm going to ask him when I get back round there."

"You can't do that."

"I can't not do it. It's unbelievable."

I've never asked anyone direct questions about their bait in my life, I don't think, but what on earth was this kid using that would induce a run out of a spooky carp after two hours of twitching? Cyclops climbed back into his bag and I retraced my steps through the still, darkened complex to the fence bank. Our man was, understandably, wide awake – and still chatty. My side of the conversation went beyond the monosyllabic for the first time.

"That's a tremendous bait you've got there. Is it one of your own?"

"No, it's the only one they'd got left in the shop. It's that Tropical Mango. That's what my mate had his fish on last Friday."

I went back to bed.

He walked up the bank to say goodbye in the morning, clearly disappointed that he hadn't had anything else during the night, then left, leaving me to reflect on the events of the night – and particularly my part in them. My manner had never been less than courteous, and co-operative, but my inner reaction had been uncharitable and I wasn't happy about it. It was an incredible capture in terms of the kid's carp fishing experience and I'd been irritated by it, because it couldn't possibly happen, and because I was having a bad time.

I blanked the week out – and it was a judgement on me.

I can't duck it; the explanation of the title of this piece is slightly indelicate. The 'Flynn' was Errol Flynn, a somewhat dashing American film star of the fifties who was rumoured to be a ladies' man. Perhaps that in itself could have been sufficient grounds for the saying, but I have a feeling there was more to it than that. There was a court case in which it was alleged that he went for it, without consent, in his socks. Thus in the fifties and sixties "in like Flynn" became an aphorism for acting precipitately when not fully prepared.

In Like Flynn

It was July, my first session of the season, and I was struggling. The wind was either blowing too strongly, or not blowing at all. It rained every day, apart from the days that it didn't, and it went dark every night. How can you be expected to catch in conditions like those? To make matters worse, Tony 'the Hound' Baskeyfield was on the water. I was in the wrong place wherever I fished, so I pursued a simple course of logic. Tony was at the west end of the lake so the fish must be at the east end; I moved there. Tony caught, my indicators did their superglued sneer, clear through feeding time, if there was still such a thing as a feeding time in the swims I fished.

Wednesday morning the Hound pulled off in the interests of staying married, assuring me that there were fish at the west end of the lake. I thought about it. "Whether 'tis nobler in the mind to suffer the slings and arrows of outrageous fortune…" and blank, or really hit the depths and go to school on Tony's efforts. I compromised. I waited till he'd left the water then moved into his swim.

Dave Phillips (no, not that Dave Phillips; yes, two in the specialist world is a bit heavy) was in the middle swim; Bri (Listen, I am the kiddie) Garner was across the bay in Reed Warblers and Bill the Hyper-eater was in the Royal Box, eating, or sleeping, or doing both. He'd caught, no one else had – especially me; I'd not caught for nearly a year. I hadn't actually fished for nearly a year but the way things were going I didn't feel it would have made much difference anyway.

Wednesday evening I was weary from moving twice in two days, and I'd heard a rumour that Mark was going to pay me another social visit, so I turned in early. Please Spirit of the Mangrove, if you can't send me a fish, don't send Garner one either. I really was worn out and died the minute my head hit the pillow, or whatever was serving as a pillow on that trip.

I came to from a million miles away, rendered half conscious by a persistent AJS telling me that we were in business, though what sort of business was not immediately clear. Whatever was causing the buzzing wasn't putting on a very convincing show. I was butt clipped with a six inch drop on the indicator. The heavy indicator was being lifted to the rod but that was as far as the action went; the line hadn't been pulled out of the clip. An eel bite I told myself as my heart thudded in my ears and I pulled on my muddy boots. Definitely an eel bite I told myself as I went forth (actually I came fifth, but that's another story – as they say) to do battle with whatever had almost woken me up. It was ten to eleven; I'd been asleep under an hour, which was proving less than adequate in the circumstances.

The AJS was still registering alarm and the heavy Micky Sly indicator was alternating between being against the rod and resuming its normal position six inches down the needle. That wasn't an eel bite, it was a roach. I still had hopes that it might turn out to be a carp (you knew that didn't you?), picked up the rod, shut the bail arm, wound down and struck. Something flapped on the surface over where the bait had been as the rod arched over – a bit. It was an eel, and I didn't play it very well. It started coming towards me and I couldn't really feel it at all. Also, it was moving towards the lily pads beyond a tree fifteen yards to my right, although that didn't dawn on me until it was in them. It had kited, and eels don't kite; they have no imagination whatsoever.

It finally occurred to me that I could be connected to a carp, and a snagged carp at that. There's promising for you. It was the first carp I'd hooked in forever and I was playing it like I was scared to death of it. Fortunately, I stayed half asleep long enough for my angling instincts to take over. The tackle was more than adequate; I was using an end-on-anti-tangle no-snag bomb; the lilies weren't the densest I'd ever seen. It's frightening watching some people with snagged fish. All they can think of is – heave!! Sometimes it works, sometimes it doesn't. If you'll let the carp find their own way out they will do so. Tighten up, ease off a bit. Keep doing it till they come tumbling clear. This one did and it gave up after that – and it was a carp. I saw it clearly before I netted it and knew if was a very golden common. It looked about eight pounds; no problem.

When it came down to it I realised that I hadn't done much planning in terms of landing fish. Presumably it was a contingency I hadn't really anticipated. I was perched on a rickety pallet with the rods between me and the fish. That wasn't a good arrangement but I hadn't wanted to bring the fish across the front of the rods because I hadn't dropped the tips. I lifted the mesh around the fish then announced to myself, the world, and any Brian Garners who happened to be listening:

"I've caught a nice little common carp."

In addition to the problem of the position of the rods, there was the boat. The swim was a little bay with just enough bare mud in it to squeeze a bivvy onto. The boat was in the bay (parked there in case a carp got snagged, so I had anticipated hooking a fish), the rods being up the left hand side of the boat, and just beyond it. Dry land was in short supply so I decided to use the boat as a platform via which I could bring the fish ashore. I eased round the back of the rod set-up into the boat, netted the fish, laid the rod down, jammed the landing net handle under one of the seats with the arms of the net clear of the water, then shakily made my way back to the muddy morass to find something suitable to lay the carp on. I spread a damp sack on the firmest available patch of mud, unearthed the near redundant Kevin Nash scales, put the sling sack in position and went back for the fish. I was out of practise but it was all coming back.

I managed to unhook the fish in the net, secured the hook in the butt ring and rested the rod out of the way against the reeds. All nice and tidy; very organised. I'd managed to achieve all the toing and froing in comparative silence and was quite pleased with the way I was coping, considering it was my first fish since the previous one. The fish had felt bigger than I'd originally thought it to be when I'd unhooked it; in fact it felt quite big for a common caught by me. All that was left to do was bring it ashore, weigh it, sack it and get back to the fishing and sleeping.

Of course I should have grasped the mesh of the landing net above the fish, thus enmeshing it and ensuring that it didn't leap back into the water.

"It didn't?"

Er, yes it did I'm afraid. I grasped the mesh in both hands, either side of the net, about halfway down. For practical purposes this halved the depth of the net, meaning that a powerful, athletic carp, timing its leap to perfection, could gracefully hurl itself out of the net… The boat didn't quite fill the little inlet, there was a three foot wide strip of water down one side, and it was into this three foot wide, foot deep strip of muddy water that the carp dived. It was a traumatic moment; a moment for decisive action. I went in like Flynn.

I didn't really have any intention at all of diving into the water until I saw the carp do it, then…well, it just seemed a good idea at the time. It was an undignified moment – or moments; quite a few moments in actual fact. The carp had no sense of occasion and appeared to be willing to go on covering me in mud and water for as long as I was willing to stay in the lake with it. I won't pretend it was easy, but eventually I managed to clutch the playful carp to my drenched, mud-plastered bosom and ease my way to the back of the swim with it. I carried it like someone doing a slow motion Groucho Marx imitation, but without the cigar, clasping the carp to my midriff.

There was a hint of desperation about the whole unnecessary exercise. I'd not been catching, then I'd caught a nice common. I mean carp men are trusting and I'm not known for distorting weights or inventing fish, but a failure to produce the claimed, largish, beautiful common for the morning's picture parade could just have aroused a certain unspoken scepticism among my angling friends thereabouts.

In Like Flynn

Bill the Hyper-eater was in the Royal Box.

Right. Brian Garner with Scaley at just under 30lb.

As it was I nearly did start acquiring a reputation for weight inflation that night. Whether it was because I had to mud wrestle it to a standstill, or because it was my first fish of the season, I did get the impression that it was bigger than it turned out to me. At that stage it was comfortably twenty plus as far as I was concerned. I put it up on the scales which read somewhere around the eighteen pound mark. If they'd been Avons I'd have given it twenty six, but as I couldn't find the torch (on account of it being dark), I had to settle for peering at the dial in disbelief and giving it 'about eighteen', subject to a morning reweighing when we all know they've lost two or three pounds anyway. I sacked it, found the torch, rebaited, re-stringered, recast and relapsed into my interrupted, soggy, muddy slumbers.

There's more. I woke up with a very acute attack of cramp in my right calf. Also the buzzer was sounding. Either event, in isolation, would have been unusual enough, but the two together was an extraordinary, if inconvenient, coincidence, although I can't recall reflecting on that at the time. Whilst I don't wish to over-dramatise the situation, the agonising pain in my calf definitely discouraged even as mundane an activity as travelling the few feet to the rods. I experienced an infuriating combination of frustration and pain; I went through the standard contortions for easing cramp, the buzzing continued, the middle rod pulled off the buzzer head as the line swung towards the pads – then the line fell slack. And the cramp went away. The fish had gone. Prior to that performance, if I'd been asked in a quiet, dispassionate manner if it was possible for an attack of cramp to stop me striking a run I would have answered with an emphatic "No!" I would have been wrong; that morning I was temporarily totally incapacitated (I've since almost convinced myself that this was a line bite, but I can't remember where the end tackle was when I reeled in).

I recast and noticed that Bri was gazing out across the water with the frustrated, quizzical look of one who cannot understand why he had just suffered another blank night.

"I'm coming round," he called quietly.

I wasn't sure whether he meant that he was just waking up, or coming to see me (the swims are over quarter of a mile apart via the land route). He came to see me. I thought it was nice of him to visit, that he had come to congratulate me on my fish. He'd come to let me congratulate him on his fish; both of them.

"I've had Scaley."

Scaley is a known fish. A beautiful, large, known fish and it rightfully took centre stage that morning – along with Bri's fourteen pound common. My fish, which I eventually weighed in at 17lb 4oz, was instantly relegated to the status it had held all along, a private minor triumph in a minor carp fishing existence, but pleasurable and memorable for all that.

My adversary going back at the spot the wrestling match took place.

This is weird, which may be about all that it's got going for it. I wrote an editorial for Carp Fisher 11 which was supposedly about writing – when all it was really about was putting words on paper, about making articles. It didn't even touch on the guts of it all, on where writing – comes from. Rereading the piece later started me thinking about writing, the carp world, carp fishing, and the extent to which so many people get involved with it all.

Carp men, percentage wise more than other anglers perhaps, are often moved to write about their experiences. Look back through twelve issues of Carp Fisher, or any angling publication, and you will find that over the years there have been a great many different contributors. At least some of these writers have contributed just one article, and it may be the only thing they will write in their entire lives. That may not strike you as being particularly odd until you really think about it. I often think about it, and to me it's very strange.

Think about it. You go through all the traumas of childhood, adolescence, growing up and adulthood. You fall in love a few times, and fall out approximately the same number of times. You have triumphs and disasters, crises and calms; you get married, have children; grow older. The years roll away and you accept it all, take it all in your stride; it's all part of life's rich pattern, and in terms of writing material it's no big deal, any of it.

Then one day you are sitting by some lake, escaping from a life that's been too long in the unmaking, and you catch a carp. Oh yeeeess! This-is-where-life-is-at. Give me that pen and let's record this for posterity. But why? Why is catching a carp so inspirational, when falling in love, getting drunk for the first time, going to a Cup Final, making a snooker break in excess of eight, or losing your virginity isn't? In fact, catching your first double and losing your virginity have a great deal in common. They are both landmarks that no one else seems to have any difficulty attaining but which can, for some, assume the epic dimensions of the quest for the Holy Grail, if you'll forgive the pun – although perhaps it's true to say that the comparison may not be a fair one as far as the female readership is concerned. If any of you ladies are having problems with either leg of the double…

It's more than that though; it's more than just the writing. I never cease to wonder at my own involvement with the carp world because it's totally untypical. I've been married, and involved, and had to go to social functions and make polite conversation; and I've tried to be nice to people I had no regard for, in the interests of trying to make a living. I couldn't handle any of that though. I can suddenly turn acid when I'm attempting to hide behind a veneer of niceness and cope with the nerve jangling gratings of some self-opinionated fool. Hard as I try I can't cope with prejudice, or snobbery, or self conceit of any sort; as a result I tend to avoid situations in which I feel exposed. And yet I attend anything from ten to fifteen carp meetings in the course of the winter and close season and fish the Skip Lake at Darenth, which is a sort of open air carp meeting with no bar.

I know I've wandered off writing, but only as part of a thought process, and I'm on my way back to it. I was talking to Jeff Denny at one of Pete Barker's Sale Society meetings last close season. We had a conversation I didn't really comprehend, but then I never did understand my conversations with Jeff, even when we were both sober. He informed me that I had become part of an elite one per cent, and had become unapproachable. Now that is a joke! Well

Isolated in Time

the bit about the elite one per cent is, for sure. I don't go for the elitist thing at all, but accepting that there is one, I will accept that there are two. One is Hutchie, the other is Yatesy. There is then a handful of very talented, very successful carp men, and there is then the rest of us. The rest of us enjoy varying degrees of success in terms of catching carp, that success often being proportionate to where we are fishing, and the amount of time we are putting in there, which is an illustrative over simplification. Occasionally I have a good result; very occasionally I have a string of good results (those were the days). I enjoy that but I don't think it's any big deal, and it certainly doesn't make me any different to the kid who is still trying to catch his first carp. It might in his eyes, but it certainly doesn't in mine. It's all a question of how significant an occurrence catching carp is in the greater scheme of things.

I think the question of approachability is something else altogether, and I think that's true of most people who attend a string of meetings. I go to meetings hoping I can relax and enjoy them. We go to these get-togethers because we have things in common, not for the differences we may imagine exist. Atmospheres differ, although that difference may be in the mind. If I'm doing a slide show, I'm usually uptight about that, because I'm always nervous in advance; then I deflate when it's over, so I'm not at my best then either! On occasions, some of that can, perhaps, add up to an apparent unapproachability, but that's on a personal level and certainly not because I see myself as part of some fictitious elitist one per cent. Hell, if I'll talk to Jeff Denny I'll talk to anyone.

I suppose there's a problem in that I'm a compulsive writer, so my name appears in print far more than it should. So I write: that's no big deal either. If I can write, and there are two schools of thought on that, then it is because I had an artistic mother. It also means that I inherited her artistic temperament, which can be a pain at times – especially for those who unwittingly trample on my numerous over-sensitive areas. Talent we are gifted with by nature is a stroke of fate; what people achieve with their gifts may be more laudable because, even given the gift, the achievement can involve graft and self-sacrifice.

Where was I? Writing and Jeff Denny, which is by way of being a fortunate coincidence. As it happens one of the best carp fishing articles I've ever read was Jeff's piece 'Mapperley' in Carp Fisher 7. I know that the article was a long time in the making because Jeff had told me the tale long before he wrote the piece. It was excellent by any standards. Apart from its unselfconscious fluidity, the writing contained some very original thoughts, *"Isn't it funny how you can still feel nervous about something six years on?"* being one of them. As it happens that was Jeff's only article (sic). He thinks he can't write another, but he's wrong. Articles don't write themselves.

Mapperley was Jeff's inspiration. Initially mine was Snowberry Lake and the whole unfolding feel of carp fishing. The need to write about it all has grown from there to the point that I don't actually need an inspiration to sit down and write. I'm not suggesting that is a virtue, but I do know that all writing can't be inspirational; if it was, we would have precious little to read and not a great deal to listen to. Inspirational pieces come from nothing; non-inspirational ones are usually about something. To start with it is the other way round.

Inspiration? Perhaps that's too strong a word for some, but its definitions are wide ranging. I mean *"the divine influence by which the sacred writers were instructed"* is perhaps a bit heavy in terms of an article about the capture of a first double figure carp. But *"something conveyed to the mind when under extraordinary influence"* is more meaningful. Mapperley had an extraordinary influence on Jeff Denny, just as the capture of a carp, or carp fishing generally, has had on many others. But the expression "extraordinary influence" can mean one of two things. It can mean that the material on which the writing is based was an extraordinary influence, or that the circumstances in which the material is written provide the necessary inspiration.

Dylan said of his songs *"They come to me when I am most isolated in time and space"*. 'Extraordinary influence' and 'isolated in time and space' can mean one and the same thing in terms of converting elusive, vague, half-formed thoughts into the written word. The thoughts, and some of the words, are often there for weeks, months, or even years until there is a moment when the mind may be under an extraordinary influence of some sort and the words start to flow. No, extraordinary influence doesn't mean drink or drugs, or it doesn't in my case. I can understand musicians and other live entertainers needing to resort to some sort of artificial stimulation, because their act of creating is immediate and urgent, but I've never taken drugs and I've never written after drinking. For me, drink gives too short a high and too long a corresponding low. In addition I think that carp fishing is too 'normal' a subject to be written about with the mind on another, artificial plane. On the other hand, I do wonder where on earth some of these pieces come from when I read them later.

I think that isolation in itself can be an extraordinary influence, provided you are able to handle the frustration and boredom that often go with it. The more blank the mind becomes, the easier it is for it to focus on a moment in time, or an event from the past. You don't know in advance how long it will be for the right state of mind to materialise to allow you to write, but distractions can be a fatal interference. Inspiration is sometimes a thing of a single moment, quite literally. You may have to seize the moment then turn the thought into something meaningful by hard work. *'Most isolated in time and space.'* For me, that moment often comes at the end of a long, tedious day of trying to find it or, more occasionally, just as I'm falling asleep. At that moment when I've stopped thinking and haven't started to dream, a clear, previously unreachable concept sometimes drops into the vacuum. If it's a vivid picture I have to get up and write a paragraph or two about it to remind me what the concept was. If it is too vague and ill-defined I leave it, hoping that time will give it definition. Explaining to women about this urgent need to get up and write a few words can be as difficult as convincing them of the necessity for spending weeks on end bivvied up miles from home. My naturalised single status has been established by means of an uneasy mutual incompatability with the opposite sex (based on the all-consuming need to carp fish and write) which I accept as being at least partly my fault!

I can't help thinking that the phrase 'isolated in time and space' is particularly significant in terms of the triggering of a first carp fishing article. We spend long periods isolated, locked up in our own thoughts, suffering crisis after crisis in our minds to the extent that when the longed-for fish does materialise, the whole inspiring experience is there, *'indelibly inscribed on the material of total recall'* as Steinbeck put it. It is that combination of circumstances that frees the

Rod Hutchinson:
exceptional.

first all-important article; from there it becomes a question of either chancing on further inspiration, or seeking it. If your main motivation is the catching of fish, then your life as a writer may be a limited one.

It's frustrating how shallow some writing is – as though the writer couldn't really be bothered. He wrote it, put it in an envelope and sent it off. It takes more sometimes; you can't possibly capture it all at the first attempt, or at least most of us can't. The process of total recall is sometimes a gradual one. Your memory can't cope with it all at once and your pen can't come up with it all first time through. It's like turning a rough sketch into a drawing, then into a painting. The first black and white sketch of how it felt brings back the colouring and detail of how it really was, and you gradually put it together, layer on layer. Sketch it quickly while the image is there, then paint it carefully with the right mix of words. Yatesy's book 'Casting at the Sun' is full of passages which are rich beyond compare; vividly descriptive and beautifully – and painstakingly – constructed.

I said at the beginning that this is weird; that's because it didn't start out in my mind as a piece about writing at all. The circumstances of a particular moment in time somehow focused my mind, and this article eventually resulted, but it was the moment I was trying to write about, not the writing. For reasons I can't explain, it brought it home to me just how temporary everything is. I used to live for tomorrow, or whatever treat life had in store for me next. I've stopped doing that, firstly because tomorrow just comes and goes in an instant and, secondly, joyfully anticipated times usually leave some sort of emptiness, a void that can only be filled by the next moment of pleasure. The passing of time has brought it home to me that there is little lasting significance, or fulfilment, in pleasure for the sake of it.

You look forward to a week's session for however long it is in prospect – and then it is gone. Sometimes there is magic; on occasions you catch what you are after; if you are as shutter happy as I am the pictures are there for posterity, as are the images of the precious moments. But in carp fishing terms alone the next session is often as meaningless as the last one was, in retrospect, and the more sessions you accumulate, the clearer it becomes that life itself is a very temporary affair. Looking back down the lengthening years causes that realisation, not looking forward across the shortening ones. I suppose I'm older than I was, but I don't feel it. There isn't anything I do now that I'm not better at than I was twenty years ago, believe it or not. I have the occasional feeling of regret that there might not be enough time left to achieve whatever I may want to achieve, but I think that's a selfish sentiment. I am well aware that my very existence is a gift; any minor regrets I've got are personal and meaningless. I write; I enjoy doing it, and if it gives pleasure to others then that is a source of pleasure in itself – a considerable one. I'm embarrassed by compliments, which means I'm rarely embarrassed but, deep down, acclaim is the consolation of those who repeatedly expose themselves to criticism.

I think the carp world is special because it is a great leveller. I tend to try and deflate those who give themselves airs and graces and champion the nobodies – as Roger Smith once described the rest of us. When you are part of the carp world you realise that no one is particularly bothered about what you do, or don't catch; you're either accepted, or you're not and catching is inclined to reduce your acceptability rather than increase it! In truth, the future of carp fishing depends more on what people are willing to put into it, rather than what they take out of it. Fortunately there seems to be an increasing number of selfless people making their much needed presence felt.

None of which quite explains what this all consuming involvement with the carp world is really about. Perhaps it is just that we all have something in common, which gives what would normally be superficial relationships an extra dimension. We have all been touched by something we don't fully understand, and probably never will, but we do understand that it's something we have in common with many others we are in contact with.

Roger once said to me, "I love articles about nothing", so this is for him. He is one of the nicest people you could ever wish to meet and I suppose this is about nothing – to some. What a depressing thought.

Roger Smith, lover of life, articles about nothing – and carp fishing.

I am very fortunate in that I get an annual invitation to fish a water that few outsiders are allowed near, although because of my involvement with publications, actually arranging the session is never anything like as simple as it should be. Last year Stoney said "Come down in October", which was exactly as I wanted it. The dates were fixed and I scheduled the production of the magazines around them; no problem. Then the Post Office, in its wisdom, lost the finished artwork for the autumn newsletter and the schedules went haywire.

Thus it was that my trip was re-arranged for late November, which was still a lovely prospect, but four or five weeks later than I'd intended. On the other hand, such was my anticipation of the session that if it had been arranged for Christmas Day I'd have been there. Late November it would have to be.

As it turned out, immediately prior to the trip I was not at ease with life. It was no big deal but I was in one of those painful situations where practicalities were becoming an unwelcome burden on my dreamer's mind. Ah well, something had to give and not for the first time reality was pushed to one side in the interests of a carp session. But I did not travel to the water with a clear mind or with my enthusiasm at fever pitch. In fact, what little anticipation I did have for the session was further dampened by the conditions prevailing on the great day. An already inclement autumn suddenly degenerated into an intense attack of winter. It isn't my imagination; all my carp fishing this season has coincided with wintry attacks.

On the drive over I wasted some badly misplaced sympathy on a group of cattle standing out in the freezing cold, horizontal rain on an exposed hillside between Baslow and Buxton. These were hardy looking beasts but they really did look blown out by it all that afternoon. Up beyond Buxton, on the moors road to Leek, the rain stopped. Well, it didn't exactly stop, it became snow, and quite picturesque, cautionary snow at that. Down through Leek and Newcastle the snow turned into roadworks and the going became tougher still, but life was receding into the background, the banality of Radio One was numbing my senses and the three day escape began to assume more welcome dimensions. Also, it finally did stop raining for a while, although later events suggested that this was simply with a view to renewing the hostilities with increased venom while we were setting up.

I arrived at Stoney's in the middle of a freezing cold afternoon; what little light the sky had held was already losing interest in the dreadful day. My fine friend and I were well met but the warmth of our greeting was slightly chilled by the thought of what lay ahead in the next couple of hours, namely setting up for a three night session half a mile from the car park on a gale ravaged, rain lashed, icy cold, bank flooded, desolate, bleak water. It is on such occasions that the distinction between carp fishing and pleasure fishing is written bold. We were there because we had to be, because of what was in the water. For certain neither of us really wanted to be there that day.

Shifting the gear from the car to the pitch took three trips, with the rain slanting across the open fields throughout. It was so awful that I was laughing much of the time – possibly hysterically. The wind was blowing straight into my chosen swim as I found while I wrestled with the bivvy and brolly, the bare trees offering little or no shelter. The nearest I could pitch to the rods was seven or eight yards away, and there was a minimum depth of water of a foot between the bivvy and the wave beaten platform which the rods eventually adorned.

Escape to Reality

Bivvy problems at Erehwon. Mine's in a swamp and Stoney's perched out in the raging gale.

Hutchie once wrote a piece called 'Good Habits' and I often think of it when I'm setting up in difficult conditions; not because he lost his landing net in the water in the course of the session he described (and couldn't land a fish until he'd swum round and found it), but because the title words somehow precisely capture the process of fishing for hard carp. Somewhere in the course of the session you hope it is going to happen, but it won't be often – if at all – and the long periods when it isn't happening usually feel very much like the brief moments when it does. So when you've got a gale force knife-edge of a north east wind cutting through you and dark is setting in, and you can't even find some semi-dry bank on which to bivvy, you still have to take the same care with bait presentation and bait application as you do on those summer days when the fish are rolling in the swim and you know the indicator is going to move.

I was shivering wet through by the time the bivvy looked as though it might survive the night, and the chore of balancing the hook baits was still to come. Good habits. I just wanted to get the stove lit, get a hot drink down me and crawl into the bag to dry out and thaw out, but this was a once a season chance and the trap had to be set with as much care as possible. For all that the water had been fishing badly, and the winter had set in with a vengeance – well, you just don't know. All you can do is try your socks off and hope that your efforts, the conditions and the fish throw together the recipe for something memorable to happen.

Interminably later, the job was done; two suspendeds fished over the fuzzy bottom weed (sic), balanced so finely that they would fly into the back teeth at even the most discreet of carply sucks. The Diablo did its best to fire the baits out into the area I was fishing but conditions were such that I had no way of judging how far they were penetrating the pitch black storm. The baits were still frozen and my left hand became increasingly numb as I fired out a couple of hundred free offerings. I had no knowledge of the swim; I was really just trying to fluke a fish from what I knew could be a producing area.

Meanwhile, thirty yards down the bank, Stoney had got troubles of his own. My platform was awash so I bivvied in the first suitable spot (suitable being strictly comparative). Stoney had chosen to bivvy on the wind torn platform of his swim, the end result being not so much a bivvy as a cross between a wigwam and a scarecrow. The set-up looked ominously precarious and it spoke volumes for my friend's willpower that it survived the night.

It was one of those occasions when just setting up is a triumph of mind over matter and by the time I squelched into the bivvy I felt quite proud of myself – and not a little relieved. There's not a great deal you can do on a night like that other than wait so I just got as organised as possible, had something to eat and a couple of hot drinks and crawled into the bag, wondering what the night would bring. It brought torrential rain, even stronger winds, and a nearly fish thirty yards up the bank.

I was awake most of the night, or that was what it felt like. I must have slept some though because a buzzer woke me at half past three; it wasn't mine. I felt I should go and see if help was needed, although the foray was a pointless one as I couldn't wade out to Ray's platform. We settled for a conversation screamed across the gale.

"You had some action?"

"Yes" (gently rural). "I've had a sixteen pounder hooked in the belly. The hook was nowhere near its mouth."

"You can't count that; put it back."

"I'll count anything on a night like this!"

I laughed and went back to patiently anticipate the balance of the fifteen hours of darkness away – and to suffer a major disappointment. I'd made a quick shopping trip on the way to the water and had stocked up with the sort of rubbish food that helps keep your mind together when it's trying to disintegrate. I'm addicted to Scottish shortbread when I'm sessioning, although I wouldn't dream of including such lovely nonsense in the boring health food diet I subject myself to at home. I would ease some of the blackness away with coffee and shortbread. The gas pressure was minimal – it always seems to be, which isn't really possible – but the cylinder had to get me through the session, which meant suffering a twenty minute wait every time I wanted something heating. Eventually I was equipped with coffee and shortbread, the highlight of the trip so far. Except that the shortbread wasn't, it was Scottish oatcakes, and struggling through the packet of them was roughly equivalent to setting up in a rain lashed gale!

Daylight was welcome, if only as a change. The water is only supposed to fish in the dark and the mixture was as before, as far as the weather went.

Ten minutes later, we were back in the dark and the land of frozen, boring expectancy. I was happier about the angling situation for the second night in that I'd put a marker out and knew that the hook baits were lying on a carpet of irresistible free offerings. I felt far from confident: hopeful, but not confident. The fish don't seem to move about much when the temperatures are down and on an eighteen acre water you hardly know, it is all too easy to spend three days nowhere near fish.

Farmer Dave fished the gravel the first two nights I was there, then Stoney moved into his swim when he moved out on the second morning. I stayed put, but it was frustrating fishing. The persistent wind made it impossible to fish at all sensitively and I had to foam or clip up at a time when I didn't really want to. I did have one out of the clip and one long, unexplained buzz on an antenna set-up, but no other signs. Two more days of growing confidence in the bait and I might have had a result; I can dream. As it was, it finished up as one among many big fish blanks. But the mental approach to session fishing is all-important and I felt I handled that session well, both in angling terms and as regards positive thinking. I felt no pressure to catch, and rarely do – but I did feel an increasing uneasiness at the thought of going back to real life.

During the last afternoon the sun made a welcome late appearance and I walked round to Stoney's side of the water to take some pictures. I felt sharp and aware and was touched by a feeling of sadness for a declining season and a departing year. Stoney had gone to get the baits and I stood around in his swim waiting to see if the sun was going to co-operate. The trees had been almost totally denuded by the rapidly falling temperatures and gale force wind combination and the tree nearest to me had very few leaves left clinging to it. For some reason I was startled that an isolated leaf should suddenly give up the ghost while I was looking at it. At times nature makes me feel very small, and that one simple moment was somehow an instant representation of the whole vast, infinite cycle. My introspection started to weaken and the glory of the setting sun breathed some peace and perspective into me.

I had to be back in Sheffield for eleven the following morning, which complicated the last night somewhat. Packing up was going to be no picnic and it would have to start early. A big fish in the night would cause all sorts of complications in terms of the photographic session, but it was a much desired complication that was not to be!

There was a sharp frost and I started breaking camp in the icy cold, pitch black of the muddy November morning. The packing up was under way by 5.30 a.m. and was made the colder because I had to keep washing my hands in the bitter water; the clinging mud was all over everything. For more than an hour it was all done by torchlight until the imperceptibly strengthening light made the torch unnecessary.

I was subdued and my thoughts were a confused jumble, but I have a recurring awareness that comparatively all my problems are always of a minor nature. Life can be inconceivably harrowing for so many that the minor oppressions my sensitivities are periodically burdened with are really not worth the inflated status the mind sometimes gives them. The introspection, and the combination of the clinging mud and the lightening sky, brought a line from one of Wilfred Owen's First World War poems into my head:

"The poignant misery of dawn begins to grow…"
The words move me because they so vividly convey a sickening dread of the new day that most of us will hopefully never feel. I dwelt on them and felt a distant, inadequate sadness. I was suffering some minor discomfort in the course of doing what I wanted to do most… I'm getting heavy and I can't catch the rest of what I'm trying to say without getting too heavy, but those of you who want to know will know. We live a freedom that Wilfred Owen, for one, was never again to taste, and perhaps too many of us abuse it in pursuit of something unattainable and meaningless. Or perhaps that is how it is meant to be and to appreciate what we have is enough.

I did my sherpa bit, bade my sleepy, long suffering friend a six or seven month farewell and returned whence I came from three days earlier, fishless but feeling strangely the richer for the whole experience. I braced myself for the roadworks, which had vanished, the snow, which had melted, and life's problems which no longer existed; all lost in a falling leaf, the setting sun, an icy dawn and the landscape of my mind.

My first trip to Redmire pool was on 10th September 1984, an event touched on briefly in Carpworld One, and at some length in 'Carp Season'. My second trip to the Herefordshire water was just four years and one week later: 17th September 1988. This time I was going to fish, although the trip wasn't strictly a fishing occasion. In fact the explanation of how I came to be going is a nice one, so I'll give it.

A blessed conspiracy of accumulating forces has thrown me into some august angling company over the last few years, and I'm suitably grateful for that. The compiling of the Dick Walker Memoir for the Carp Society necessitated me spending some time in the company of the splendid Fred J. Taylor, and through those meetings we have become friendly. Surprisingly we have a number of things in common. We are both past it; we both married girls from Fleetwood; we both visited the stone city of Petra (in Jordan) when we were in the forces; we both have a drink problem (we can't afford to drink as much as we'd like to), and we are both overweight. Some of the things Fred and I don't have in common are ferrets (he's an expert), angling (he's an expert), cooking (he's an expert) and staying married (he still is).

At one of our meetings during the compilation of the Memoir, I confided in Fred that the Society was on the verge of obtaining Redmire. Fred is a man who can hold a confidence, which makes him almost unique in the carp world (if he'll excuse me lumping him in with the rest of us). He has fond memories of Redmire.

"If you do get it I'd like to spend a weekend there – if you wouldn't mind putting up with me."

What a disarming request! I hadn't actually planned on going at all; the water just didn't mean enough to me, but the thought of going there with a part of Redmire's past was a different proposition. On the other hand, it must be said that I did have reservations. I'd read Len Arbery's account of Fred's previous nostalgia trip to the water (Carp Fisher 13) and I didn't know if I was up to Fred's rather cavalier attitude to carp fishing. I'm a somewhat intense carp angler; my time on the water is limited so when I'm there I live it. A weekend at Redmire with Fred J. wouldn't be like that; it would be all wining and dining, nostalgia and reminiscences. I would have to mentally prepare myself for that, and in the special circumstances I would take someone who would appreciate Redmire, and Fred J. Taylor for their own sakes. I invited Colin Dyson, editor of Coarse Angler, to make up the cast list of three, which later became a cast list of four when Len Arbery was enlisted to chauffeur Fred, act as his fishing caddy, take pictures and generally look after us all. Like me, I think Len wanted to be there if and when Fred broke his thirty year Redmire blank!

Thus it was that Colin called for me and my mountain of tackle on the morning of Friday the seventeenth of September. Apart from a couple of minor disasters en route, like a kettle emptying itself over my AJS control box, and my thumb almost being broken during the premature closure of the estate's back door, the journey was an uneventful one. We made it to Redmire at just after one o'clock, a bit nervous that we would be intruding on the fishing of the week's anglers, but they had already gone, leaving details of their five day blank in the new Redmire Log.

I hadn't given much thought to the emotions involved in going back to Redmire. I'd been there the once, on a cold, grey interview-haunted day and

Redmire Revisited

had barely been touched by the place. It had been devoid of atmosphere that day.

This time the occasion was a happy one and I was going fishing: it was different from a long way out. The lanes of the last mile or so to the water have not been touched by progress or the passage of time and we could have been in the 50's, 60's or 70's as Colin negotiated the narrow, banked, hedged lanes. I felt a rising surge of excitement – and hope. Hope! Can there be any other recreational field into which as much unfounded optimism and expectation is poured as into the pursuit of carp? And what must the arriving hopefuls have felt like in the fifties, in the period it produced the 44 and the other big fish, and was known to hold bigger carp? It was one of just two known twenties waters in the whole country at the time. Is it any wonder that Maurice Ingham says he rarely slept at all during a week's Redmire session? It's easier now (I'm told) but how many hearts has Redmire broken in the past? You've only got to browse through the old Redmire Log to understand the extent to which blank weeks at Redmire have always been very much a part of the fishing there. I don't know how many hours, or days, or weeks fishing, the few carp caught in the fifties represented, but it doesn't really matter how long a blank is, does it? Be it a few hours, a few days or a few weeks, you still have the same build up of hope and the same gradual, and eventual acceptance of defeat.

We travelled in hope, but it was a journey on which it was enough to arrive – because we just wanted to be there. We beat the southern contingent to it and conditions were lovely, which was a social blessing. I tried not to get wound up about the fishing, to play it cool, but I couldn't help getting excited at the prospect. I felt a bit ignorant about the names of the swims, but we peopled the east bank in deference to the festive nature of the occasion. We left the Evening Swim to Fred, so he could cook and fish at the same time. Col. took the Stumps Swim, and I chose the one in between. I think this is now known as the Boathouse Pitch, although it seems sad that there is no longer a swim named after 'B.B.'. Pitchford's Pit is between the Boathouse Pitch and the Stumps, a swim that is now overgrown, but it really doesn't take much effort to drop a bait in the deep spot that is Pitchford's Pit from either swim. Colin commented, and later put in print, that it is strange that there is no swim named after Richard Walker, and I'll echo the sentiment – but with reservations. We all know that the 44 was caught from the Willow Pitch, which makes the Willow Pitch historic, but it wouldn't be changing the course of history for the swim to be renamed Walker's Willow Pitch. Perhaps the Carp Society can strike a small, discreet, brass plaque to mark Walker's Willow Pitch as the birthplace of modern carp fishing.

I was indulging in a long, leisurely setting up process when the Arbery estate arrived, laden down with Len - and Fred, his pantry, his cellar and his al fresco cooking facilities. They arrived at four o' clock and the next few hours represent one of my happier carp fishing memories. My resolve not to be intense about the fishing was still unshaken: it was lovely to meet old friends in that setting: Fred was at his entertaining best.

At some stage in the dim and distant past Fred was a chef, and he loves preparing and providing food and drink. The lengths he goes to would be a chore to me, but are a labour of love to him. He got stuck straight into the preparation of the evening meal while Len tackled up for him and erected his

Left to right: Fred J. Taylor, Colin Dyson, Len Arbery and the author drinking a toast to Redmire past… Fred J. and Len have, between them, fished Redmire in five different decades. A memorable occasion.

bivvy. There was considerable bustle, and a toing and froing, but it wasn't really an angling occasion – so hopefully the carp forgave us our lack of consideration. We finally gathered for the celebratory repast in the slowly fading light of the car park at seven on the dot. We ate a meal of considerable quality and proportions and drank a toast to Redmire past; then drank one to Redmire present, then Redmire future, then Black Dog, then anything else that seemed to fit into the scheme of things – and most things did.

The dusk gave way to night; Fred stoked up the fire and regaled us with stories of the pool and its fifties, and sixties, cast list, the Upper Ouse, America, and the great Australian Outback – where he learned much of his outdoor cooking skill and how to make his amazing damper bread.

It was like Christmas Day in September, but better, because there was no washing up, no mother-in-law, and no television to numb our minds and stem the flow of banter. By the time we retired for the night our minds WERE numb, but it was the welcome fatigued aftermath of a day's anticipation, travelling and celebrating - and it was lightened by the weekend's fishing still to come.

The atmosphere of a still Redmire at night is stunning. If the fish are less likely to feed heavily enough to get caught while there are numbers of people present, they don't seem to be the least bit inhibited by the bankside presence. Both nights we were there they were very noisy, swirling and leaping. We all had some indicator action, but nothing strong enough for the hook to be set. One of Fred's runs sounded like the real thing, but it stopped just as Fred was emerging from his bivvy. One of Col's sounded like a goer; so much so that I even walked down to see if our man was 'in'. He was, in bed and sound asleep: I must have disturbed him and my interest resulted in me being written up as a ghost in Col's Coarse Angler feature about the weekend!

Saturday was a day of breakfast and recovering from it. The carp were flaunting themselves. They were clearly feeding on the baits and the far margin spot I was baiting heavily with flake maize and rape seed was turning red from their attentions. They weren't preoccupied enough to trigger the indicators though, and the occasional signs of action I had came from a point two thirds of the way across. This was a hot spot Len had taken three twenties from when he fished the water earlier in he season, and he kindly pinpointed it for me.

I suppose it's one sad aspect of Redmire now that you can go there for a weekend's fishing not just hoping, but half expecting to catch. There was a time when carp fishing was about guts; a triumph of mind over matter. Now it's becoming an increasingly technical, do it by numbers exercise. No, I think I'm overstating that. I'm describing how most of us want it to be, not how it actually is. Inventiveness and individual angling technique and ability will always be a basis for success.

Black Dog appeared whenever the hypothetical meal gong sounded: dinner Friday night, breakfast Sunday morning, and a couple of other Saturday visits "in case". Seven o' clock Saturday night and we were all ready to go again. Friday it had been game-burgers; Saturday night it was game stew; game on, you might say. Black Dog was slow to appear, as were Messrs. Arbery and Dyson. Fred and I were sitting with our backs towards the car park gate and Fred had just remarked "Black Dog's late tonight", when he was there, lying behind Fred's chair, looking up adoringly at our provider. He couldn't believe his luck when he was given the stew pan to clean out when we'd all cried "enough". He wasn't late for breakfast next morning.

"We used to come up for a couple of weekends each year, but conditions were usually against us. Nine times out of ten the pool was a mass of weed, covered with a thick scum. If you cleared some of it you set the whole lot moving. The lines were constantly being fouled and the baits dragged out of position. You never felt you were really in control of the fishing. We enjoyed it though. We had our camp fires, the meals, the wine, and the friendships."

Aye, the friendships. I touched on that aspect in the Introduction to the Dick Walker Memoir. How many enduring partnerships and friendships can you bring to mind among the top angling writers of today? I know of a couple of temporary ones, but few have lasted. The group comprising Dick Walker, Maurice Ingham, Pete Thomas, the Taylors and 'B.B.' was unique and had a stature of its own. It didn't end there though, because if you look back through the fifties, and sixties, angling books it's surprising how many other writers on the fringe of the group were inspired by that stunning line up.

I think 'privileged' and 'legendary' are sadly overworked adjectives in the angling press of today; careless use of them diminishes true privilege and real greatness, so if I don't refer to Fred in over the top journalese it is not through any lack of regard for him. I believe that a good friend of mine has referred to Fred in print as being "past it". Grief! He's still out there; he's still fishing, and he's still travelling the globe to do it. He still can't get enough of angling meetings, and charity events, and he's still willing to give his fascinating talks to appreciative audiences. Fred was at the top thirty to forty years ago: he has nothing to prove. Past it? If I'm still around at seventy plus I pray that I am past it to the extent that Fred is. He's part of our past, but a part that's still with us, and still willing to give it a go. If you get the chance to meet the man, do so, but don't get drawn into a carousing session: he sure as hell isn't past it at that!

The magic of the weekend evaporated into the mundane chores of a Sunday morning's resigned acceptance of the inevitable. It was sunny and the carp visibly relished it, unconcerned. All traces of our excesses were gently erased and the six of us, Fred J., Len, Colin, Black Dog, Redmire and I faced the return to our separate realities. Late morning brought the first of the following session's anglers in the form of Mike Kavanagh from Essex, and saw the departure of Len and Fred J. The past departed in a mood of defeated contentment and the future burst in on a wave of anticipation. The Redmire atmosphere is a mixture of three and a half decades of tangled emotions – but it's ninety per cent hope. Shortly after Colin and I departed – hoping to go back.

The magic lives on, and we were fortunate enough to taste it in very special circumstances.

I started fishing the Shropshire mere known as the Mangrove in 1983, so presumably that was the year I first set eyes on Birch Grove. I'd been visited by John Bloomfield, Steve Corbett and Tim Stent on the Mangrove and they went on about this water just up the road where Steve and John had caught twenty doubles to 19lb+ the previous weekend… It was a day ticket water, clearly quite prolific, and Mangrove action was spasmodic, to say the least. I went up to Birch to have a look – like you would!

Thinking back to that first visit is like reflecting on a different water to the Birch we know now. It was day ticket – and it showed. There was a party of Sea Scouts using the water as a training ground. It was hot, and scorched, and there was a bit of a litter problem. Not to put too fine a point on it, the water did little for me, and while I called in from time to time to have a look, that first impression of the place *became* the place in my mind.

* * *

A couple of years later, Tony Murtagh took over the exclusive fishing rights to Birch – and kept it exclusive to himself and a couple of friends. He installed a small caravan, and a boat, and presumably Birch became his escape from the world. The water no longer existed as an available fishery, a loss that was – understandably – mourned by those who'd had access to it during the early part of the 80's. I still called in occasionally, but the water suffered by comparison to the Mangrove and I had no real desire to fish it.

* * *

Rumour was that Tony hadn't renewed for the 87/88 season, although the owner, Bill Gwilt, wasn't left with enough time to make alternative arrangements and didn't want to go back to day tickets. The lake was fished very little during that season and came on the market during the following close season. At the same time, the escalating aggro attending the fishing of the Mangrove – which was actually a day ticket water till then – finally decided Bill to let the water on an official syndicate basis. On a trip across to talk Mangrove terms, I went to have a look at Birch. Actually, I had become 'we', because Mary and I had got together shortly before.

Birch hadn't been trampled on for some time, it was that most lovely time of late spring/early summer, and the water and its surroundings looked more peaceful and verdant – radiant even – than I had remembered them. And those fish… They were on top, inviting inspection. I think we started to fall in love with the place and, rightly or wrongly, we decided to bid for the Mangrove and Birch. I put it like that because I later found out that the locals had bid for the water on a syndicate basis, but I didn't know that at the time, and I did know that a representative of Tony had been in touch with the owner expressing a desire to re-rent the water. I knew what Tony had been paying, thought that was too much, pulled a figure out of the hat and bid for both waters. We got them both which, of course, displeased those who'd bid for the Mangrove, and miffed the local syndicate which had tried for Birch. The only comment I'll make on that is that I didn't know there was a local bid, and that if I hadn't taken the water over, Tony would have got it back - and no one would have

Fragments
of Birch

Opening night party, Birch 1989.

Our first Birch carp and Mary's first carp. Common, 10.06.

been able to fish it.

We didn't actually know what to do with Birch once we'd got it. Reasonable fishing access was limited. For normal purposes, four anglers on the water at any one time is more than enough, so how could we make the fishing available to others and limit the number of anglers to four? Let the water by the week to a maximum of four anglers? That first season the fishing ended at the end of August and resumed at the end of January. The letting system seemed a good idea at the time – and it worked out well: Birch's reputation as a doubles water didn't make it a viable proposition as a syndicate water on the terms that would have to be applied.

* * *

The start of our fishing of Birch coincided with the start of the new Mangrove syndicate. The first entry in the Birch Grove log reads:

'*Opening. Dinner at Birch served by Mary. Present John Lilley, Brian Garner, Bob Tapken, Eric Green, Tim and Mary*'.

Our first Birch fish fell to Mary's rods at 3.00 a.m. opening morning. She was asleep in the caravan so I struck the run for her, put the rod back on the rests and went and informed her that she'd got a carp on. It was duly landed and was a common of 10.06.

Opening was Thursday midnight and we gave way to the first official visiting party midday Sunday. Our two and a half days of fishing were memorable in their way, bearing in mind that Birch was a fun water, and our time there was just for fun.

'Easy doubles water', was Birch's tag and that assessment seemed about right to start with. For instance, in the misty stillness of the second morning, the carp took floaters very strongly off the Cattle Drink: I hooked six and landed five, biggest sixteen pounds. There is a lovely, naive log entry for later that day.

'More fish in the evening and a number lost. Not sure of numbers but biggest of the day 17+'.

It was hot, it was lovely, and the surface fishing was a throwback to Snowberry days, and very exciting – but it was only for fun and I was anxious to get stuck into the Mangrove just down the road.

The results of the visiting parties were more or less what we'd expected to start with. Colin McNeil's party had some good doubles, although they didn't find it quite as prolific as we'd expected in terms of numbers of fish on the bank – but they suffered heatwave conditions, which probably explained why the fish didn't surrender themselves.

* * *

Clive Gibbins and party fished the second full week. The heat wave broke, mild westerlies and showers changed the fish completely and they bagged up. This was what we'd been expecting of Birch. "60 plus hard fighting fish" was the final statistic. Sadly, the statistic was right, but the methods were unsatisfactory and the result was not one that was to be repeated. But it did show that the fish were there, and what it was possible to achieve if you got it really right.

We were told that up to that time a twenty out of Birch was a very rare animal, and they were certainly few and far between during that first season. I had a 20.10 on floater while fishing shoulder to shoulder with John Lilley and Brian Garner. One of Clive's party, Cockney Brian, had one – but that was one out of sixty, which made landing one pretty long odds. There were perhaps half a dozen twenties out of Birch that first summer.

* * *

Mary loved the carp atmosphere from the start, and enjoyed floater fishing, but she found the remote control fishing of putting the baits out and waiting for the buzzer to sound uninteresting. That changed mid-August. She declared that she wanted to catch a big fish. Floater results were slowing down, so we were talking bottom fishing. I was breaking in an HNV bait, but I thought that would be too slow for her. The fish had been taking Ener-Vite all summer – if a bit cautiously at times – so we made up some Ener-Vite bricked baits for chopping up, flavoured with Strawberry and Juniper Berry Oil. I wanted to be on the Mangrove, but if Mary had a run I'd have to be around, so I settled for Birch.

I was bivvied in the Cattle Drink, fishing across; Mary was in the Fence Pitch, fishing to a 70 yard marker. She'd got a big bed of hemp and two mixes of bait out so there wasn't much prospect of action till the early hours/next morning – I thought. I'd just got into the sleeping bag when one of Mary's buzzers sounded. Four beeps, then nothing. I waited for sounds of panic-stricken activity, but nothing happened. I shot across.

One indicator was at the bottom of the needle, and Mary was lying in her bag, propped up on one elbow, watching it.

"Your indicator's moved."

"I know. I'm waiting for it to roar off."

"It's already roared off – in this direction! That's a drop back."

It was a mirror of 17lb 8oz.

The next take, at 1.30 a.m. did roar off, and Mary did well with it – till it decided to get involved with the fence to the right of the swim. I had to take the rod, climb out along the fence, and clear the line. The fish had had enough by this time and just wallowed on top as I climbed back.

"It's finished love. Just stick the net under it."

It was her fish and I could have handed her the rod back, but there might have been a chance of a slip up that way…

There was a slip up anyway. The fish had surrendered long before, but Mary couldn't see it too clearly in the dark and knocked the hook out of the fish's mouth with the net right at the death. Her consolation prize was a common of 18.02 the next afternoon.

* * *

The party theme launched by the modest gathering on June 15th added a dimension when Fred J. Taylor came to visit the water early in August. That lovely man… I can picture him now, bounding down the field from John Mason's car, playful as a puppy and as welcome as the spring.

There was fishing to hand and we limited our celebrations that first night. Late in the evening, Fred and I were standing talking on the Cattle Drink and he became increasingly aware of a hawthorn bush to his left. Now that particular hawthorn bush grows at the foot of a magnificent, isolated Sequoia tree that towers 70 or 80 feet into the air. Fred fingered the leaves of the hawthorn and craned his neck to study the outline of the tree towering above him against the night sky.

"This must be the biggest hawthorn I've ever seen," he opined! It was Fred who was able to identify the main tree as a Sequoia though.

The main party in honour of Fred's visit took place the following afternoon, and it was attended by the Mangrove lads, the Liverpool layabouts and Stoney. The Stoke boys are hardened drinkers and soon disposed of the available resources. The off licence was unburdened, the home made wine provided by Fred J. was quaffed. It was an occasion to match the significance of Fred's visit – and at the height of the celebrations, Fred had a run on his nearby rods! The run was greeted by a big enough cheer. What a moment it would have been if he'd landed the fish – but it was not to be. The carp had made the sanctuary of the nearby snags by the time Fred got a bend in his rod – and his line parted. That afternoon would almost certainly have been the highlight of the Birch summer had it not been for another event on a gentle September evening…

* * *

We got back for a two nighter at the death, the close down having been extended to September 10th. The Liverpool lads – namely Alan Young, Eric,

200

Gary and anyone else who would make up the party – were invited to the close. I was ill all week and almost couldn't travel (yes – that ill!), but Mary and I made it for the party on the Saturday and fished Saturday and Sunday night – the latter being an extra night just for us. We were both bivvied in the Cattle Drink.

The comings and goings faded away, leaving just Mary and me to savour Birch's special summer atmosphere for the one last night. We'd had a good fish apiece on the Saturday night but the going was slow.

The nights were drawing in and Mary feels the cold so she was in the bag for nine. I sat in the entrance to my bivvy, listening to the sounds of the night and hoping for evening action – a rare occurrence.

Twenty past nine brought Stoney for a chat. I had a twitchy take while we were talking and struck into fresh water. Half nine and a couple of bleeps to Mary's right hand rod preceded a blistering run, turmoil in the sleeping bag and a protracted scrap in the dark, which ended when the hook length parted under the rod tip. Mary takes these things far more calmly than I do...

We repaired to the caravan to tie a new hook length, balance the bait to the four inch hook length, have a consoling coffee, and a last toast to the fading summer.

It was ten o' clock by the time we went out to recast, and as we came out of the van there was a single bleep to Mary's remaining rod. Single bleeps are common on four inch hook links over heavy beds of bait. They mean "I have just inadvertently pulled a hook into myself and will try to remain calm for a second or two before I panic." Beeep. Panic set in.

There were no fireworks. There was no typical, protracted Birch scrap in the edge. There was no distant fanfare of trumpets to announce that here was a moment among moments in Birch's history. Mary played the fish, did everything right, it came up on its side at the first time of asking and one grateful angler led the fish into the net.

I murmured an admiring "Well done, love," grasped the mesh and lifted – and laughed. "You won't believe what's in this net. Go and get the scales and sling."

The fish felt huge and in my mind immediately registered as 25lb plus – which in national terms is big enough, but in Birch Grove terms was massive.

25lb 12oz was the verdict and the euphoria on the darkened Cattle Drink that mild September night can be imagined. And what a magnificent first 25+ for a water. A male, we think, and a big framed fish that must make thirty, if it hasn't already done so. Our last nostalgia night at the water.

* * *

That was nearly two years ago as I write. I think the combination of that hot summer and HNV baits going into the water caused a weight explosion that had been suppressed by particle fishing for too long. Some of the fish looked almost anaemic that first summer – a typical aftermath to the use of peanuts – but now...

Well, the water produced fifty twenties the second season, including two new twenty five pluses, and it's already produced two new twenty fives and a number of new twenties this summer. It's an exciting carp water with an air of mystery to it, because we don't know the weights of some of the fish – but more important, it's just a lovely place to be.

The other memories are fragments. The weekly groups of hopefuls coming and going... The Seal family; Elliott's party; Steve Colclough's group and the lovely painting Steve did of the water which now graces our living room wall. The video sessions – and Mary twice catching twenties for the cameras. John and I struggling to catch for four days in what seemed like ideal conditions. The parties, the people, the fish... and the place. Almost everyone who visits Birch loves it. It feels friendly, which waters in that part of the world tend to. In the long term, it's people who spoil them

Birch scene as Mary poses with a 20lb+.

202

The easy doubles water tag has long gone. Four fish in a week to four anglers isn't an easy anything water – and that's the return for last week's party of four as I write. It's moody. It switches on and off and none of us have a clue what good conditions are for these fish. Some very good, experienced anglers have struggled on here: some beginners have scored unusually well. I've become so involved with the place that it now rivals the Mangrove in my affections, with an added novelty value that has me fishing the water whenever the chance presents itself.

We're waiting for the water's first thirty, which will come as unexpectedly and out of the blue – or dark – as Mary's great fish. But it's more than the sum total of the fish and the fishing. It's one of those carp waters where just being there is enough and almost everyone goes away delighted with the place, whether they've caught or not. It doesn't quite have the beauty and rarefied atmosphere of Snowberry, but it's in that league, and the fish are a lot bigger. It's just a lovely place to be.

The Birch fish were not co-operating. It was the fourth week of the season and I had the water to myself – for a few days. I'd started in the Fence Pitch so I could combine some writing with some fishing, but the lack of activity at the caravan end of the lake had forced me down to my favourite Planks Swim.

By Wednesday night I'd had one fish – and I'd caught that on the Sunday, within a couple of hours of arriving. I was trying, working at it, adjusting the end tackle, altering the hooklink material – all with the same end result; no result.

I was fishing maize to my left against the snag tree. The fish were there in numbers, as they insisted on reminding every few minutes with their crashing and swirling. We've learnt that Birch fish crashing and swirling doesn't mean they're feeding – or not on your baits anyway – it just means you've got a swim full of very active fish which have no intention of getting caught. Yes, I know; you would catch them: you can't fail to catch leaping, swirling fish. Everyone who goes to Birch thinks that – and most go home sadder and wiser.

Wednesday night the fish were particularly active around the snag tree. They woke me up before first light, and I was expecting action any minute. Nothing. Mixture as before. I was fishing a heavy bed of maize with a light scattering of boilies, and a boilie hookbait, on one rod, with a one-off pop up attractor bait on the other. It was one of those mornings that screamed carp – or fish, to be more precise. Whatever your chosen species you would be expecting to catch that morning.

The fitful dozing during the night left me worn out and I stuck to the bedchair longer than I should have. It was seven o' clock by the time I managed to stir myself sufficiently to put the kettle on, sit up and assess the situation. When I did I could have kicked myself: the whole area of the snag tree was a mass of bubbles. I reeled in, rearranged the end tackle, dropped down to a one ounce lead, dispensed with the tubing, changed the hook bait to maize and recast. The feeding time was almost over, but I managed a twelve pound common at 8.15, knowing that I should have had two or three chances that morning. My awful ineptitude set my mood for the day. I was frustrated, thinking badly, and starting to get confused by too many alternatives and too many wrong decisions.

The morning faded away without further action, but conditions got better as the day progressed. Not better for carp fishing, perhaps, but certainly better from the point of view of sitting out in the scorching sun watching the fish enjoying the heat on their backs. On the other hand, sun was what the water needed. Birch is deep and takes some warming through, which is presumably why the fish spend so much time in the margins and can only spasmodically be caught from the main bed of the lake.

When we first fished Birch it was a joyful venue for surface fishing, but since then very few fish had been caught off the top – perhaps half a dozen, top whack in the previous season and a half. All new floater offerings were being met with the same apathy; a couple of free offerings sampled and no follow through. Isolated hookbaits were treated with scornful indifference. Fish that couldn't be fooled on the bottom were not going to be taken in by a floating bait quite patently tethered and spelling out danger.

By early afternoon there were dozens of carp on top. It was humidly hot, but a gentle breeze was keeping some of the fish on the move – and they looked like possible feeders. I tried again with a few more pouchfuls of the latest

version of Chum Mixers – laced with Maple flavour and Juniper Berry Oil – but the carp yet again just didn't seem to recognise the offerings as food. Ron and Ron did though. With the first thwack of the catapult they descended menacingly from their dead tree roosting spots, swam irritatingly across, and fed with an obstinate, irritating voracity that didn't abate until there wasn't a single little orange ball to be seen. Thanks a bunch. My mood of disenchantment deepened and I had quite an animated discussion with the feeding geese.

Ron and Ron are two ornamental geese who are as much a part of the Birch set up as the scenery and the carp. They are male and female, inseparable, as dumb as geese tend to be, and an absolute menace when it comes to devouring floaters. The thwack of the catapult acts like a dinner gong, they are totally immune to insults and supposedly terrifying gymnastics, think that "shoo shoo" means "Food", and are much loved by Birch regulars. They mate in the close season and lay a succession of eggs which the crows devour the second the eggs are left exposed. We love Ron and Ron in the close season – and feel sorry for them. We could cheerfully blow them away during the floater fishing season.

This particular day the sun must have increased their appetite by mega lumps. They moved to my side of the lake so they could keep an eye on my every move and a weather ear open for the catapult. It was frustrating, but not terminally so because the carp were showing no interest in the floaters anyway… Still, it would at least have been nice to have had some baits out there in case the carp got suicidally hungry during the course of the afternoon.

I'd been putting off eating as long as possible, but at one o' clock I reeled in and shot up to the caravan for fresh supplies. I'd got some bait making materials with me - would the carp respond to a different smell in the Mixers? I chucked what Mixers I'd got left into a bag, poured twenty mils of Nutramino onto them, added twelve drops of Cassia Terpenes, topped up with water (160 mils per pound) and gave the mix a good shaking for a few minutes. The new bait would probably be regarded with the customary studied indifference by the carp, but briefly it would give me renewed hope in my surface fishing frustrations.

Ron and Ron eyed me with interest as I returned to the swim. There was an increasing number of carp mulling round on top and conditions looked increasingly promising. The Mixers wouldn't really be ready for use for some time, but I couldn't wait to see the carp's reaction to them. I waited till Ron and Ron's attention wandered for a moment, and fired a pouchful of baits towards a couple of carp that were bow waving around ten yards out. They didn't hesitate: they started eating the baits: in open water. I hadn't seen that happen in almost two years – unrestrained feeding on floaters in open water! I dived on the bag of baits to see if any were ready for the hook. They were still a bit softish but some of them would do. I sat on the boards at the front of the swim, cast out and had a strong offer almost immediately. It didn't result in a hooked fish, but certainly instilled an increasingly weary angler with renewed optimism.

I surreptitiously fired out another pouch of floaters, but this time Ron and Ron twigged it and gratefully set off for my swim. Then it started raining, rather heavily. I had been so engrossed in what I was doing that I just hadn't noticed the change in the weather creeping up over the trees behind me. The lovely blue and white was pushed east and a sombre bank of grey sat on the tree tops and roofed in the pool. I was gutted. I'd been on the verge of catching, then

within minutes there wasn't a carp left on top. And Ron and Ron were happily mopping up the remaining rain splashed free offerings. I offered the disturbing duo a few words of friendly advice – which they didn't act on until every last Mixer had gone – and retired to the shelter of my temporary home. Disenchantment and irritation consumed me. The weather had been so changeable that that could be the end of any floater chances for the session – just when I'd got a going bait. The sky of grey offered no hope, which accurately reflected the dark depths of my mood.

Although the beauty of the early part of the day had gone conditions were not totally uncarpy between showers. But Ron and Ron had shown the same reaction to the new baits as the carp had done, and were well keen for more. For a while, temporarily at least, they gave me the breathing space of going back to their favourite perch on the far side of the lake. Such was their effect on me that I was mentally talking to them all the time by now. When they were on their perch I was exhorting them to stay away – and while they were in the swim I was making it quite clear that their presence was less than welcome.

Some carp came up on top as the rain eased – so it increased again. I fretted. I didn't dare risk any free offerings, so I cast a single hookbait out into the area of greatest carp activity. The carp were definitely interested. If only I could achieve some measure of preoccupation, or a mild feeding rhythm even. The trouble was that while ever I was sitting on the boards at the front of the platform, Ron and Ron knew there was a prospect of another snack. My anxiety increased with the certain knowledge that the carp wouldn't stay on top indefinitely. There were already fewer showing than there had been earlier.

Conditions improved briefly and half a dozen carp showed up on the inside line. They were high in the water and moving with some purpose. Potential feeders. The controller was drifting round on the outside line and nearing the area of greatest carp activity. I'd still got no free offerings out but urgently needed some. I sneaked a look in the direction of the deadly duo. They were asleep! I had a chat with them, the spirit of Birch, and possibly even the Almighty, such was my desperation for a carp at that moment – and fired a single pouch of floaters halfway out to the hook bait. Two carp immediately started feeding on the free offerings. I didn't dare risk adding to the baits: Ron and Ron would occasionally sleep through one pouchful, but not two.

I stuck the rod tip under water and eased the controller and bait back towards the feeding activity, leaving it six feet beyond the meagre scattering of free offerings. The two carp continued feeding. I can't say I was excited because my mental state was still fairly negative as regards catching a fish off the top, but I must have been hopeful... The muted optimism was not unfounded. A third head appeared at the back of the floaters and joined in the feeding. The first floater it made for was the one with the hook in it. There was a swirl at the back of the controller... Had it taken the bait? Surely not... The controller stabbed down, the rod swung right – and locked solid! I was in! Please, Spirit of Birch Grove which has given me this take, don't let it come off.

The fish fought so powerfully that I thought it must be foul hooked and felt a rising anxiety about the ability of the size 10 Drennan Super Specialist to cope. The scrap went on, and I wondered why no one came to help me, which, in retrospect, was acutely dumb thinking seeing I was the only one on the

*A typical chunk of a
Birch mirror –
off the top.*

water! I can only think that I'd spent so much time talking to Ron and Ron that afternoon that my subconscious had registered them as company; or perhaps it was the spirit of Birch that had guided the hook to its secure hold deep in the carp's mouth I was sensing… Whatever it was, my subconscious registered a benign presence which didn't materialise in the form of assistance with the netting!

Five minutes, ten minutes perhaps: I don't know how long the scrap took, but the carp agreed to be netted at the third or fourth time of asking, and a chunk of a mirror weighing 22lb 4oz joined me on the bank. It was the first of four fish in twenty four hours, my first Birch fish off the top in almost two years, my biggest floater caught carp and, as far as I know, the biggest Birch floater caught carp. And not for the first time in my carp fishing life it was a carp that arrived when my carp fishing was seemingly at its lowest point.

I'm not the most relaxed of carp anglers and I don't take kindly to the inevitable blank periods – but isn't it pointless, all that fretting and anxiety? In this instance there was a useful side product though. Ron and Ron, with occasional animated assistance from the dozen or so resident ducks on the water, reduced me to such a state of paranoia when the carp were willing to feed on top that I decided to do something about them – in the nicest possible way. I fed them off. I put half a bucket of maize in their favourite grazing area – and had no further interference from them all week.

I had no further takes off the top that session either, but the relationship between Ron and Ron and me was a far happier one! And they got their come uppance shortly after. Mary joined me on the Friday and we were sitting savouring the peace of a Birch Grove dusk when we had a rare visit from a heron. They are regular visitors to the Mangrove but rarely fish at Birch. It chose to occupy one of the branches of Ron and Ron's favourite roosting tree – just after they had settled for the night. To say they weren't happy about the intrusion is an understatement: they were distraught, and after a sharp exchange of the verbals and a long cold stare from the heron, they opted for the middle of the lake until the fierce looking intruder moved on. The visit had a traumatic effect on them and they steered clear of that particular roosting tree for some weeks after the heron's intrusion.

Terry Eustace once said that someone else once said, about fishing – "You start out wanting to catch one, then you want to catch lots, then you want to catch a big one, then you want to catch the biggest, then you want to get selective and catch in a special place, or at a particular time, then, if it's really got hold of you, you just want to catch" I am one of a great many carp men who just want to catch. More than that, there are times when it is enough just to be there. Why? What is the attraction? Why does carp fishing effect men the way it does?

My carp life has been typical of a hundred, or a thousand others. The first time I went to a carp water I could reach out and touch the atmosphere with the tips of my fingers. Over the years that atmosphere has been there on almost every lake I've visited, sometimes representing no more than a vague feeling, sometimes as tangible as that first visit and at the tips of my fingers, and on rare, privileged occasions, real enough to almost grasp in the palm of my hand. Almost… And it is those who are sensitive to the feel of it all who look on carp fishing as far more than trying to catch carp, who stick around through good and bad and become men who habitually fish for carp, as Ransome referred to the addicted. The really addicted will tell you that life is too short to allow time for fishing for anything else.

But even the addicted lose the compulsion. Few fish for carp for ever, or till they die. And it's not even difficult to understand why some people become disillusioned with carp fishing. Among them are those who are never true carp anglers, but principally carp catchers. Many run themselves into the ground in their sudden rush up the big fish league, then find they have nowhere to go, and have, by then, forgotten what it was they felt about it all in the first place – if they ever felt it: anglers who must catch doubles, then twenties, then thirties, then run out of ambitions because, to them, carp fishing is about size and size alone. Others are never addicted. They go along with their friends and dabble until something else comes along to capture their interest. None of these are ever involved with the carp themselves, with the actual feel of carp fishing.

I can't help feeling that for some there comes a stage where carp fishing reality cannot match the anticipation. That the memories of past scenes and past events are so deeply etched on the mind that actual experiences are but pale imitations which can no longer satisfy an addiction to something that never existed, something that imagination has coloured beyond reality.

Did 'BB' ever return to Beechmere and sit in contemplation of those 'sinister dark waters brooding and waiting' and recall the feelings they stirred within him in those days now long gone? Or are those feelings themselves now so long forgotten that they are recalled with a tolerant smile as with a youthful indiscretion? Or perhaps, in that case the memory was accepted for what it was, as of a love affair that had died but which left a gentle, warm memory. Much of the prose written about carp fishing is on the verge of being poetry, which suggests that in some it can be a love affair rather than an addiction. Or are they one and the same thing?

But addicts are cured, habits are broken and carp men go on to pastures new. 'BB' turned to sea trout and there must be as much excitement and mystery in their pursuit – and tranquillity? But that doesn't answer the question why that initial passion for carp fishing dies in all but a limited few. Perhaps it is that most addictions are temporary, or are but passions, and that in some carp fishing is elevated to the level of a love affair for which the passion never dims.

Hymns of Mystery

Most carp men are nomadic, restless creatures. Most have got to have roots, but paradoxically they have got to have freedom and independence.

Perhaps it's all to do with life itself. 'B.B.' tried to categorise different types of anglers into trades, but I think he was writing figuratively. I know what he meant, but I feel he was equating trades, or professions, with mental attitudes; a man who thinks in a certain way is more likely to take up a certain trade and become a certain type of angler.

Perhaps the major problem lies in the fact that a carp fishing involvement is very anti-social. It strains relationships, and only when the compulsion is at its most potent is the game worth the damage it can cause. Most distractions of late youth and early manhood allow a compromise with life. Two games of football a week and the odd practise session leave plenty of time for conscience appeasing chores and family social occasions. Cricket is a very social game, provided the wife enjoys making sandwiches; it rarely endangers marriages, except at the highest levels. Rugby tends to be a relationship strainer, but is workable. Mountaineering and pot-holing must stretch marriages to the limit but because of their very physical nature they are, to some extent, of necessity of limited life span. But they must come closer to carp fishing; they must be a passion. There is a mystery to mountains and potholes which takes them beyond the pursuit category and into the realms of passion, and addiction, and compulsion.

Then there's golf. Those who haven't played golf won't understand about it, but it is an ideal subject for addiction. There is beauty, for golf courses are beautiful. There is companionship, and loneliness. There is competition, and social life, and there is mystery. Mystery? Very much so; golf of all addictions is a battle of mind over matter. Theoretically, it is possible to achieve perfection, and to most beginners achieving that end is only a matter of time. The ball is stationary, the objective predetermined, the movements reasonably elementary and the equipment provided infallible – in the right hands. But perfection, or even adequacy, is an illusion. Practised golfers who achieve scores of seventy five in the morning are rendered suicidal by their inability to get within fifteen strokes of that score in the afternoon in identical conditions. And once the mystery has gone and the mind accepts that perfection cannot be achieved, it becomes habitual. A very nice, lifelong habit, but a habit rather than a passion, or addiction, nonetheless.

Thus with fishing. Men with well ordered lives and little imagination are able to treat fishing as a pursuit. There is a minor element of mystery and they dream of catching a big fish, much as many of us would dream of winning the pools. And pleasure fishing, as most of us would define it, can be practised within the definitions of social acceptance. But there's fishing, and carp fishing, and even to many men of little imagination there is mystery and excitement in carp fishing. And to men with imagination, and sensitivity, carp fishing is, within the restricting confines of our society and legality, the ultimate in mystery and excitement. To anyone who is not an addicted carp angler that will be a pure flight of fancy, or even fantasy; that I accept and them I would not even try to convince. On the other hand, no one could satisfactorily explain to me the urge that drives men to lose their lives on Everest, Nanga Parbat or K2 – and I think we must accept that carp fishing is small beer compared to their involvement. To die for one's passion hints at a mental unbalance rarely encountered even in the notoriously extreme carp fisherman's ranks. Yes, there has been the odd sad loss through drowning, but it is not a risk we are consciously running.

But the fact of the matter is that to many of us there is mystery and great beauty, and something almost primeval in carp fishing. And it is also a fact that men who are able to accommodate marriage and one of life's more sociable pursuits, have great problems in combining marriage and carp fishing.

I think that for carp fishing to really retain its mystery, the very big carp should be occasional captures, rather than the norm. It's been written that specimen hunting is a young man's game, but I do not necessarily equate specimen hunting with carp fishing: it's all a matter of degree. The moment you start comparing your results with other people's and start letting it matter you cease to fish for the reasons that motivated you in the first place. I don't mean the friendly rivalry that exists on many waters, but the jealous rivalry that starts driving carp men further afield and onto other people's waters in pursuit of the bigger fish, just because someone else is catching them. The moment catching big carp becomes a competition, you start to struggle, because you can't compete for ever.

I've taken a long, long time with carp fishing. I wanted to catch a double figure carp. I'd been carp fishing for four years locally before I ventured further afield in its pursuit, and even then it took me over twelve months at Snowberry to achieve that modest objective. Of course I wanted a double figure fish that first season, then a twenty the second, but it became a double the second season and a twenty the fourth, and the time element seemed totally unimportant because the landmark fish had less significance than the fishing itself. It was nice to catch them eventually, but there became less and less hurry, and there was always this thirst to understand. There was mystery all around me and I was just a helpless, ignorant, infinitesimal part of it, not comprehending anything about the environment, the fish, the bait, or, I suddenly realised, myself. Is it necessary to understand any of it? Possibly not, but acquiring an understanding strengthens the involvement for me, as it seems to with others. Why? Why? I cannot stop asking myself questions about what is going on. A great deal of it does not fit in with what the text books teach us, and some of it contradicts them; I knew that from the first. I think that has probably added to the excitement because I knew that much of what I was seeing had not been seen before; or seen through unenquiring, uncomprehending eyes. There are too many sciences involved and no one person had all the sciences and understood the carp. So even to the scientists the whole thing was a mystery, which made it more mysterious still.

The first time you catch a carp the mystery starts to devalue. No, not the first time. When you get to the stage that you think you are beginning to comprehend some of whatever is happening in front of you, that is when it starts to devalue; but then, somewhere along the path to understanding, the mystery heightens. You half understand that you have no understanding. You draw breath sharply and realise that an involvement with a fish has led you to an insight into the unbelievable complexity of the workings of nature and its creatures.

Should you draw back at that point? Is the mystery going to be devalued by the knowledge you are acquiring, or the insight you think you have? No, because you will never understand the mystery; but awareness of it and some knowledge of it intensifies the feel of it. The more knowledge you acquire, the more evident your ignorance becomes because every 'answer' creates more questions. You will almost certainly understand the basic problem that was in your mind when you started searching, but eventually you will finish up asking yourself increasingly unanswerable questions. If it were possible to understand every single scientific aspect of it all you would find that two and two do not necessarily make four. There is more to it than that. But if ever you are granted a half glimpse of the answer to one of the unanswerable questions it will be a stunning moment, because the glimpse will be of something that may never be known, and that no one else has ever seen.

I used to read Jack Hilton's references to "that feeling" and envy him. I knew what he meant by that feeling, because I used to get it, but it never lead to the capture of a carp and in the end I dismissed it as a figment of my imagination. I was feeling it because I wanted to feel it and it wasn't there. Then suddenly it did start to happen. I would sit there and know for certain that an indicator was about to move, and within minutes I'd be away. Or I'd be travelling to a water and know which pitch I'd got to fish, and I started to follow the instincts even if they flew in the face of all other considerations in terms of weather and fish movement.

Perhaps some kind of communication with the carp develops when you've been fishing for them for a long time; or perhaps you just have a long run of coincidences. I don't honestly like to have any definite knowledge of what is happening out there in the lake. That is personal, but it is one of the things about carp fishing that I enjoy, perhaps because I've done so much of that type of fishing. Having no prior warning of a take, apart from the occasional premonition, heightens the mystery and excitement for me. I'll sit for hours, gazing at the water, wondering what is happening out there. How many times has the bait been picked up without a sign at my end of the line? Is there a big fish mouthing the bait at that very moment? Of course it's better fishing to actually find fish and watch them and then get one of them to take the bait, and it's exciting fishing too.

But I prefer it my way. Out there somewhere, unseen, unknown and apparently totally unco-operative, they are mysterious, alien creatures: idling round the margins picking up baits in full view, or taking floating particles under the rod tip where I can clearly see them the excitement is increased, but the mystery diminished.

"For God's sake," most of you are thinking, "what is this fruitcake rambling on about now?" You may well ask, but then one day you'll be sitting there, studying your navel, and nothing will have happened for a couple of days; suddenly, you'll have trouble breathing, excitement will flood through you, and you'll think "That indicator's about to move." And it will. A couple of days later it will happen again, at a completely different time of day, and then you will start to wonder. Whether you like it or not you will have become part of the mystery.

Enough. For all the words, I haven't really touched it. All I have managed to do is touch lightly on some aspects of it. Perhaps there is no mystery. Many carp men cease to carp fish because of the changing scene. The change from the placid, gentle early days of carp fishing towards the present day competitive, commercial atmosphere, slowly turned the Walkers, the B.B.'s, the Jim Gibbinsons, and others away from the scene they had unwittingly helped to create by their writings. There are many aspects of the carp scene that leave much to be desired, but I would have thought that is no more than a sad reflection of life generally.

I know many carp men, and beyond our common interest in carp, I find them individually more acceptable company than most acquaintances from the real world. It's not we who are out of step; temporarily it's the others. We see our normality reflected in each other and cling to other carp men's company for reassurance and understanding. We are secretive, persecuted creatures, collectively seeking that carp fishing peace amid the storm of everyday life – and the less satisfactory life seems, the more necessary the escape becomes. It's as normal as that.

> *"…it just held hymns of mystery,*
> *An' mystery's all too involved,*
> *It can't be understood, or solved."*
>
> Bob Dylan

Tim
'91

I get a feeling of great sadness when I'm putting the finishing touches to a book, and that's particularly true of this one. The pages of "Carp Amid the Storm" represent a lot of hours of fishing and writing, and a great range of emotions and changes of fortune. Rereading the book I know that over the years the greatest change in my own carp fishing has been in my commitment. I don't know if it's disillusionment, age, or just increasing apathy but my craziest carp fishing spells now cannot match the wild infatuation I felt for carp fishing in my first couple of Snowberry seasons. It hurt in those days, and if that is how you feel about it now I half envy you. All I wanted to do then was carp fish, catch carp, dream carp, live carp…

And here I am, fifteen years on from the first words of the book being committed to paper, living carp. All my life is carp. Reading about them, writing about them, publishing magazines about them, publishing books about them. And still crazy about them – but not all the time any more. Not crazy to the extent that I will drive 140 miles to find the water frozen over any more; not to the extent that I will make a round trip of nearly three hundred miles for a night's fishing; not often to the extent that I can't sleep the night before I go fishing now; not to the extent that anything and everything has to go in the interests of being out there fishing for carp.

Occasionally I even think that I'm losing it altogether, that the carp fishing connection is weakening, but that temporary apathy usually coincides with the dark, shortening days of late November and December and starts to lift as the nights begin to draw out. I suppose I know that carp can be caught in winter but have every sympathy with the fifties' carp fishing philosophy that you hang your rods up at the end of October at the latest!

But one thing doesn't change. I love session fishing; the "ecstatic immobility" (Ransome's words) of just being at the water, living with carp. Leaving the water at the end of a session is still the awful prospect it always was. The need to escape to carp fishing may be nothing like as strong as it once was, but when I'm there the need to remain there is usually as compelling as ever. Mary and I drive through a golf course on our way to work, and the pull of the fairways is still there, buried not far beneath the surface. I still have a great nostalgia for golf, and the thought of combining a five mile walk with an enjoyable pursuit is healthily attractive at my advancing age – but I know it wouldn't be the same. Arriving in the swim with my world on my back and a week severed from the real world in prospect is as attractive a proposition as ever it was. I still find the waiting as fretful. I still go through the full range of emotions from giving up to wanting to stay there for ever in almost every session; from the dejection of not catching and the despair at losing a fish to the euphoria of the dawns and dusks, and the anticipation of the coming feeding time and the indicator being away. The need to session fish you either understand, or you don't. To me it is carp fishing.

I find carp and all its attendant glories a humbling experience, but I would hesitate to use the word humble to describe some of the carp world glory seekers who seem to think our waters have been stocked with carp so they can prove how great they are. If you are just starting out in carp fishing cherish what you have ahead of you. If carp fishing matters to you then you matter to carp fishing. "Thirties is where it's at" is the philosophy of those with ready access to them, those on the fringes of carp fishing, and some of those on the outside looking in. To the great majority of carp anglers they are fish other people spend their lives pursuing, and occasionally catch – which is how it really is. The majority go carp fishing because they want to, or have to, depending on the degree of involvement, or addiction. If you can retain the attitude that a carp is an event, a double an achievement, a twenty a major success, and a thirty a fish of a lifetime for the rest of your carp fishing days, then they will be a joy. If you reach a point where the big fish matter too much you may become a liability to yourself and those around you, both on and off the water

When I first felt the carp fishing compulsion I was mystified that Dick Walker, "B.B." and other carp fishing pioneers and writers no longer carp fished. Surely that overwhelming need to be carp fishing at every possible opportunity could never die? Well, it did for them, and I now accept that one day it may for me, which is the reason for the slightly high flown title of this little chapter. Because of the context from which they are taken "At the going down of the sun we will remember them," the words have a nostalgic, despairing evocative sadness all of their own. They spell out the passing of time and the passing of lives: in this context carp fishing past, and carp fishing passing. We all live in the shadow of the great men who have gone before, and in the shadow of carp and carp fishing, try as we might to impose our own small temporary existences on it. I can claim no greater significance for this book than that it chronicles something of the feel of the rapidly changing face of carp fishing from the early seventies to the early nineties. Hopefully my words speak for at least a significant percentage of a generation of carp anglers which has shared the dreams, hopes, successes, disappointments and experiences on which "Carp Amid the Storm" has been based.

"Patient at morn, at evening patient still –
Peace, if not fish, was theirs, and peace is best."

Richard le Galliene

Tim Paisley
January 1992

Addendum

Travelling On

Written late 1991 for the book. It's a sort of crib of Bob Dylan's 'My Life in a Stolen Moment'. In case the early references confuse you I lived in the Preston area till my early twenties, when I moved to Sheffield.

Disturbing Affinity

I'm not sure when I wrote this, but I've a feeling this is the second or third version. The original was probably late seventies.

Conversion

Written late 70s and frequently revised over the years. The background to fishing Snowberry was that the Loxley Valley water became polluted. Snowberry was advertised in Angling Times, which is how I came to join.

Snowberry Season

Written late 70s but rewritten fairly recently judging by some of the comments.
Nigel and Ken. Nigel Talling and Ken Payne(?) two successful local anglers.
Lenny, Keith and Kevin. Lenny Middleton, Keith Gillings and Kevin Maddocks, who were developing the boiled bait/exposed hook rigs at about that time.
Kit-e-Kat. One of the most popular specials of the seventies.
Confessions. Confessions of a Carp Fisher, the first book to be published exclusively about carp fishing.
Jim Gibbinson's 'Carp'. The mid seventies Osprey version.
Sheringham. The references are to Hugh Sheringham's book 'Coarse Fishing' published in 1912.

First Day – First Double

Again written in the late 70s and changed very little over the years.
King Edwards. Cigars.
Old Spencer Tracy film. I've no idea what the film is called.
First double. Weighed 11lb 8oz and is the fish I'm holding in the picture.

Midnight Runners

Written late 70s with frequent revisions.
Jack Hilton's description… In Quest for Carp I would guess.

Twitcher Hitting

Written for the book late 70s but published in Coarse Angler in the early 80s under the title "Don't Worry They're Here," in reply to a Jim Gibbinson article "Bring in the Clones."
The first article I ever wrote… CAA Newsletter, January 1977. "Bite Indicators and Bait Presentation." How naive!
The Jim Gibbinson article I'm referring to appeared in Coarse Fisherman in the mid seventies.
Smoking. Frequent references until May 1983, when I managed to give up for good.

Black Majician Dick Weale. Successful Norfolk anglers Dick Weale and Lenny Bunn invented one of the first commercially available bait mixes and called it Black Majic.

Wednesday. Sheffield Wednesday.

The One That Got Away

One of my favourite pieces. Written late 70s, possibly early 80s. Slightly revised since.

Kasparov is the chess world champion and his name is known to most people. The earliest version was Korchnoi, and I almost finished up using the name of former champion Karpov, which means 'of carp'!

Herons. The universal buzzers until the appearance of the Optonics in the late 70s.

Cuttle Mill Revisited

I've got bitter sweet feelings about this piece. It's an exaggerated collection of experiences based loosely round the combined efforts of the late Pat Brady and our mate Bob Sellars. Sadly Pat died shortly before the article was published in Coarse Angler, August 1981.

Deeppocket. My mate Greg Fletcher is presumed to be Deeppocket, which is true on occasions, but the Deeppocket character was born before Fletch and I became friendly. It's actually a characterisation of a carp world trait.

Duncan. Duncan Kay was one of the first suppliers of commercially available baits and was very high profile at the time. *"Duncan's stuff"* is a bit ambiguous.

Spud Alley, Pontoon etc. Cuttle Mill swims.

Red Slyme. Duncan's best known bait mix.

Severn Bore. Ambiguous. Refers to the Severn tidal wave and a prominent carp angler who resided in the Bristol area.

Technical Piece

Written for the book in the early 80s, possibly late 70s. Published in David Hall's Coarse Fishing magazine in August 1987.

CAA. Carp Anglers Association, now defunct.

Attitudes Campaign

Published in Carp Fisher One in November 1981.

Trev Moss. A tackle dealer from Gainsborough.

Mike. Mike Wilson, original advertising man for Carp Fisher and the angler on the front cover of Carp Fisher One. The early magazine meetings were at his house in High Wycombe.

We'd been East. The capital E was because we'd been to Rod Hutchinson's!

...open coffee bar. The Little Chef on the road out of Grimsby.

Lounge Lizard. Jim Fielding, one time Bryan Ferry clone. I once wrote about the Lizard that "his shoes cost more than my cars." This statistic was rewritten by the stock market slide in the late 80s.

Waverley Lakes. Waveney. I used to change all the names in the Matthew Black pieces to maintain an illusion of fiction.

Paul from York. Paul Thorpe, high profile at the time.

Rod (Hutchinson).
Bob (Davies), first chairman of The Carp Society.

Nostalgia and Atmosphere

Published in Coarse Angler in 1981.
Water at Little Brickhill. Snowberry.
…at his water. The Conservative Club, a very exclusive restricted membership club in the Colne Valley. At the time I wanted to call this piece Carp Valley but Bob thought that would give too much away!
Lloyd Bent. Ran the Carp Cellar at Watford at the time.
Gary (Harrow). *Ritchie* (McDonald), the first time I met him. Geoff (Rendell). Keith (Gillings).
…recasting is a very private occurrence… The hair wasn't common knowledge at that time and you had to leave the swim when an angler had his end tackle out of the water. It probably still happens.
Bob (Morris). *Rod* (Hutchinson). *Andy* (Little). *Kev* (Maddocks). *Cliff* (Webb). *Bob* (Davies) ran the Savay syndicate at the time.

Twenty Four Hours

First published Coarse Angler May 1983. About Elsecar Reservoir. I've included it because this was one of the most memorable day sessions I've ever had. The first of a series of two about the water.

Yatesy

First published in Coarse Angler in October 1982. Chris lived in Surrey at the time.
Three of the current Top Twenty reported big fish. Now three of the top 200 I would guess.
Chris's account at the time. Appeared in the First BCSG Book, but an account later appeared in Casting at the Sun.
Tom Mintram. Leader of the Redmire syndicate at the time.
Leney. Donald Leney, son of the founder of the Leney strain. Yatesy was friendly with him up until the time of Leney's death.
The wrath of Tom and the Syndicate committee. Someone started a rumour that the 51 shouldn't be accepted as a record because it was dropsical. I wrote two articles in defence of Chris, the Syndicate and the fish "For the Record" and "Beyond all Reasonable Doubt." Tom and the committee somehow misinterpreted my defence as an attack and there was a lively exchange of correspondence on the subject in Coarse Angler late 81 early 82.

Beep-Crack – Wait There

First published in Coarse Angler in September 1983 as "Margin of Error" and rewritten for inclusion in here – because I wanted a chapter about Roman Lakes. This my favourite of the half dozen or so I have written about the water.
References to shift work and loads are to my seven years as a loader/fork lift truck driver/foreman with British Tissues.
…to Cheshire. Roman Lakes is near Glossop, just in Cheshire.
Kev's book. Carp Fever.

Roman Lakes at the weekend in the close season is a very busy water!

Blank at Fox Pool

First published in Carp Fisher 2, the piece was rewritten for inclusion in Ritchie McDonald's book "Ritchie on Carp." Included here because it's one of my favourites, and because the week described had such an impact on my life.

Fox Pool was Longfield, which was in turn a code name for Staines. After this piece appeared in Carp Fisher the name Fox Pool stuck and Rob Maylin's second book carried that title. The water closed down early in 1990 and the great fish were moved to Horton.

Mike's Billingsgate shots. Mike (Wilson). Multiple carp shots. Billingsgate is the famous fish market.

Clive and Malc. Clive Diedrich and Malcom Winkworth.

…one of the biggest names in carp fishing… Bruce Ashby. I think Bob James was there, too.

…notorious trip to the Welsh border. A close season visit to Redmire.

Big Kev. Kevin Andrews.

Arthur Ransome. Rod and Line.

Interview with Roger Smith. Two part interview in Carp Fishers 6 & 7.

Enter a Tall Dark Stranger

First published in Carp Fisher 4 and rewritten for inclusion here.

The Lizard and a close friend. Jim Fielding and his now wife Marie.

The Crafty Cockney. Derek Cunnington.

Martin Symonds. Son of the then proprietor Norman Symonds.

On the Tenth Day of Christmas

Written early 80s.

John O'Hara. One of my favourite authors. Published a collection of short stories under the title "Hell Box." Rereading the book later I discovered that the Hell box was the box to which printers consigned incorrect plates. I preferred my mistaken version and left it!

Norman (Symonds).

Hutchie wrote a good piece… In Rod Hutchinson's Carp Book, the chapter about his winter twenty from E Lake.

I was foamed up etc. The butt ring was crammed with foam to increase the resistance to a taking carp and an indicator included in front of the foam for drop back indications.

Lovely Bill (Whiting).

…play table tennis… There was a games room fifty yards behind the swim.

…some crazy woman. A slightly unkind (possibly justified) reference to the then departed Julie.

New Year. In the Snowberry days I caught a carp at literally five minutes after midnight into the new year, to end a two month blank. I wrote an article about the incident "To Celebrate New Year," which was published in Coarse Angler and stuck in Mark Summers' memory.

Col Dyson. Editor of Coarse Angler until early 1991.

Coincidence

I don't know when I wrote this! Mid 80s I would guess. I've dropped it in at about the time of Greg's visit to Cuttle.

Baz (Griffiths).

Mrs Brewer. Albert and Mrs Brewer ran the Mill until the mid 80s. One of them used to blow the whistle at dusk to signify the end of fishing for the day.

George Whitaker is still around. *Ken Selvey* died in a car accident in the 80s.

Some evil smell. Butyric acid. Very successful but so unpleasant that Fletch stopped using it – because it made him feel sick!

The Longest Day

Written for the book and first published in Carp Fisher 5.

Dave is a Maddocks man. Neither of them believed in bivvies.

Bill's mere. Referring to the owner, Bill Gwilt.

Mangrove Swamp. I gave it that name. In parts it is reminiscent of the Everglades.

Richly Undeserved Success

Written for the book at the same time as the other Mangrove 83 pieces. These chapters were written before the material for Carp Season was written.

Hooked in Reed Warblers

Originally written for the book as two chapters, "Blow Out" and "Hooked in Reed Warblers." I ran them together and published them as one chapter when I was compiling "For the Love of Carp" for The Carp Society. One of my favourite memories and pieces.

Blackadder. Dave Preston. His friends called him that because of his likeness to the TV character of the same name. Or perhaps it was Paul Roberts (Dia-wa).

I listen to the radio a lot… I haven't done so for a few years now, although I don't know why I stopped.

Jeux Sans Frontiers. A TV programme of that period. Eddie Waring, also famous for rugby league commentaries, and Stuart Hall were the presenters.

I was standing playing this fish… The back cover painting is based on this indelible memory.

Ritchie's eel tale. Ritchie caught an eel on his first night at Redmire and used to tell an hysterically funny tale about the incident.

Steve (Corbett). A friend from thereabouts.

Mangrove Finale

Written at the same time as the other Mangrove chapters and a clear follow on from Hooked in Reed Warblers.

Frank. A work mate. A lovely bloke who died suddenly in his forties in 1991.

Ray Moore. Early morning Radio 2 DJ who died suddenly in the mid 80s.

JY. Jimmy Young.

Jim Gibbinson's book 'Carp'. Again the Osprey version.

"Sh… you know where." A play on the Schweppes advert of the time.

Near Blank at the Tip

Written late 83 for the book.

Brooklands. Dartford Club Lakes.

Peter the Eater. Peter Woodhouse.

Cockney Poison Dwarf. My mate Mark Summers, also known as Slapper Summers and the Sidcup Assassin. Had an aggressive streak!

Little Jimmy. Jimmy Burns, I think.

Lockie. Martin Locke. Now proprietor of Solar Tackle and designer of the Savay Seed Mixes.

The old Cortina. Died in Carp Season!

Brummer Gummer. Paul Gummer. Went to Australia but now back in England.

Past Preferred?

Written for the book then used in David Hall's Coarse Fishing magazine in September 1987.

To An Unknown Angler

Published in Carp Fisher 11 and described by Jim Gibbinson as his favourite anecdotal piece of all time! What a lovely man.

Peter the Eater's splendid tale. There was an article about the Skip Lake (Tip Lake) by Peter the Eater in Carp Fisher 11. As I was the editor I suspect that Peter's article was probably the trigger for this one. I'd been trying to write it for nearly a year when I finally managed to do so.

Godfather. Alan Smith.

Three of us. Bill Cottam, Nick Elliott and I.

Cyclops. Nick Elliott; he had lost an eye.

Phil (Turner) (see Carp Season).

Malcolm Winkworth clone. In the original Richworth videos Malcolm spent a great deal of time hammering.

Rockin' Ronnie (Middleton).

Finishing this tale stretches credibility, but the kid came back on the Friday night just as I was packing up to leave. He looked at me as though I was mentally retarded when I told him I'd blanked! I've never been back… This was a year or two after the Carp Season sessions.

In Like Flynn

Written at the time describing a 1987 session. Published in David Hall's Coarse Fishing in December 1987.

Bill the Hyper-eater (Cottam).

AJS. Type of buzzer.

Mickey Sly indicators (see picture on page 172).

Isolated in Time

Written in the mid 80s and published in David Hall's Coarse Fishing in January 1988. One of my own favourites.

Pete Barker's Sale Society meetings. Carp Society regional meetings run by then regional organiser Pete Barker and held at Sale, Manchester. Sadly Pete died suddenly in the late 80s.

Uneasy mutual incompatability with the opposite sex. The failure of two previous apparently permanent relationships triggered this phrase. Ken and Carole Townley interpreted it as implying that I'm a ginger beer. I'm not and my current permanent relationship – with Mary – is still permanent!

Steinbeck, John. Another of my favourite writers.

Escape to Reality

A bit introverted, but it says something I wanted to put across so I've included it. Published in David Hall's Coarse Fishing in February 1988.

Stoney. Ray Stone.

Diablo. Barnett Diablo slingshot.

Farmer Dave. Dave Morgan, another good friend from those parts (see Big Carp).

We live a freedom… A recurrent thought reflected in the title of the final chapter.

Redmire Revisited

Written for Carpworld 3, late 1988.

Dick Walker Memoir. Published by The Carp Society.

…a small discreet plaque. The Society has since struck two close to the Willow Pitch, one to the memory of Dick Walker and one to 'B.B.'.

Fragments of Birch

Written at Birch Grove in July 1991.

Come Uppance for Ron and Ron

Written in the autumn of 1991.

Hymns of Mystery

Written late 70s for the book and subject to frequent revisions. Took it out of the book, then put it back in, having edited out about quarter of the original text. I think it expresses much of what I felt then, rather than now.

Beechmere. In Confessions of a Carp Fisher.

'B.B.' tried to categorise… Confessions again.

Jack Hilton's references to "that feeling." Quest for Carp. See interview in Carp Season.

The original version of Hymns of Mystery was written a long time before Yatesy started writing about the sixth sense. The title comes from the Dylan quote on the first page of the book.

Going Down of the Sun

Written January 1992, a few months after the final deadline!

Ecstatic immobility. Arthur Ransome's book "Mainly About Fishing."